New Men, New Minds

Breaking Male Tradition

How Today's Men Are Changing
The Traditional Roles of Masculinity

New Men, New Minds

Breaking Male Tradition

How Today's Men Are Changing
The Traditional Roles of Masculinity

Edited by Franklin Abbott

The Crossing Press/Freedom, CA 95019

Copyright © 1987 by Franklin Abbott

Printed in the U.S.A.

Cover by Betsy Bayley

Library of Congress Cataloging-in-Publication Data

New men, new minds.

   1. Men—United States—Psychology.   1. Sex Role—
United States.   3. Masculinity (Psychology) I. Abbott,
Franklin.
HQ1090.5.U5N48   1987   305.3'1   86-32866

ISBN 0-89594-220-8

ISBN 0-89594-219-4 (pbk.)

DEDICATION

For those men with whom I have shared moments of tenderness and moments of courage and for the men whose lives their lives have touched in our ever expanding embrace we call circle and know to be movement toward human liberation.

ACKNOWLEDGEMENTS

Many of these writings originally appeared in two small journals: *Changing Men* and *RFD*. Both have unusual histories and editorial practices. *Changing Men: Issues in Gender, Sex and Politics* appeared first as *M.: Gentle Men for Gender Justice* and is a child of the pro-feminist men's movement. The original editorial collective formed in 1979 consisted of Tom Mosmiller, Rick Cote, Timm Peterson, Mark W. Sherman, Eric Johnson, Michael Biernbaum and Jonathan Mesinger. I have been privileged to work with the collective as poetry editor since 1983. In the making of this book I am especially appreciative of the support and assistance I have from managing editors Rick Cote and Michael Biernbaum.

RFD: A Country Journal for Gay Men Everywhere has a longer history beginning in Iowa in 1974 and moving soon after to rural Oregon. The issues done by the ever changing Wolf Creek Collective are among the essential documents of contemporary gay journalism. *RFD* moved to the Southeast in 1978 and under the guidance first of Faygele Ben Miriam and in recent years Ron Lambe has continued to be a voice for gay men living outside the mainstream. As with *Changing Men* I serve as poetry editor for *RFD*. In my work on this book I am grateful for the encouragement and support of Ron Lambe.

I also wish to thank Len Richardson, Yervah Orstein, and Sy Safransky for their help in tracking down contributors. I especially appreciate assistance from Daniel Garrett in recommending writings from Black men.

Most of all, I'm thankful to John Gill, publisher at The Crossing Press, for his critical support, advice, editorial assistance, and for taking a chance in publishing the book. Finally I am grateful for my circle of friends, in particular Charles Haver, my partner and lover, who had held my hand throughout the process.

It is my hope that readers of this book will support the journals through which the book has been made possible.

Franklin Abbott

TABLE OF CONTENTS

III ISSUES

IV SPIRIT AND SOUL

INTRODUCTION

New Men:
Changing Minds, Hearts and Lives

Sometimes a Man...

by Rainer Maria Rilke

Sometimes a man stands up during supper
and walks outside, and keeps on walking.
because of a church that stands somewhere
in the East.

And his children say blessings on him as if
he were dead.

And another man, remains in his own house,
stays there, inside the dishes and in the glasses,
so that his children have to go far out into
   the world
toward that same church, which he forgot.

It is significant, perhaps prophetic, that Rilke refers to "a church that stands somewhere in the East." The influence of East on West has been increasingly felt in the 20th century. Mahatma Gandhi's model of non-violent social change inspired the first effective social movement of the second half of the 20th century in the U.S., the Civil Rights Movement. Martin Luther King, Jr., prime symbol of that movement, employed non-violence in such an eloquent manner that racial segregation, the U.S. equivalent of apartheid, is now illegal. The Civil Rights Movement inspired the contemporary Women's and Gay Liberation Movements. Its influence was keenly felt in the movement that ended the war in Viet Nam. Its influence is still felt in the anti-nuclear movement and in the pro-feminist men's movement.

Of equal though more subtle influence on the West have been the Eastern mystical traditions. D.T. Suzuki and Yogananda, J. Krishnamurti and the Western Zen adept Alan Watts brought to the West a new concept of mind. For them there was MIND where the divine, the immanent made contact with the world and there was mind that was limited and frought with illusion, similar to what Freud called the ego. Carl Jung, deeply influenced by his study of the East, speculated that what the ego lacked was the collective unconscious, a repository of all we do not yet know about ourselves. The task of both psychotherapy and meditation is to help us in the process of knowing ourselves fully (MIND) by way of introducing the ego to the collective unconscious. In learning to do this we are ever more deeply understanding the archetypes (Jung's term for the forces of tradition) that underpin our behavior. Through dialogue with these archetypes we are understanding they are not fixed, they can change (+ or -), and we can change with them.

One such archetype under close scrutiny by both women and men is the archetype of father, the patriarch/wise old man, the Emperor of the Tarot. He has been called God, Moses, Mars, Allah. He always has a son of sorts—Jesus, Isaac, Eros, Muhammed; in Tarot he is The Fool. The son is another archetype under close scrutiny, especially by men. The journey of the son to his own wisdom is an old story of initiation, the hero's story. Joseph Campbell calls the son the hero with a thousand faces.

Some men in their internal dialogue, in their mutual support and non-violent cooperation for gender justice and peace, have recognized that the father archetype can change and so can the son and so can the journey. Through MIND where East meets West, reason meets mystery and yin meets yang these men are learning something new. They are learning there are possibilities that are not war, competition or domination. It's been women's wisdom for milennia and as men tune into mystery, to yin, to the East, a new way of seeing reality opens to them. It is the way of forgiveness, the way of compassion. The spiritual teacher Patricia Sun speaks of this understanding, this change of mind to MIND, when she says, "Love is for giving." Sidney Miller, poet laureate of the changing men's movement puts it closer to earth: "The quest for perfection is a fool's game." That brings us back to The Fool, the son and what he is learning about imperfection and mercy.

To learn what he must learn The Fool, the son, must leave what he already knows. Native Americans call this a vision quest. In his vision quest the son grows nostalgic for his father's house, his father's land. Rilke understood, again almost prophetically, the odds against a son (or daughter) who leaves the father's land and yet there are many who do leave.

This is a book about those men who have left their father's houses "because of a church that stands somewhere in the East" (where day breaks, where the sun rises). It is a book about how these men came to decide to leave, how they left, what they found and what they are making of what they found. This is a book about men finding themselves and finding each other. It is a book about pain, support, violence, eroticism, change and love.

The force of tradition is one of the strongest gravities in the human psyche. While it may be fundamentally true that all that really makes men and women different are chromasomes and genitalia that is not the way differences in gender are experienced by human beings. We have traditions that are thousands of years old and these traditions are often where we find ourselves when we are challenged or confused. Some of the traditions a father knows are traditions of hunting, planting and building. He has been told by his father to protect his family and raise his sons to be men. Whether he succeeds or fails, he measures himself against tradition, and perhaps on deeper levels against the father archetype.

A son learns not only from his father's instruction but from his example. The less a son sees of his father the more he fills in the blanks with his imagination. He may image his father as a saint or an ogre, often taking unconscious cue from mother whose presence may offset (but not balance out) his father's absence. In these ways, through instruction, imagination and example a son answers the question of how to be his father's son. In adolescence, he may show his father his loyalty directly through doing his best to approximate what he figures consciously/unconsciously his father wants (he may even fail in order to support his father's need for dominance). He may also show his father his loyalty through rebellion. In this way he is true to his father in the same way a negative is true to a photograph. Whether or not the son aims to please or displease, he is still his father's son and not yet his own person. Autonomy, the realization of self (the heart of the matter), is always hard won. Many men leave their father's houses but few go far and many quickly return.

In each of our father's lives there is a gift. In our anger or our obsession to please, the gift is often hard to notice. It is there for us just as for each of us there is a gift from our mothers. The gifts can be real or magical: a genetic link to an ancestor or a psychic link to an arechtype. Perhaps our mother's gift is laughter and our father's gift is honesty. Perhaps our fathers taught us how machines work and our mothers showed us cooking (or vice versa nowadays). Whatever the gifts they are ours and as an act of power we must learn to take them. Otherwise we will be unable to leave our fathers' houses or always be returning. Unless we take our gifts part of us will be missing and in our incompleteness we will fear the world. In fear we can only continue the tradition that calls domination power and confuses freedom with hierarchy.

With the gifts we take from our parents we can take the first step into the world and toward realizing ourselves. As men we may find our hearts through acts of beauty: making music, making bread, making love, making a garden. We may find our hearts through acts of courage: refusing to continue harmful traditions we may organize against injustice, practice civil disobedience, confront in ourselves the fear of change. We may also find our hearts through acts of truth: honest emotion, forgiveness, and faith in our inner knowing. In acts of power and beauty and in acts of courage and truth, as men, we may come to know in our hearts a necessary but not sufficient condition to change our lives. As men, once our minds are changed, our gifts are claimed and our hearts are known we can direct our life force with greater clarity and precision. This does not mean we now know it all. It means we are ever more present in our sharing of ourselves in an ongoing dialogue with others. Perhaps it is at this point we can truly begin to hear the wisdom of women, the truths of other cultures, the music of the spheres.

The book reflects the process of bringing insight into action in its organization. We begin with sections on fathers and men's stories (journeys). We conclude with sections on social change and spiritual deepening.

The first section of the book focuses on the struggles of fathers and sons to know each other, to connect through painful and stifling traditions and to change a relationship that for centuries has been framed by idealism and competition.

Stories of changing men comprise the next section. Explored here are the private joys and sorrows of men questioning the rules of masculinity: competition, stoicism, the work ethic, the taboo on closeness, the fear of death. These men and the writers of the section that follows on Issues are rejecting the burden of male privilege and are working collectively and individually to understand and challenge rape, battery, war, misogyny, homophobia and dehumanizing pornography. Their struggle is to find a positive way to be men, one that honors women and that enhances their capacity to live long, lovingly and well.

The book concludes with a deeper look into how men are becoming whole. Is there a passion that men can find in and among themselves that is healing and affirming? What are the special qualities of that journey for men who are Black and men who are gay? How can men support each other in overcoming their separateness, their fears, their need for control? How can men touch their own deeper longings, find each other, find themselves and co-create equally with women a safe and peaceful home on earth?

This is a book of some of those men who remained in their own houses "inside the dishes and in the glasses" so their sons "have to go far out into the world." It is a book about men beginning to see and act in new ways. It is an invitation to sunrise, to the dawn of gender justice in the minds, hearts and lives of a few "new" men whose works and words will hopefully touch the lives of many more.

Franklin Abbott
Atlanta, Georgia

I FATHERS

American Family

by Essex Hemphill

If there were seven blind men
one of them unable to hear
would be father.
He would be the one
promising to deliver
what never arrives.
He is the bridge
which on one side
I stand feeling doomed
to never forgive him
for the violence in our past,
while on the other side
he vigorously waves to me
to cross over,
but he doesn't know
the bridge has fallen through.

If there were seven blind men
the deaf one would be father.
The mute, his son.

Healing the Wounded Father

by Joseph H. Pleck

Recently, I was stunned to learn that long before he died, my father had two heart attacks that he kept secret from his family, including my mother. They both occurred on business trips. He extended the trips, swore his business friends to secrecy and the secret came out only twenty years after he died. He never faced up to how sick he was. To him, illness was a sign of weakness, something to be denied.

I lived my first five years during what was probably the time of the greatest security and happiness in my father's life. In his early 50s, he was increasingly successful in his work (the law) and his health was still good. In his office, he kept a framed set of photographs of his four children. I am about 3, sitting, holding an apple; my oldest brother (now over 50) is a teen. These photos seem to capture a moment in his life that he wanted to keep; he never updated them.

But things did change. I was about 5 and he was about 55 when he had his first heart attack. Though no one told me what happened, I think I knew something had changed. He stopped picking me up to hug me when he came home from work. Perhaps he felt physically weak, or feared the exertion of picking me up would bring on another attack. He had a second heart attack at 60, again a secret he kept to himself. He developed painful calcifications in his shoulders, and later, a golfball-sized cyst on his neck.

During his last several years, he looked so bad that my mother destroyed all the pictures taken of him then. About a year before he died, when I was a high school freshman, I told a teacher that I knew my father would not live to see me graduate. It must have been terribly apparent, though otherwise never openly acknowleged, how physically sick he was.

In this period, he seemed to feel increasingly embittered by how his health, his family, and the world itself were changing around him. He spent his last years working on a case involving highly technical engineering matters which he never really understood, something terribly difficult and frustrating to him. He seemed to work all the time. He became chronically irritable and depressed, undergoing what textbooks call the "personality changes of later life." Perhaps he was having small strokes in his hardened arteries toward the end. Those years, especially when I was an adolescent, were hard for the family.

He also began drinking much more. I clearly remember his telling me when I was about 11 (after the second heart attack) that his doctor had said if he stopped drinking he would live another twenty years, but if he continued drinking he would only live another five years. In my 11-year-old way, I wanted very much to heal him, especially to stop his drinking, but I couldn't. He in fact died suddenly just four years later, when he was 64 and I was 15.

Recently I've come to understand more deeply some of the hurts and disappointments of his life. Growing up in a small town, German-Irish Catholic culture in the upper Midwest, he went to Chicago and became a partner in a major Chicago law firm in the 1920s. In any organization, before there is the first black, the first woman, the first Jew, there is always the first Catholic. In most of the things he was involved with, that is who he was. It was not easy.

My father worked in his own father's ice cream business until he was 18 and went to college. I remember him talking about his own father once, describing him as "a good man, but he was a Prussian, he was strict. It wasn't that he refused to give me a vacation from making ice cream every day of my life, it just never occurred to him that a boy might not want to make ice cream every day, it just never occurred to him." His voice expressed not so much resentment as an almost unbearable sadness. He left his family with a strong desire to succeed.

I've also learned more about the losses he had in his family. He had a beloved older brother who died shortly before World War I, of some infection that today would be cured by a dollar's worth of antibiotics. My father had in fact had a premonitory dream, completely accurate in all details, of his family receiving the telegram notifiying them of his brother's death. I remember him weeping, nearly five decades later, while reading aloud the poem at the end of Thomas Merton's *The Seven-Storey Mountain* in which Merton says good-bye to his own brother who had died young. Several of his younger siblings died of scarlet fever or rheumatic fever in infancy. My father, as a teen, was usually the one sent to get the doctor, to get the priest, as they died. His mother never really recovered, and he was the one who had to comfort her.

Once when I was about 10, I became very sick, vomiting uncontrollably all night and running a high fever. The next morning he told me he had been certain that I was going to die during the night. During acupuncture, I re-experienced this incident, and recognized how concrete this fear must have been for him. He was fatalistically convinced that I, his youngest child, and the one named after him, would die just as his siblings had. The realization of how deeply he must have feared losing me made me weep. Perhaps his fear of losing me (and mine of losing him) was what the tension during my adolescence and his last years was really about.

He was greatly interested in literature and music, and when he was young had aspired to be a college professor. But he felt he couldn't support a family that way. Of his daily ride on the commuter train, he said, "If everyone else is reading a newspaper, you do not read a book." (This was the 1950s.) I remember him spending several years reading *War and Peace*, a few pages a day, secretly.

He and I felt closest around music. He played the piano a bit, and I took after him. My involvement in music seemed to express a repressed part in himself. When I showed some talent, he wanted to take me to an audition for professional study at a local conservatory. He especially liked to walk around in the back yard in the summer listening to the sounds of my piano practicing coming through the back windows. This seemed to be a way I could give him something he needed.

I am struck by how many men and women describe fathers who are psychologically wounded, often physically disabled. At a cultural level, too, the wounded father is one of the great themes. I think especially of Arthur Miller's *Death of a Salesman*. Feminism, too, has made us aware, not alway with sufficient compassion, of the sexism and homophobia which have crippled so many of our fathers. Are these tragic defects part of our fathers' wounded legacy to us?

We all know the mythic pattern in which the father is supposed to do something to bring his children, especially sons, into adulthood. But this relationship takes another form: the child, especially the son, must heal the father's wounds. In one of the central mysteries of the Grail myth, the King lies ill, and the kingdom languishes, until healed by the virtuous acts of a knight-son who is spiritually pure.

The title of Robert Bly's *New Age* interview asks: "What Do Men Really Want?" At least one answer is clear: the unwounded, healed, whole father. Men—and women—want this not only for what this would mean for their fathers' lives, but also for themselves.

What to do? We have to help heal our fathers' actual wounds, when we can, and to realize honestly when we cannot. We need to heal the so-often destructive and alienated images of masculinity which surround us, the wounded father-images of our culture. And, most important, we have to heal the wounded fathers we carry in our hearts.

The Lost Father

by Thomas Moore

The day before I sat down to write this essay on the father, I dreamed that I had stuck my hand into a glass container and it broke, cutting my hand in two places. The bloody tendons and muscles were hanging out from my entire hand. I felt the nausea of seeing my insides dripping out of my skin. At that moment my father appeared. He dislodged the glass and touched the bigger wound in my hand. It healed immediately. He left the smaller wound for me, saying without actual words that I could heal that part myself.

Not only in my own life, but in the lives of many of my patients, men and women, I see the potential for healing on the part of the father. By "father," I mean a particular attitude, perspective, or fantasy that is best represented in the image of the father. The father may be an inner figure of the sort who appears in dreams, or he may be a quality in a person or in a cultural institution. A school or a church can itself serve as a father, for instance.

Specifically, the father offers direction, authority, understanding, governance, tradition, and protection. These days we tend to denigrate the notion of patriarchy, but, in spite of its problems and exaggerations, patriarchy in the sense of a deep, solid fatherly capacity is a psychological virtue. The father also provides what I would call "procreativity," which is somewhat different from the usual idea of creativity. When a person is procreative, he or she can generate a life, work, ideas, and relationships that are particular and unique, a product of the person's own talent and character. The father, as a figure of the psyche, offers life a sense of meaning and form.

This image of the father I draw not only from the character of actual fathers, but also from fathers in myth, literature, and religion. There are as many different kinds of fathering as there are literary and mythic images of father. Zeus, for example, is a father who rules and governs, while Odysseus is a father who wanders and longs for his son. Hamlet's father is a ghostly presence who is demanding and relentless. Dreams reveal an infinite array of fatherly qualities.

The need for a father never goes away, but the need is fulfilled in many different ways. In the best of circumstances a person's actual father provides a solid base for the father fantasy that will last throughout life. But what is psychologically important is the father complex, or the capacity to father. The source of this capacity is not limited to a person's actual father but may derive from other people, from experience, or from imagination.

What stands out sharply to me is a noticeable absence of father in the lives of many of my patients regardless of their age, gender, or family background. A woman comes into therapy who has raised her children well, who is full of feeling and sensitivity, and who has given her attention and her heart to deepening her relationships. In other words, her "mother" is highly developed. But she doesn't know where her life is going. She can't get any project finished. She doesn't know what to do for a career, or simply for some fulfilling way to spend her time and energy. She always expected her husband to provide that kind of direction in her life. Her actual father, she says, was an alcoholic and never seemed to be there when she was a child to give her some love.

As a therapist, you notice the missing father in the subtle manner in which the patient relates to you. She asks for direction and approval. She sees you as an authority and as a guide, and she may quickly develop intense feelings for that father who is constellated in the therapy. She may also spend a great deal of her time talking about the men in her life. You ask about her experience, and she tells you about one of her men. The father is missing in her own style, but he looms in her fantasy. She remains in touch with the father through powerful feelings for many different representatives of him.

On the other side, a man comes into therapy who also quickly betrays a painful disconnection from the father. As a man he is a boy, what Jungian psychologists call "puer." He looks young, he has boyish habits, he seems sensitive to women and yet he is ruled by them. He feels his years passing by, and he hasn't accomplished what he expected. He can't seem to get life into gear. He's embarrassed by his adolescent feelings and his unestablished life. He feels he hasn't grown up.

This psychological boyishness can be found in both men and women. Patients will say that in the family they were close to the mother, perhaps her confidant. They look at the world largely through a mother's eyes, full of care and responsibility. These mothers' sons and daughters have a strong maternal sensibility, what I would call a maternal superego that requires of them an intense compassion for the world. The "boy" is also often in flight from the mother to whom he is so attached. He may live at a great distance from her and yet long for her. He may literalize the need for flight by traveling the world, trying to get distance. But this sharply felt need to flee the mother is only a signal of an attachment to her. As a result, the boy sides with the mother in the oedipal triangle so that the father is felt as foreign or alien. Patients say: "How can I be so selfish and worry about my own career when I should be taking care of my home or the children?" There is nothing wrong with this actual concern for the home, but the fantasy of maternal care can dominate so that the father has no place.

Another sign that the father fantasy has been lost is the tendency to project the father onto others. Projection always implies a symptomatic preoccupation with what is missing, along with an obvious and painful loss. Psychology students tend to fix their attention, for instance, on a founder of a theory or on a remarkable teacher. In Jungian circles familiar to me, I notice that the old man from Zurich is a figure of mythic proportions, a sainted senex (the Old-Man fantasy), a man full of wisdom who seems as free from error as the Pope. This kind of projection of the father has its useful side, just as any apprenticeship can serve as an effective initiation into learning. But its negative effect is to ban the father from the psyche of the apprentice. Then the individual feels no personal authority, no inner source of wisdom. You ask such a student what he or she thinks, and the reply is, "Well, Jung says . . ."

A hearty sense of father gives birth to independent thought and to a style of life that is one's own. Without the psychological father, men and women go off in frantic search of a father-guide, and there is no dearth of psychologists and gurus who deal with their own missing father by playing the part for others. It's no accident that the young puer followers of the Reverend Moon always refer to him as "Father."

In therapy I deal with the missing father is several ways. For example, I myself imagine the father as an imaginal figure. It's important that I don't get confused and focus too much on the patient's personal father, or worse, assume the role of father in myself. I feel the therapy itself in its fatherly tones, and I encourage faltering attempts at fathering on the part of the patient. I try not to get caught in praise or condemnation of the maternal, a posture that indirectly keeps the father away by making the maternal dominant. Most important, I watch the dreams of my patients and notice the father figures, or actions and events that have a fatherly quality. Often dreams show clear father-child interactions, or father-ego relationships. If a person shoots his or her father in a dream, it doesn't take great powers of understanding to sense the hostile attitude of the ego. What that hostility implies is a more complicated matter. I also watch for erotic movement in relation to the father in dreams, or in life. When a woman dreams she has a penis, not unusual at all, or when she dreams of making love with her father, I don't take these images literally. I consider the move toward reconciliation with the fathering capacity in her psyche. Outside the dream, I pay attention to fascinations and attractions to fatherly figures, such as teachers and older men. Both men and women betray their father needs in attractions such as these.

Therapy for the missing father is necessarily subtle, and it has to follow the particular psychological inheritance and direction of the patient. So, I let the patient father the therapy as much as possible, and I let the dream and fate itself father the psychological work. The point of the therapy is to see the father in imagination—in dreams, projections, identifications, and so on. The patient has to begin to see the value in his father, eventually loving him enough to give him a place of prominence in the psychological economy.

Another strategy in therapy is to feel barriers that are set up against the father. A man or woman whose dominant fantasy is the mother or the puer, full of idealism and compassion, might resist the traditionalism and authority of the fatherly way of being. The fatherly mode may appear as a threat to the spirit of youthfulness or to the mother's sensitivity. In therapy it's possible to feel the resistence sharply, thereby noticing ways in which the father is lost. And, in therapy the patient can discover that it's possible to reconcile with the father without loss of the spirit of youth or of the mother's sensitivity.

Yet another resistence to the father has to do with the feeling of responsibility that comes with fatherly authority and power. We get nervous about own own progeny: our ideas, our relationships, our achievements. I'm nervous about this little piece of writing that I am procreating. Do I have to take responsibility for it? Do I have to claim it as my child?

It is particularly difficult to love the father and give him a place in your own personal life when the society at large has its father problems. Our culture craves a deep feeling of tradition and authority that is not neurotic and egotistic, that is not defensive and self-serving. The fathers we see in the newspapers, the old men who decide our laws and our fate, often seem to lack the wisdom of the deep psychological father. They play the role and seem to enjoy the power, but our world suffers from the need of a greater fatherly direction, protection, and wisdom. Superficial productivity takes the place of soulful procreativity. The dominant myth of our culture tells the story of a puer, Jesus, whose father spoke from the heavens at the son's baptism. Then when the idealistic son was suffering his torment on the cross he cried: "Why have you forsaken me?" This is a loud cry shouted in symptoms and suffering today if not in words. Why is the father not here to attend to us in our need?

My dream is hopeful to me. Just when I see my insides torn and bloody, when I am most aware of the pain in my hands—perhaps the suffering of not being able to "handle" my affairs or "get a hand on" my life, or simply get to work, just then the father appears to heal the wound. I wonder if it isn't important to me to give attention to a solid sense of fathering in my own life at this moment and to discover the healing powers of the old patriarch.

Letter To My Father

by Steven Riel

You are the one who leaves
me speechless, cold   We can't diagnose what to say
to each other sometimes   or can't bring ourselves
to begin   What is our history
of disrepair   You changing a tire
on a flat Saturday morning in February
me inside   vacuuming, reading   a mama's boy
Go outside and help your father
Bring him his gloves
Outside, I freeze next to you
my hands deflate in their pockets
as I try to jack up
this imposed shame
I must disown   dislodge myself from
pinned in our impotence
together   as you tighten the bolts

Restraint can be sparing
I've watched you bite cutting words in half
shield us from your edge
but whom do you protect
whom do you respect
your tongue cut out
your heart's murmur stalled to a cough
you have no spare
fingernails gnawed to the quick
bluntly betray you with blood

Is indifference ever lenient
to move off   a lost cause   let what must be
drown   pain washed away
but bodies float up   selfishly
insistent as inner tubes
as dreams   bloated and blue
but recognizable

Would you recognize these relics
as yourself, or me
as I begin to see   the scars
the stitches   you in me
wanting to have your hairy arms
hold me together until I heal
tell me all
they are able to
salvage

I don't despise you anymore
the once reflexive *No*   has another side
I've found what fuels
my pistons   my muffled rage:
love revved between two men
with nowhere to go   and the black spot
in the driveway   oil leaking through the night
drop after drop echoes like a pulse
through my dreams

calls me to you
after I've assumed for years
that indifferent distance
you taught me unawares   that selfish lack
of curiosity I pretended to have
about what happens under the hood
of another   did you try to know me

can I ever know
you   in all fairness
can silence be paraphrased
                    as a wound
                    without drawing blood
or only written upon
                    with a razor

in all fairness
did you have the tools
the right screwdriver   the antifreeze
stocked up from a lifetime
of tuning oneself
that precise and exacting word that tightens
like a wrench   that improvisation of wire
for a flashlight

others took care of that
for you   sutured the slipcovers
after your nap   noted on the calendar
the last time we went to confession

I had to take care of myself
ask more of myself
than you

and so take care
to come back to you now
with a new respect
for what we let go
what duty must be undertaken
by a sissy and a son   the lawn needs mowing
the wood needs splitting
Let's step outside
that dishonest proximity
Go outside and help your father
and ask of each other
Is the battery dead   Maybe if I hurry
I can still find you there   Here
are your gloves   *Connect this*
to the negative   And this to
the positive?   We can't go inside
until we jump-start what should have been
charged all along

Fathers

by Sy Safransky

I dreamt last night my father had died. Waking up, I felt thankful it was only a dream. I reached out to him, across that twilight space that separates dreaming from waking. Then I opened my eyes. Fully awake now, I realized he *was* dead.

I wept, reliving the pain of his dying four years ago. When I was a teenager, we were each other's best friends; I'd spend my weekends with him, driving in the car, helping him deliver the encyclopedias he sold, rather than play with the kids on my block.

In my dream we were in a car, and I remember his hands on the wheel—big, strong, a symbol of that strength in him which was genuine and not boastful. He was a huge man, with an enormous belly and even more enormous chest. At the age of eighteen, he was six feet two inches tall, weighed 275 pounds, and was "all muscle," the doctor said. He boxed and played football and ate sandwiches made from *whole* loaves of bread. The muscle went to fat, as sports became something to watch on television, but those hands and forearms! Thick and uncontestably *earned*. If his advice and his "experience" sometimes seemed dubious, I could at least trust his hands.

His triumphs were mine, and so were his disappointments. I knew his sales pitch by heart, could anticipate as readily as he a "yes" or a "no," a good day or bad day. He let me, at twelve or thirteen be a *man*, telling me, as best he could, his own fears and aspirations, trusting me to understand. The irony was that as I became a man, thinking for myself, questioning his values, our relationship turned sour.

When I fell in love, at nineteen, with the woman who was to be my first wife, we began drifting away from one another. No, drift is the wrong word; it suggests indifference, but our new inability to communicate bound us as passionately as our camaraderie. Not having a vocabulary for my new emotions, nor he, for his sadness that I no longer idolized him, we watched our closeness die like a beloved animal neither of us knew how to save. Eventually, I found the words, but I was nearly thirty then, and he was dying.

Sartre says you're not a man until your father dies. But accepting my father's death has been less of a challenge than accepting his *life,* and the strange and beautiful ways our lives twisted around one another, like the gnarled roots of an old tree.

To let our parents be, to accept them as people, human and therefore imperfect, rather than as gods—that is the challenge. They *were* gods for us when we were small, their approval and disapproval roping us in, their love our meat and bone. How hard to let go, in all the cells of the body and folds of the mind.

A friend told me he couldn't love his father until—well into *his* thirties—he said to him, "You're a son of a bitch." But feeling our pain—hard as it is—isn't enough; we need to understand we can't blame anyone for who we are, including our parents.

We fear becoming that within them which we most abhor, we fear everything unrealized in them which got projected onto us—all the longing, and the greed for acceptance, or money, or power, or sex, or goodness. But my father's idol, Franklin Delano Roosevelt, was right; there's nothing to fear but fear itself (hear that, Dad?). We live out the dramas that most compel us—being powerful; being powerless; being *someone.* Pain itself can become an identity easier than joy to bear, because it's familiar, a lumpy old mattress shot through with knives, but with *our* name on it, and therefore more to be trusted than the unknown— and madness? ecstasy? the disapproval of our friends? more life than we know what to do with?

Notes of An Instant Father

by Robert E. Price

Nothing prepares a man to move instantly from bachelorhood to parenthood. I married a divorcee with two children a little over three years ago, so I'm speaking from firsthand experience.

Each year, thousands of Black men with little or no experience in child rearing become instant fathers through marriage because of custody decisions in divorce cases, paternity law and other sociological conditions. Statistics show there is a good chance that the woman a Black man chooses to marry will already have children. In 1973, according to one study, nearly 28 percent of the Black women who married already had children; while less than three percent of the Black men who married had children living with them.

While the instant-father phenomenon is spreading, it can, and often does, place an added burden on new marriages. Childen play a major role in any husband-wife relationship, and if one parent is not prepared to take on the responsibilities of parenthood, the results can be traumatic and can jeopardize an otherwise solid marriage.

I met my wife-to-be, Barbara, at a social gathering. I was a 28-year-old bachelor who had lived alone most of his adult life. She was a divorcee, who had married at 16, and had an 11-year-old son, Mshinda, and a nine-year-old daughter, Makini. She told me about her children during our first conversation and made it clear that the children were an integral part of her life. I didn't pay much attention. I had dated sisters with children before, but they had always remained in the background. I didn't really expect this relationship to be any different.

Our first date changed my smugness. I had to work late, so Barb picked me up, and we went to catch a drive-in movie. When I saw she had the children with her, I was stunned!

I spent the early part of the evening trying to be gracious and nonchalant. But my mind reeled: Was this a test to see if I really liked children? Was this a ploy designed to cut down any aggressiveness on my part? Was I being scrutinized by the children?

Surprisingly, the evening went well. When it was over, I told Barb that I had enjoyed the evening, and I meant it. But on my way home, I couldn't help wondering if I was ready to court a woman while her two childen looked over my shoulder. And, I still felt a bit resentful about her testing me by bringing the children on our first date.

Later, I realized it had not been a test at all. It was part of Barbara's logic. After all, we are only going to the movies, and it saved the expense of a baby-sitter. This was my first hint that winning the heart of a lady with children was going to present problems.

I soon knew that I loved Barbara and believed that little else mattered. When the subject of her children came up, I always tried to dismiss it. I saw them when I picked her up. We played, told jokes and got along fine. But Barb insisted that we discuss details. I wanted to spend my life with this woman, and if *her* children were part of the package, then that was OK, too. But Barbara is a very wise woman and even though I assured her time and again that I loved children and that I could not help but love anything that was a part of her, she was still hesitant. The children would be allowed to see their biological father whenever practical, she'd say. "Sure, why not?" I'd reply. "They would be *our* children, not just *my* children," she cautioned.

Barbara and I had many soul-searching discussions before making a final decision about marriage. We had little trouble resolving questions about our careers, where we would live or how we would handle our money; but the subject of the children hung us up.

Finally, she insisted that I consider three questions, and if I could honestly answer yes to all three, then we would set the date for the wedding. The questions were: 1) Are you ready to take the sudden responsibility not for one but for three people? 2) Do you realize that marrying a woman with children will subtract from the amount of attention most new husbands receive from their brides? 3) Are you sure that you won't resent the fact that you are not the children's biological father? My first impulse was, of course, to say yes and get on with it. But, I knew that Barbara would ask about the grounds on which I had based my answers. So, I gave them some real thought. The first question seemed easy to deal with, but the more I thought about it, the more complex it became. Yes, I was prepared to pay the bills, love and respect all three people, but then I began to realize that responsibility meant a lot more than money. It meant seeing that the children were emotionally and physically cared for, educated, as well as provided with a proper male image. The more I thought about it, the longer my list grew. I began to doubt whether anyone could do it.

Finally, I spoke with a friend who had three children and another on the way. Although his situation was not exactly like mine, I wondered how he viewed fatherhood and its awesome responsibilities. He smiled and told me to forget the list and just decide whether I was willing to sacrifice some of my comfort for the good of the total family. I finally decided that I was.

I'm a romantic at heart, and used to daydream about standing on the deck of some luxury liner with my new bride, feeling the salt spray on our faces as we sailed 'round the world on our honeymoon. Needless to say, my dream had never included keeping a watchful eye on two children who might wander overboard. So the second question did pose a problem—how was I to avoid resenting the children for spoiling my picture of newlyweds?

I sought advice from three couples who had recently married with children involved. Two of the marriages were not going very smoothly. But the couples didn't attribute their problems to the children, or to a lack of time for each other. In fact, they said that some of their happiest moments had been the result of time spent as a family. One sister told me, "When you're in love, you find time." and I believed her. Besides, my real desire was to have Barbara by my side and that was more important than any daydream.

Finally, I approached the question of biological parenthood. Consciously, I didn't think it mattered to me. But, I wasn't taking any chances with my subconscious, so I talked it over with my family doctor. He asked if we planned to have other children. When I said yes, he said that he couldn't see any problems. He added that problems sometimes arise when a woman who has had children by another man either refused to or could not have children by her new husband. But even then, this had to be coupled with other basic problems before it became a major issue. So, at last, I was able to tell Barbara that I had carefully considered each question and felt we were ready to tell the children about our plans.

They took the news of our getting married calmly, and seemed intrigued by the idea of having someone new live with them. It was different with relatives and friends.

My mother, a devout Catholic, was eager for me to "settle down," but had church-related reservations about my marrying a divorcee. And Barb's parents weren't eager for her to "rush into" another marriage, especially when this stranger was going to be the new father of *their* beloved grandchildren.

Friends offered a lot of advice—most of it bad. Besides the usual comments about my "getting hooked," my buddies, both married and single, described in detail the horrors of a "ready-made family." I heard stories of biological fathers who ruled the house through their children. I was advised to adopt Makini and Mshinda "cause you can't do nothin' if they ain't legally yours."

As I was being advised by friends, Barb heard every horrible stepfather story imaginable. I must never be allowed to spank the children because stepfathers are sadists. Makini was never to be left alone with me since stepfathers automatically turn into child molesters. We assured all concerned that we had carefully considered what we were doing and with my new son at my side and my new daughter at her mother's side, we were married that next Sunday afternoon.

My wife and I went on a one-day honeymoon (there was no one to keep the children longer), and upon our return I instantly became head of a household—father as well as husband. At this point, though, these were merely titles. The actual transition was something else. Let me tell you now that *none* of my worldly experiences had prepared me to deal with what was to come.

On many occasions during those months Barbara and I dated, Makini and Mshinda accompanied us. Other times, I had taken them on outings without their mother, so I felt that the children and I knew each other fairly well. Wrong! I soon discovered that those experiences were no indication of what our parent-child relationship was going to be. Up to this point, I had always been the nice guy who took them to the movies and then went home. No scolding about the spilled ice cream on clothes or bad manners. Sure, they could have a second candy bar. Eager to please and be liked, I had been overindulgent with them. But this was before I knew that a 9-year-old could need a thousand dollars worth of dental work. Before, when they saw me, I was always well rested, so wrestling and tumbling had been the order of the day. Now, suddenly the children had to adjust to the fact that I was no longer their mother's date, that I was not going to leave and go home in a few hours, and that I was not a perpetual rough-and-tumble machine; quite the contrary. I got tired, was concerned with what they ate and was in their house to stay. While the children were trying to adjust to this shift, I was coping with jelly-smeared counters and doorknobs and toys in hazardous places.

There were many other aspects of instant-family life that I had not taken into consideration. Money, or the lack of it, was one. The old axiom that says "two can live as cheaply as one" may still be true, but it definitely doesn't extend to a family of four.

Although my salary is adequate, I found that I had to make many severe adjustments in my spending habits. I had never been a spendthrift but, as a bachelor, I had been accustomed to dining out whenever I wished and to purchasing a new shirt or jacket on a whim. Now, my new responsibilities as a father demanded that the needs of my family take precedence over my own. As a result, the money I would have spent on a new jacket ended up being used for dance lessons or a birthday party.

I must be honest and admit I was at first irritated by the sudden need to be more concerned about my money. But this was before the satisfaction I gained from watching my son's face as he opened his birthday presents, or before I sat as a proud parent observing my daughter's dance class perform. Moments like those made me realize that while I had less money for myself, I was compensated with the priceless joy of children.

In other areas of adjustment, we made it over hurdles that brought us closer together without realizing it. And at other times, our progress was painfully slow. For example, it took months to decide what the children should call me. Originally, at their mother's instruction, they called me "Mr. Price." But, after our first outing, I asked her to have them stop that. I wanted them to call me Robert; "Mr." was too formal and it made me feel like a stranger. This worked fine as long as I was only dating their mother. When I moved in, the situation became more complex. In fact, it was downright irritating when Mshinda used to refer to me as "he," or "him"—"The phone's for him." Since they both knew and corresponded with their biological father, whom they called "Daddy," what were they to call me? I wasn't sure myself, so I decided to let it work itself out—and it did.

I'd hear their playmates ask if I was their father. They'd answer yes, but it took awhile for me to earn my title directly. Makini finally broke the ice; she asked Barbara if I would mind if she called me Daddy, too. Barb told her to try it and see. For weeks I was bombarded with "Daddy this" and "Daddy that," but it sounded and felt very good. Mshinda, however, remained aloof awhile longer. It was all worth the wait, however, when, one night, he startled me by saying, "The phone's for you, Daddy." I felt like I'd been voted "Father of the Year."

Most of the adjustments were mine, though, not the childrens'. For all practical purposes, I'm an only child. I grew up accustomed to quiet surroundings and, as an adult, I'd never shared my apartment for any length of time. Yet, I had always said that I would never raise an only child; that I looked forward to having a house full of kids. Suddenly, I was constantly surrounded by people, and the fact that I loved them didn't always make it easier for me. Where once I was met by a cool, quiet room, music and a drink when I came home from work, I now opened my door just in time to referee a fight while the TV and radio blasted in the background.

Through all of this, Barbara was my salvation. I had grown up believing it wasn't very cool to yell, so I hadn't had any practice at it since I was a child. Consequently, when I tried to make myself heard in the middle of a fight and ear-piercing music, my voice faded. Barbara laughed, but I knew she was proud that I was at least attempting to assert myself.

Self-assertion can be a very touchy problem, especially if your children try to be preteen lawyers. In most instances, parents work out their differences in opinion on child rearing through compromise. But children are very shrewd at playing both ends against the middle by singling out the weaker parent and playing on his weakness. I found myself in long debates on dishwashing, homework and bedtime. And I lost most of those debates because their arguments were usually prefaced by such things as "Mama said . . ." or "We always used to . . ."

This ploy worked for weeks, until it finally dawned on me that, as head of my house, I had to establish my own procedures. I felt as if a ton of bricks had been lifted off my back the first time I told them, very firmly, "This is the way I want it done." My wife smiled and said I was learning faster than she had.

Giving orders didn't always work. Some things required a little more tact. One such problem was with Mshinda. When my wife divorced, Mshinda became "man of the house." He was in charge of protecting his sister, securing the house at night and handling any other manly jobs around the house that arose. He took his responsibilities very seriously and was not about to relinquish them to me. In fact, there were times when he made his resentment toward my intrusion very clear.

It took awhile to figure out what the problem was and to finally sit down and talk about it with him. I explained how proud I was of the fact that he could and did assume so much responsibility. I assured him that I did not want to take his place. Instead, I explained that, as two men, we should share in the work. From then on, I made it a point to seek his advice on matters pertaining to the house and our duties in it. The result was a much stronger relationship.

Being the third parent posed still other problems. My children are in communication with their biological father, and though he lives out of state, they are free to write, call or visit him whenever the opportunity arises. I didn't admit it, but I was extremely uneasy about this situation. I was afraid that if I put any real pressure on the children, they would label me the bad guy and give all of their love to their biological father.

This was particularly true during a period when Mshinda and I were trying to weather the storms of incomplete homework assignments and calls from teachers. After one especially heated session, I looked in his room and found him going through letters and pictures from his "other" father. I didn't say anything to him, but I almost panicked. "Now I've done it," I thought. "He wants to leave me; I've driven him away." I told all this to Barb, who reminded me how we all, at one time or another, fantasized about an aunt, uncle or friend who would treat us better and be more understanding than our parents. She added that, usually, a few days spent with that person changed their minds.

I reluctantly accepted her advice and never mentioned this matter to my son. But, I was still uneasy, and the first time the children went to visit their "other" father, I worried for a whole week, certain that I had lost them forever. Then came their first letter, which was the turning point for me. "Dear Mommy and Daddy..." It said "Daddy"! That was me! From then on, I knew there was nothing to worry about.

My two older children now have a baby brother. At first, I didn't know how to hold him or what to do when he cried. But my leap into instant fatherhood had taught me that nothing really prepares you for such a task.

I am extremely proud of my family and my role in it. But I would be less than candid if I tried to pretend that our relationship is like that of a TV family, with all problems solved before the 11 o'clock news. I must admit that there are times when, like many fathers, I consider walking away from braces, homework, diapers and discipline problems. But, the ancestors have provided me with a woman who is willing to share her life and her children with me, who has always managed to find the balance that brings us back into harmony. I cold never turn my back on her. So, I never go any farther than the library, where I write poems about the day when I'll become an instant grandfather.

To those brothers who are about to marry a sister who has children, I warn you that winning that special woman's love and respect is only half the job.

To those sisters about to bring home a "new daddy," remember that that is what he is. It's all new to him—guide him gently and give him room to make mistakes. Assure him that your children are his children, too. Rearing a family in America can be a tremendously frustrating experience but it's one I wouldn't trade for anything in the world. It's difficult for me and Barbara to find time to be alone. There's always a bruised knee, a lost sock or a PTA meeting just when we'd planned for the two of us to sneak a few hours. I sometimes envy those childless couples and their late mornings spent in bed without interruptions. But about that time, Makini kisses me, says "Good morning, Daddy," and it's no contest. I'm happily hooked on fatherhood.

The Co-Parenting Father

by Lewis Rich-Shea

The last twenty years have produced significant changes in attitude toward birth exemplified by the recent pregnancies of media super stars who command the resources to integrate childbearing into their lives and work. The vast majority of women have become subject to the same expectations but find little support to meet them, and even less understanding if they do not.

Under such circumstances, the man who makes parenting a priority can find continual opportunities to strengthen his relationship with his mate while building one with his child. In fact, I have found that co-parenting not only builds a relationship between father and child, but also furnishes much needed support to a woman during pregnancy, birth, and even breastfeeding.

The Pregnant Father

Since, for women, parenting begins at conception, then why not begin co-parenting then as well?

In this context, one of the first indications of mothering is nausea and the first assignment of fathering is to deal with it in order to avoid cleaning up its consequences. The purpose of pregnancy nausea is not to encourage small families, but to remind the woman that building a baby requires a constant supply of raw (or cooked) materials. Morning sickness is often the result of not having eaten since the night before. It takes a minimum of culinary skill to fix a snack or light meal for your partner just before bed, and particularly important, first thing in the A.M.

As the baby increases in size, so does the mother. Unfortunately, few rules in our culture are enforced as vigorously as cruelly as the one stating that women should be thin. A man who shows a pregnant woman that she is still attractive, romantic, and exciting to him will not only help her maintain a positive self-image, but will also do himself a big favor by liberating his idea of beauty from the air-brushed world of Playboy magazine.

In addition to psychological discomfort, pregnancy weight gain produces plain old aches and pains. A man does not need to be a chiropractor to massage a woman's back or a reflexologist to rub her feet. And, of course, he can also knead away the strain on her stomach muscles and supporting ligaments and tendons.

Sometime during the fifth or sixth month of pregnancy, the co-parenting father can begin to relate directly to his child. Although we have been conditioned to believe that the baby is somehow not really present until birth and possesses no intelligence until she begins talking, more and more parents are discovering that they can interact with their child in utero. Suspended in amniotic fluid, your child has control over his limbs that he will not regain for many months after birth. When you push in, your child will respond and push back. The more you try this, the more fascinated you will become with the variety of motions your child is capable of. This basic form of communication, coupled with simply feeling the baby, will help a father to build a concept of the unborn as a separate person, instead of just a nebulous growth inside his partner.

Men at Birth

In addition to being involved with the pregnancy, a man can plan with his partner the type of birth they would like, a freedom that was denied most of our parents. You will be amazed at all the options that you will encounter in reading, visiting hospitals and birthing centers, researching home birth, shopping around for a midwife and/or doctor, and talking to people who have recently had children.

On the other hand, do not waste too much energy on being outraged at doctors and hospitals who try to limit birthing alternatives in your area. Put the energy into finding a way to have a medically safe birth that meets your own personal criteria. The entrenched medical community has the resources and credibility to fight and delay any challenge except the economic pressure of consumers making truly informed choices.

While most childbirth choices are rightfully the woman's (let's not forget who is going to push that baby out), there are some key considerations for the father. It is up to the man to make sure that there are no restrictions on him during labor, birth, and post-partum. The easiest, but not the only, way to ensure complete freedom to participate is to have a home birth. If you decide on a birthing center or hospital, however, there is no medically justified reason for a man to be separated during the birth, even if the woman must undergo a Caesarean. Since not all hospitals and physicians share this view, discuss the issue with your medical professional beforehand.

With all this newly-gained liberty in hand, what can a father-in-process do? Bear in mind that coaching his partner in LaMaze breathing techniques is not the only way for a man to play a part in the labor. Certainly thousands of couples have used this method successfully, since deep breathing during each contraction helps the woman relax and provides oxygen needed for the strenuous muscular activity of the uterus. But the deep breathing can be done quite simply, without worrying about the difference between shallow chest breathing and panting, or whether to say "hoo hah" or "fah fah".

During the births of our two children, I found the best labor support to be an experienced and trusted midwife, who can quell any concerns about how the labor is progressing, and who knows how to handle any aspect of labor directly, instead of trying to block it out by focusing on an object in the room. With such professional support, I was free to respond to my wife's special needs instead of wondering if I was following some method correctly.

A compelling reason to enlist a midwife to direct the delivery of the baby is to avoid an episiotomy. I am astounded by the number of women who accept this procedure, which, to me, seems like the obstetrical equivalent of a dentist slitting the corners of your mouth to remove your wisdom teeth. A competent midwife knows how to massage the perineum and manage the presentation of the baby's head to avoid vaginal tears. Ninety-five percent of obstetricians know only how to cut. Of course, most doctors will tell you that they do episiotomies just when necessary, which turns out to be nearly all the time.

The hard core male oriented justification for episiotomy is that the woman can be sewn up nice and tight for her husband's pleasure, and more than one woman has had her episiotomy re-done because her doctor took one tuck too many the first time.

A non-barbaric approach is to maximize the flexibility of the pelvic floor muscles with the kegel exercise. A concerned partner can give his partner feedback on the strength of her kegels, which is one of the rewards of being involved so intimately in the birth process.

Once the baby is born, a key thing for the father to remember is that the child has come to him and his wife, not the hospital, the doctor, the nurse, or anyone else who might try to take the newborn away in the name of rules and regulations.

The best time to discuss standard post-partum procedures is well ahead of time, not while they are about to be invoked.

Avoiding Post-Partum Depression

There is also no reason for a man to leave the mother and child once the birth is over. What a lonesome feeling it must be for a man to come home to an empty house or apartment, eat by himself, and go to sleep alone. Many hospitals, and almost all birthing centers, will allow a healthy mother and baby to leave within a few hours after the birth. Another alternative is for the man to stay in the mother's hospital room, along with the baby. Remember to ask about and arrange for such options during the pre-partum period.

The first weeks of a newborn's life are unique, and a growing number of men are taking time off work to enjoy them. It is also a time of rest and recovery for the new mother, whether she has just given birth at home or has spent the previous five days under hospital care. A resourceful man will find more than enough friends and relatives to help out with food, laundry, and such, so that he can spend time with his partner and child. He can also make guests feel welcome but let them know that he is not there to make tea and wait on them while they enjoy what he stayed home from work for.

While nature is kind enough to present us with children who do not move around on their own for several months, it is never too early to consider the child's safety in the car and the home, where the vast majority of accidents happen to youngsters. Federally-approved, crash-tested children's car seats are considered so effective that their use is mandated by law in many states and foreign countries. For more information, contact: The Child Passenger Safety Resource Center, Room 705, 600 Washington Street, Boston, MA 02111; for more thorough guidelines on making your home child-safe, contact: The Statewide Childhood Injury Prevention Project, Sixth Floor, 39 Boylston Street, Boston, MA 02116.

The Breastfeeding Father

If the baby's mother chooses to nurse, there is a great deal that a father can do to facilitate it. Especially in the beginning, he can bring the nursing mother something to drink when she feeds the baby. While a woman does not need cow's milk to make her own milk, she does need plenty of fluids.

Although breastfeeding is certainly a natural process, it is not something that comes naturally. It takes a bit of time and learning, particularly with the first baby. An observant husband is invaluable to a new mother, because he can more clearly see and provide feedback on the mechanics and positioning of nursing.

The best advice any man can give to a new mother who wants to nurse is to contact a local chapter of La Leche League, whose leaders have a wealth of knowledge that comes from rigorous training and breastfeeding their own children. People in the League will also be aware of the birthing alternatives in your area, so it makes sense to talk with them in early pregnancy.

Despite being the most widely-reaching and successful women's self-help group in existence, they are sometimes criticized as fanatical middle-class proponents of God-fearing and child-rearing. The fact of the matter is that the women in La Leche League are your neighbors and contemporaries, and will help any woman successfully breastfeed, whether she is married, single, working at a paid job, or working at home. In addition to their regular meetings for women only, the League holds couples meetings, where men have the rare opportunity to take part in discussions about raising and nourishing children.

Bringing Up Baby

One of the traps of nursing is to resort to it as the only way to calm the baby down each time he cries. As a prospective parent, my greatest fear was to be with a baby who would not stop crying. We have all heard about (or heard) the little one who wails from 6 to 10 in the evening or from 2 to 4 in the morning (the parental graveyard shift). Needless to say, breastfeeding seemed like the panacea I had hoped for, since all I had to do was hand the baby to my wife and, voila!, instant peace. It soon became clear that this approach would produce a four month old child who weighed 185 pounds and a mother who would give her child a bottle of anything just so she could button her blouse all the way.

With a large amount of encouragement, and a moderate dose of coercion, I found that even I was able to quiet my crying child, and without sticking one of my nipples in her mouth. In fact, I soon discovered that our baby did not cry just to exercise her lungs, or all the other rationalizations I had heard for letting an infant bawl to exhaustion, but to express a real need, such as:

—Hunger
—Burping
—Diaper needs changing
—Other physical discomfort
—Need to suck
—Tired
—Need for human closenes
—Need for specific human closeness (sometimes the baby wants Mummy and sometimes Daddy)

Clearly, a father can satisfy all the above, except for hunger in a nursing baby, and need not wait for the child to cry before doing something. The most constantly-expressed and pleasant to satisfy is the infant's desire for human closeness. It is also the most difficult one for parents, especially fathers, to accept in a culture that expects rugged individualism and emotional self-sufficiency by the age of six weeks.

My experience, and the experience of many others, is that a man will not spoil his baby if he picks her up when she fusses any more than he will spoil his mate if he consoles her when she is upset, or vice versa. An infant is a perfectly clear person—without deception—eager to accept all the love you can offer and return even more. By holding your child and looking him straight in the eye you will be communicating in the child's own language. What could be more basic to establishing a relationship than communication?

A Co-Parenting Father Needs His Partner's Support

The co-parenting father is a member of a growing, but still very small, minority. He will not find many other men interested in the pros and cons of cloth diapers vs. disposables. He is not free to go out with the boys any night of the week. He is not likely to be on the fast track at work. He has already committed his nights and weekends to the work of raising children, building family, and taking an accelerated course in life.

He needs his partner's support to do things he never conceived of when people asked him what he would be when he grew up. He needs to be allowed to diaper the baby, even if it leaks once in a while. He needs to be allowed to dress the baby, even if it takes him half an hour.

He needs to be allowed to become a father and stop being just one of the boys.

An Older Father's Letter To His Young Son

by Lou Becker

Dear Jacob:

When I was a little boy, as you are now, my daddy—your grandpa—died. For a long, long time, I thought that he had done that on purpose, and I guess I thought that he did it just to get away from me. I didn't know why he wanted to, but that's the only reason I could think of for him leaving me. I tried to remember him, but I never could. I knew what he looked like, from pictures, but I couldn't *remember* him. I couldn't remember if he hugged me and kissed me; couldn't remember his voice, or his smell, and how he tasted when I kissed him. I missed him a lot, but I was also very angry at him for going away forever. So when I grew up, I though that it was a good idea to try to be a person who didn't love other people a lot, because if you love someone a lot and he or she goes away forever, it hurts so much. But as I got older I discovered that you can't just *choose* to not love other people; if you love them, well, you just *love* them, that's all. But do you know what else I discovered? I discovered that you can *pretend* that you don't love other people, and you can make it very hard for them to love *you*. You can make up a lot of reasons why people *shouldn't* love you. You can pretend that people don't need you to hug them a lot, and talk to them about how you're feeling or about how *they're* feeling, and share private things. You can pretend that you don't ever feel like crying, because if someone sees you cry then that person might decide to make you cry by hurting you. You can pretend that you could live in a tree house, all by yourself, and be happy there because no one could hurt your feelings, or not like you, or go away forever and you wouldn't be able to remember them. I pretended all that stuff to your sisters and their momma, and to my momma and my sisters, and I even pretended it to *your* mom for a long time.

But then something happened to me, and slowly I began to change. You know how when spring is just beginning and we see our daffodils start to change? First the stem gets green, and then the buds appear, still wrapped tight in their leaves. And then some morning, almost like magic, the yellow blossoms are there when we go outside. That's sort of how I was. My life had a new spring, and very slowly I began to change, too. I began to feel like a daffodil: just as the daffodil *knows* that it wants to open itself to the hugs and kisses of the sun and rain, and to give its pollen to the bees and its color and shape and smell to people to make them feel good about things starting to grow again after a brown winter, I also wanted to be like that. I wanted to open *myself*—to love and be loved, to grow, to *be* beautiful and to *feel* beautiful, to give myself because I had good things inside me to give to other people. Our daffodils act like they love us because they open up to us and give us pleasure and do their own natural things. They don't pretend that they're *weeds;* they don't hide their blossoms and their pollen so people and bees can't share them. They open up and grow because that's what daffodils are *for:* for loving the rain and sun, for loving the bees' hairy legs and tiny feet, for loving being cared for and needed and loved just as they are.

My spring began when you were born. That was the first warm day after my long brown winter: Even though it was cold and snowing that day, it was the beginning of my spring. I had pretended for so long that I could be alone that it wasn't easy for me to change. I had forgotton how to be loved, so I had also forgotton how to be loving. And at first I still pretended. I pretended that you needed me because you were so little and couldn't do things for yourself. I pretended that I wouldn't love you too much, because you might go away. I pretended that you shouldn't love me because *I* might go away—and that anyway you *wouldn't* love me because there wasn't much about me to love.

But I was wrong. For the nearly five years that you and I have been together, we have loved each other as hard as we could. Why do you suppose that is? Some of it, I think, is because I've been lucky enough to get to take care of you all day every day. When your sisters were little, I went away to work every day, so I didn't get to be with them all the time. And when I *was* with them I guess I thought I was supposed to *teach* them things, and be the one who knew everything. That was just more pretending, though. I never spent much time finding out what they knew so I imagined that they—and all little people—probably really didn't know very much at all.

With you, however, I just let myself be loved. And that made all the difference. Because you loved me, slowly I began to imagine that I could be loved. So I stopped hiding and pretending, and loved you back. I let you be my teacher. I learned to sing because if I sang like a crow you didn't make fun of me. I learned to cry because we sometimes cried together about the same thing. I learned to listen, because you had lots of things to say that we needed to think and talk about. I learned that the most important thing I had to do while we were together was to *be* with you and to *do* things with you. Work and play got to be the same thing: When we worked together building something, what we built wasn't very important, but the fun we had doing it together *was* very important. When we play baseball it really doesn't ever matter if we hit the ball; what matters is that we're having fun with each other. I guess that learning new things with you has been the most fun of all: One minute neither of us knows a certain thing, and the next minute we both know that new thing at exactly the same time!

I wanted you to know all this stuff for two reasons. First, if when you're big you decide that you'd like to be a daddy, I hope you'll remember that the best part of that is to arrange it so that you can be with your child all day. If you can do that, if you're anything like me, you'll find that your special loving muscles get bigger and bigger and stronger and stronger, and you'll almost explode with love, like a big pudding!

The second thing is that even though I tell you that I love you, and we snuggle a lot, and sit on laps, some day I'll be gone, and you might wonder why, or be angry, the way I used to be. If that happens, I want you to be able to unfold this paper and sort of listen to me while I tell you this special story about myself, and about how your magic turned me into a beautiful daffodil.

I love you very much.

Dad

Stories to Antonio

by Jimmy Santiago Baca

I lie in bed and he runs after me,
jumps onto my bed, and says,
"Tell me a story papi."

Rather than open a book,
I turn what we did together
into a magical story.

"A man builds a patio. A little boy
digs next to his papi. He find a worm.
The worm decides to turn into
a great, big butterfly. How are you
the worm says to the little boy.
The little boy closes his eyes
and the worm takes him down
into the earth, to his home.
It is dark. Things shine.
The little boy asks, what are those
shiny things?
The worm replies, those are baby suns.
When they are ready, they will walk
the long journey to the end of the earth,
and there, they will work to shine across
the sky..."

As my son listens to the story,
his eyes glow. He is the little boy
beneath the earth. He picks up the baby sun,
and slowly, falls asleep in its glow.

II STORIES

Having Sons

by John Gill

the fish-eye of comparison will not hold.
catapulted out of the tower they sing another
flight. different birds. different music. yet.
one feather from each son drifts down to match
our plumage.

it may be the lucky feather of good looks. or
the black feather of night. the feather of making
money. or the idle feather of a fool. whatever it
is it's the wrong one and it's not enough. this
particular feather of ours.

surely. we're mocked. the very presence of our
sons is an itch we have to scratch. our voices get
tense and shrill. we grow red in the face. what
did our sons do in their harmless way to provoke
us but repeat every one of our failures. and when
they are through. the list empty. the terms
exhausted. with tender love they will plow us
under where we have plowed.

and one feather of ours will cling to them. they
will wear it the rest of their lives.

Some Scars Don't Show:
a coming-out story

by Ken Fremont-Smith

I can't remember the child-that-was, before the fire. He's a stranger to me. My father tells me he was a scamp—bright, active, intently curious and totally fearless. Which makes sense, because one day that child climbed onto a kitchen stove and started playing with all the attractive buttons. The flames went up, and in seconds he was burning, screaming as his clothes and skin were eaten away with frightening speed. It lasted only seconds (thanks to the quick reaction of his mother, wrapping the boy in a nearby scatterrug), but the damage was deep—third-degree burns on chest and back.

There followed the weeks in the hospital, where the skin grafts were taken from his legs to replace the destroyed areas of skin. And then, nothing but time—time for the long and painful healing process to take place. But children are wellsprings of vitality and resiliency, and in a year he had recovered—or rather, "I" had recovered, since here is where memory kicks in. Scarred on parts of my chest and back, with some lighter scars on my thighs, but completely healed. No twisted joints, no tenderness, no lack of mobility or of sensation. It takes more than fire to keep an active child down!

As it turns out, though—there was more. What fire couldn't do, taunts and rejection by others could. With my scars I was different, and children learn at an early age that different is bad—ugly. Typically, it was worst in sports, with other boys—swimming, or playing "shirts and skins." Sometimes the stares and comments were of simple curiosity, but more often they were combined with the easy cruelty young children pick up and use against each other. And the assumption was that my scars meant I was physically inferior, and *that* meant I was fair game. P.E. went from bad to worse.

At home there was love and support, and that made a difference. But my parents were afraid *for* me—for what I had been through and what I had yet to face—and the fear mixed in with the love. My mother gave me *too much* protection (was I so frail?). My father gave me *too much* encouragement to be physically strong (was there something I had to prove?). Through these messages, through my peers, I learned what fire had not been able to teach me—I learned fear. And I grew to despise the source of my fear, this frail, ugly, incapable body of mine. If others rejected it, I would too. My powerful energy turned inwards, away from the physical world and into the world of the mind. As I grew up I "became" an intellectual, where bodies didn't matter. Where I could curl up my lip in scorn at "jocks" and competitive sports. I hid my fear behind my intellect, just as I hid my body behind clothes and a caved-in, unobtrusive posture. I gave up swimming—which I loved. I would have willingly cut off an arm in order to fit in. Failing that, I cut myself off from my body.

Coming Out

But there's a limit as to how small you can compress yourself; it's hard to offer your other arm to the hatchet when one's already been chopped off. For me the turning point came when my sexuality rose up fully in me and I recognized my gayness. Unable to deny still more of my life, I "came out"—the gay phrase that refers to the simple but profound act of standing up and shouting out, *my life is worth living.* That simple declaration has changed many people's lives.

But this isn't a coming-out story about my gayness It's a coming-out story about my scars.

Coming out as a gay man first took place when I was 19—almost 10 years ago. Coming out as a scarred man is a far more recent story. As with my first coming out, there was a flash of insight, a moment when I understood my situation in the world and determined to turn it around. That happened at a gestalt group workshop, where, with the therapist's encouragement, I took off my shirt and "introduced" my scars to the others. I was scared/excited/defiant/hopeful—so many reactions that in seconds I was drenched in sweat from the energy exploding inside me. As I sat down, it hit me—this was just like coming out! Here was another closet I was hiding inside of, trying to conform to the outside world of "nice" bodies. Here was the same pressure to be invisible, to not embarrass others with my "differences." And here was the same opportunity to reclaim a part of myself (or in this case, my whole body, which had stubbornly stuck by me all those years I was ignoring it).

"Coming out" is a gay term, but it's not limited to the gay experience. It's an act of wholeness; a rejection of meaningless sacrifice. (Who benefits by my being straight? Who benefits by my being embarrassed and afraid?) Coming out is anger: fighting back against bigotry and senseless fear. Coming out is pride: finding dignity and joy in who I am. Coming out is strength: standing tall and taking risks in the world, no longer divided against myself. And coming out is compassion. For if I can celebrate *my* uniqueness, surely can I celebrate the uniqueness of others. If I can name *my* pain and acknowledge its truth, then can I listen to the pain of others. And only then can we join together in *common cause.* Make no mistake: a single person's coming out shakes the chains of the world.

Taking Heart

I've still got a ways to go. Now that I've found there's more than one closet to come out of, I'm that much more aware of how easy it is to hide. Being in a closet, after all, is safe. The only thing safer is being in a coffin.

But I've made the commitment. I'm learning to love my body—to see it not as a source of my fear, but as having been the victim of my fear. It's a *good* body. I'm back into swimming again. I'm encouraging myself to deal with group sports. And sex turns out to be a whole lot more fun with a body! The more I came out, the more strength I find to call on. Instead of denying myself options in life, I'm learning to open up to them.

The thing is, we *all* have closets to come out of, and coming-out stories to share. We all have pieces of ourselves we gave up in the face of accusation of being different. As boys we worried—did we fit in? Were we accepted? Did we have the "right stuff"? (Not only did we have to fit in, but, bewilderingly, we also had to be *better*. Our peers were our competitors, against whom we proved ourselves.) Then we come to manhood to find nothing changed. The stress drives us on: outwardly we conform with our competitive peers; inwardly, we deny our confusion, our fears, our dreams. How many men bury their "unmanly" dreams, their "unacceptable" feelings, and never understand what they've sacrificed? It is a kind of living death that no human being deserves.

Coming out is a refusal of that living death, an affirmation of life and self. That is why it is so important to gays. But is affirmation of life and self any less important to my brothers who are straight, or bisexual, or just plain sexual? I believe our common history as men reaches beyond our sexual preference. All of us have stories to share. And through that sharing—of pain, of coming out, of pride—we can reach toward a common strength.

That small child who was so fearless before the fire, he's still inside me. I haven't met him yet, or made amends with him. But I feel him coming closer. He feels me reaching out. And on the day when *he* comes out, you'll hear the sound of crashing iron. It will be the sound a chain makes—when its broken.

Ah, Ya Throw Like a Girl!

by Mike Messner

Although the sociology department at U.C. Berkeley is situated on the fourth floor of a very ugly post-war building, the place does have one thing going for it: the fourth floor balcony overlooks the women's softball field. There I have spent not a few fine afternoons in the past few years basking in the sunshine and watching some of the most talented softball players in the nation.

When I am joined on the balcony (usually only briefly) by my hard-working friends and colleagues who kid me about "taking the day off in the sun," I retort that I am actually doing *research* at this very moment. After all, I *am* doing my dissertation on "sports and male identity" (great thing about sociology: everything is data).

One spring day I was enjoying a beautifully played pitchers' duel between Cal's women and another top-ranked team. It was late in the game, with the score tied 1-1 when I was joined in my personal left field pavillion by a friendly and gentle man who is nearing the end of a very successful career as a sociologist at U.C.B. Suddenly, with a runner on first via a rare base-on-balls from the Cal pitcher, the batter drove the ball on a line into left-center field. The left fielder managed to run the ball down, turn, and fire a strike to the shortstop just at the edge of the infield, who in turn spun and threw perfectly, laser-like, to the plate, nailing the lead runner. What precision teamwork and execution! And the game was still tied!

My fellow fan smiled, as did I, and shook his head. "You know, it amazes me to see a woman throw like that. I always thought that there was something about the female arm that made it impossible to throw like a man."

* * * * *

I'm 8 years old and I'm playing Little League Baseball for the first time and my dad's the coach! It's my first tryout/practice and it's an exciting, confusing, scary affair, with what seems like hundreds of boys, all with identical green caps and leather mitts facing each other in two long lines, throwing balls back and forth as fathers furiously race around coaching, criticizing, encouraging, demonstrating, and scrawling mysterious things on clipboards.

Later at home, my father informs me that there are two boys on the team who throw like girls, and that I, unfortunately, am one of them! By the next practice, he tells me, we will have corrected that problem. That evening, with glove and cap securely in place, I anxiously face my father on the front lawn. And we play catch. For quite a while. I am concentrating, working hard to throw correctly ("like a *man*"), pulling my arm back as far as I can and snapping the ball overhand, just past my ear. When I do this, it feels very strange—I really have very little control over the flight of the ball, and it hurts my shoulder a bit—but I am rewarded with the knowledge that *this is how men throw the ball.* If I learn this, I won't embarrass either myself or my father. When at times I inadvertently revert to what feels like a more natural and more easily controllable throwing style (more of a shot-put style, with hand and ball starting just behind the ear, and elbow leading the way), I immediately am rewarded with a return throw that sails far over my head and lands two or three houses down. "Run! *Run* after that ball! You won't have to chase it anymore when you quit throwing like a girl!"

Simple behavior-modification, actually. And it worked—I learned very rapidly how to throw properly. But it wasn't really the having to run after the ball that taught me: it was the threat to my very fragile sense of maleness. The *fear*—oh, the fear of being thought a sissy—a *girl!*

* * * * *

I was momentarily taken aback that a renowned sociologist would have such a "biological" explanation for gender differences between women and men. I explained to him that, indeed, "throwing like a girl" is actually a more anatomically natural motion for the human arm. "Throwing like a man" is a learned action which can, repeated over time, actually seriously damage the arm.

A few years ago, a sportswriter did an informal survey of major league pitchers, asking of those who had played Little League as youngsters just how many of them had been pitchers in their youth. The astounding answer: *zero.* Stories of Little Leaguers burning their arms out for life are common. The destruction of young shoulders and elbows has led to some Little Leagues outlawing curve balls. Others have even instituted systems in which adults do all the pitching for 8- and 9-year-olds.

"Throwing like a man" is an unnatural act, an act that (like most aspects of "masculinity") must be learned. Indeed, I learned it at a very young age, as did most of my male peers. And while I was on the front lawn with Dad, my older sister Linda was God-knows-where, but certainly not playing ball. Only this past summer did she join a softball team and learn how to throw a ball. She's a natural athlete who had to wait until the age of 31 to get some simple coaching.

* * * * *

Things change far too slowly for most of us, but it is a fact that things are changing. People are changing. As we men begin to question the traditional meaning of "maleness" and reject those aspects of the traditional male role which have been oppressive to others and destructive to ourselves, we discover new ways to be men. After a 15-year break, I, for one, have taken up pitching a baseball to a friend who used to be a catcher. I throw exclusively submarine-style (almost underhand) which does not hurt my shoulder like overhand throwing always has. And we do it just for the simple joy of throwing and catching the ball.

As women become more and more visible and competent at tasks (including sports) that are traditionally "male territory," our conceptions of masculinity and femininity are being challenged. While watching women play softball, my professor friend learned something about the social basis for traditional differences between men and women. My sister not only plays softball, but coaches her 9-year-old daughter Jennifer's team, where she is determined to teach the girls how to throw a ball accurately and safely, among other things. And with this kind of role model and a changing social context, Jennifer is a girl who plays with a sense of enjoyment and confidence that was never allowed her mother. She loves to play. And she even loves to be the "bat-girl" for her father's city-league softball team. The first time she went to clear a bat away from home plate, she was confronted by a boy about her age who said to her derisively, "There's no such *thing* as a bat-*girl!*"

"Watch me," she replied.

Backwoods Boyhood

by Jim Long

My first memory of an attractive man was during my fifth year, when I saw my fourteen year old neighbor (the only other boy in my little town) go walking past my house, shirtless. I loved his body for years, secretly, watching him and his every muscle and move.

Rural areas make for unusual circumstances, and the very circumstance of being the only small boy in a small town had its own rewards and hazards. The rewards were attention, even camaraderie, from the older folks, sharing their ideas, opinions. The hazards were more numerous. First and foremost, I was the only one available to pick on, and so I was the favorite to pick on constantly. One old man delighted in holding me down and pulling my nipples every time he caught me shirtless. Another "kindly" old troll always hung around the only little grocery store in town (I would have sworn at age five that he lived there, waiting just for me), and whenever I would walk in, my father beside me, he would stop me for his little game. The game consisted of his pulling out his pocket knife, reaching down into my cut-offs and grabbing me by the balls saying "I'm going to cut those off and get rid of them for you" and then he and my father would nearly roll in laughter. Of course, I would laugh too, a sick little laugh, so as not to let them know how terrified I was of their game. The fear came from their game and an event of the same Summer. The only other child in my entire town of 98 people was a girl, one year older than myself. One day while playing some game or other with her, I undressed her, washed her clothes in a water hole, and to my horror discovered that the mean old troll had already gotten to her. So, in my 5-year-old mind, I believed she had been bad, the old man or someone else had castrated her, therefore she was a girl! That was the difference then, between boys and girls—girls were just boys that had been bad and had received their punishment. Needless to say, I was a perfect child, gave no one any trouble, never stole, lied, or did things I wasn't supposed to. I didn't even think bad thoughts and that was to be a problem in itself, later.

Coming from a rural area, I was privileged to experience a one-room school for my first three years of school (although I was the *only* kid in my class), along with outhouses, a big school bell, two mile hiking trips to other nearby schools for all-day baseball games, etc. (I graduated from high school in 1964, so this happened not that long ago, just a VERY backwoods area). This education system came equipped with a travelling music teacher, coming to our school two afternoons a month for a two-hour session of singing while he played the piano, always ending with my constant request for the "Chariot Race" and his playing it like it was the "12th Street Rag". I loved that man and his music. Actually I adored him, to be truthful.

With the fourth grade, the elections were over, bad feelings were still high and the school district had "consolidated"—been voted "in" by a neighboring town against our will, made to pay taxes and go to their larger school. Also with the fourth grade were boys, nearly as many in our room as there were kids in the entire school where I came from. Everyone did everything together, including go to the bathroom together, and of course, measure each others' cocks. I'd never been afraid in a bathroom, but suddenly someone measuring my cock became a fear-inspiring activity. Why measure? Some secret I didn't know about, or just seeing if everyone had one and if it was normal? What if mine wasn't "normal"? No one was going to measure mine. But they did, with their eyes, every time I hung it out at the urinal. The fear grew. In a short time I could no longer bring myself to piss with someone else watching (measuring... remembrances of the troll and his knife). Eventually I was not physically able, no matter how hard I tried or how badly I needed to piss, to do it with someone watching. I became quiet, anti-social, had imaginary friends, spent my time alone.

My seventh and eighth grade years were great. The old travelling music teacher was now my all-day teacher, for both of those years. He was witty, intelligent, interesting. I livened up, became more social, although I tried every scheme possible to avoid playing games with the other boys, since they were still a threat. I really enjoyed those two years, due to the teacher.

The Fall after leaving eighth grade for high school, I returned to my old school, my old room for a visit with "my old teach," who I still admired. It was late afternoon, we were alone, and with two sentences about copulation, ovulation and sex glands he unzipped my pants, reached into my shorts and pulled out my cock in one swift move. Here was a man I idolized, trusted, beating me off—my first time at masturbation as well as my first time with someone else doing it for me. I was in total shock. He was doing something "dirty," horrible to me, something I didn't understand, and him wanting to know all the while if it was "feeling good." I was too scared to know. When I came it felt like I was coming all over him. It made me angry that he had taken advantage of my trust. He had just finished wiping me off and was cleaning up the floor when my father drove up right beside the window where we were standing... my father who laughed at the old troll's castration-type games. No way I would ever tell my father what happened that day. No one would know for years and no one would would get that close to me again for years.

In high school the restrooms were even more crowded, threatening. Gym class was worse. All those assorted cocks dangling, all so different, all so intriguing. I became self-conscious even dressing, rather, undressing. What if I got an erection in the midst of all that, I would think. They'd know for sure I was liking what I saw, would they know the terrible thing the music teacher made me do? I was so naive, such a typical only-child.

My Summers were filled with swimming and fooling around doing Summer things. I'd get guys naked at every opportunity, just to see their bodies. It became a game, the one I became very good at, that of getting someone to willingly take their clothes off. I wrestled, poked around, but never any sex. Around age 16, I became very interested in a 13-year-old new neighbor boy. We swam and fished together a lot, and one day while swimming in my father's pond with my friend's older brother diving off the other end of the boat, the 13-year-old pulled his very hard cock up between my toes in the water. I got into the water and we played around, attempting to fuck each other, while keeping the very near-sighted brother diving at the other end of the boat. I was scared to death, felt guilty, but enjoyed it. On other occasions he would try to talk me into giving him a blow job, and though I fantasized about it, I couldn't bring myself to do it. The closest we came was nearly two years later on a camping trip, played around a lot, talked some, and finished off with a beat-off race. I fantasized about him for a couple of years, yearned to complete what he had started.

At no point did I ever admit to myself that I was gay. I felt it necessary to keep proving to everyone, and myself, that I wasn't "queer." I dated, took out an "easy lay" at about 19, laid her, except she just lay there, like a dumb log. I never got it up for her, didn't prove myself a man.

I went off to war, Viet Nam war, became lonely so far away from home, still trying to prove myself a man, still in love with the pretty boy back home. I met a woman, married to have a companion, one that "proved" I was a man. She had an affair with a friend of mine, and at age 25, I *consciously* realized that I craved a man. The guilt, the horror of that first thought. I was, I am, have always been "queer." My wife and I lived together ten years before we were divorced, and although the last three years of those ten my wife knew I was gay or bisexual, we eventually parted on very bitter terms. My children are 4 and 5 now, deprived of a father because I admitted I was gay. The children, the house, the cars, the business, all gone now. I'm allowed only two-hour visits with my girls, due to her bitterness and the 750 miles between us. The courts, the lawyers, family and friends, most all on her side.

I'm gay; I'm proud to be, for I've tried the alternatives, I've paid the prices. I've chosen, either in this lifetime or one before, that this life I'll spend loving people regardless of race or sex. Love is timeless and sexless and it's taken me 33 years of my life to discover it. Growing up gay in the backwoods is different than in any place in the world, but I'm not sorry that I experienced any of those things.

I grew up in these beautiful hills, left them for city life, city people, came out there, then returned to the land where I'd always *been* out, just never knew it. I'm home now, in the backwoods, searching out others who are trying to come out, making it easier maybe, for them than it was for me.

Pigskin, Patriarchy and Pain

by Don Sabo

I am sitting down to write as I've done thousands of times over the last decade. But today there's something very different. I'm not in pain.

A half-year ago I underwent back surgery. My physician removed two disks from the lumbar region of my spine and fused three vertebrae using bone scrapings from my right hip. The surgery is called a "spinal fusion." For seventy-two hours I was completely immobilized. On the fifth day, I took a few faltering first steps with one of those aluminum walkers that are usually associated with the elderly in nursing homes. I progressed rapidly and left the hospital after nine days completely free of pain for the first time in years.

How did I, a well-intending and reasonably gentle boy from western Pennsylvania ever get into so much pain? At a simple level, I ended up in pain because I played a sport that brutalizes men's (and now sometimes women's) bodies. *Why* I played football and bit the bullet of pain, however, is more complicated. Like a young child who learns to dance or sing for a piece of candy, I played for rewards and payoffs. Winning at sport meant winning friends and carving a place for myself within the male pecking order. Success at the "game" would make me less like myself and more like the older boys and my hero, Dick Butkus. Pictures of his hulking and snarling form filled my head and hung over my bed, beckoning me forward like like a mythic Siren. If I could be like Butkus, I told myself, people would adore me as much as I adored him. I might even adore myself. As an adolescent I hoped sport would get me attention from the girls. Later, I became more practical-minded and I worried more about my future. What kind of work would I do for a living? Football became my ticket to a college scholarship which, in western Pennsylvania during the early 'sixties, meant a career instead of getting stuck in the steelmills.

The Road to Surgery

My bout with pain and spinal "pathology" began with a decision I made in 1955 when I was 8 years old. I "went out" for football. At the time, I felt uncomfortable inside my body—too fat, too short, too weak. Freckles and glasses, too! I wanted to change my image, and I felt that changing my body was one place to begin. My parents bought me a set of weights, and one of the older boys in the neighborhood was solicited to demonstrate their use. I can still remember the ease with which he lifted the barbell, the veins popping through his bulging biceps in the summer sun, and the sated look of strength and accomplishment on his face. This was to be the image of my future.

That Fall I made a dinner-table announcement that I was going out for football. What followed was a rather inauspicious beginning. First, the initiation rites. Pricking the flesh with thorns until blood was drawn and having hot peppers rubbed in my eyes. Getting punched in the gut again and again. Being forced to wear a jockstrap around my nose and not knowing what was funny. Then came what was to be an endless series of proving myself: calisthenics until my arms ached; hitting hard and fast and knocking the other guy down; getting hit in the groin and not crying. I learned that pain and injury are "part of the game."

I "played" through grade school, co-captained my high school team, and went on to become an inside linebacker and defensive captain at the NCAA Division I level. I learned to be an animal. Coaches took notice of animals. Animals made first team. Being an animal meant being fanatically aggressive and ruthlessly competitive. If I saw an arm in front of me, I trampled it. Whenever blood was spilled, I nodded approval. Broken bones (not mine of course) were secretly seen as little victories within the bigger struggle. The coaches taught me to "punish the other man," but little did I suspect that I was devastating my own body at the same time. There were broken noses, ribs, fingers, toes and teeth, torn muscles and ligaments, bruises, bad knees, and busted lips, and the gradual pulverizing of my spinal column that, by the time my jock career was long over at age 30, had resulted in seven years of near-constant pain. It was a long road to the surgeon's office.

Now surgically freed from its grip, my understanding of pain has changed. Pain had gnawed away at my insides. Pain turned my awareness inward. I blamed myself for my predicament; I thought that I was solely responsible for every twinge and sleepless night. But this view was an illusion. My pain, each individual's pain, is really an expression of a linkage to an outer world of people, events, and forces. The origins of our pain are rooted *outside,* not inside, our skins.

The Pain Principle

Sport is just one of the many areas in our culture where pain is more important than pleasure. Boys are taught that to endure pain is courageous, to survive pain is manly. The principle that pain is "good" and pleasure is "bad" is crudely evident in the "no pain, no gain" philosophy of so many coaches and athletes. The "pain principle" weaves its way into the lives and psyches of male athletes in two fundamental ways. It stifles men's awareness of their bodies and limits our emotional expression. We learn to ignore personal hurts and injuries because they interfere with the "efficiency" and "goals" of the "team." We become adept at taking the feelings that boil up inside us—feelings of insecurity and stress from striving so hard for success—and channeling them in a bundle of rage which is directed at opponents and enemies. This posture toward oneself and the world is not limited to "jocks." It is evident in the lives of many nonathletic men who, as tough guys, deny their authentic physical or emotional needs and develop health problems as a result.

Today, I no longer perceive myself as an *individual* ripped off by athletic injury. Rather, I see myself as just *one more man among many men* who got swallowed up by a social system predicated on male domination. Patriarchy has two structural aspects. First, it is an hierarchical system in which men dominate women in crude and debased, slick and subtle ways. Feminists have made great progress exposing and analyzing this dimension of the edifice of sexism. But it is also a system of *intermale dominance*, in which a minority of men dominates the masses of men. This intermale dominance hierarchy exploits the majority of those it beckons to climb its heights. Patriarchy's mythos of heroism and its morality of power-worship implant visions of ecstasy and masculine excellence in the minds of the boys who ultimately will defend its inequities and ridicule its victims. It is inside this institutional framework that I have begun to explore the essence and scope of "the pain principle."

Taking It

Patriarchy is a form of social hierarchy. Hierarchy breeds inequity and inequity breeds pain. To remain stable, the hierarchy must either justify the pain or explain it away. In a patriarchy, women and the masses of men are fed the cultural message that pain is inevitable and that pain enhances one's character and moral worth. This principle is expressed in Judeo-Christian beliefs. The Judeo-Christian god inflicts or permits pain, yet "the Father" is still revered and loved. Likewise, a chief disciplinarian in the patriarchal family, the father has the right to inflict pain. The "pain principle" also echoes throughout traditional western sexual morality; it is better to experience the pain of *not* having sexual pleasure than it is to have sexual pleasure.

Most men learn to heed these cultural messages and take their "cues for survival" from the patriarchy. The Willie Lomans of the economy pander to the profit and the American Dream. Soldiers, young and old, salute their neo-Hun generals. Right-wing Christians genuflect before the idols of righteousness, affluence, and conformity. And male athletes adopt the visions and values that coaches are offering: to take orders, to take pain, to "take out" opponents, to take the game seriously, to take women, and to take their place on the team. And if they can't "take it," then the rewards of athletic camaraderie, prestige, scholarship, pro contracts, and community recognition are not forthcoming.

Becoming a football player fosters conformity to male-chauvinistic values and self-abusing lifestyles. It contributes to the legitimacy of a social structure based on patriarchal power. Male competition for prestige and status in sport and elsewhere leads to identification with the relatively few males who control resources and are able to bestow rewards and inflict punishment. Male supremacists are not born, they are made, and traditional athletic socialization is a fundamental contribution to this complex social-psychological and political process. Through sport, many males, indeed, learn to "take it"—that is, to internalize patriarchal values which, in turn, become part of their gender identity and conception of women and society.

My high school coach once evoked the pain principle during a pre-game peptalk. For what seemed an eternity, he paced frenetically and silently before us with fists clenched and head bowed. He suddenly stopped and faced us with a smile. It was as though he had approached a podium to begin a long-awaited lecture. "Boys," he began, "people who say that football is a 'contact sport' are dead wrong. Dancing is a contact sport. Football is a game of pain and violence! Now get the hell out of here and kick some ass." We practically ran through the wall of the locker room, surging in unison to fight the coach's war. I see now that the coach was right but for all the wrong reasons. I should have taken him at his word and never played the game!

A Month in the Life of a High School Homo

by Eric Peterson

I moved to Roseburg from North Hollywood about a week before Thanksgiving because I thought the change of atmosphere would do me good. In N.H. I was a full closet case. I did the whole trip of looking up homosexuality in the library and being afraid I'd be caught. About two months after I moved here, I met Billy and adopted the more political side of being gay and came out to my family and then at school. I went the whole hog. I put GALA Hotline stockers on my notebooks and on teachers' bulletin boards and whenever anyone made a comment about me being gay I challenged them to argue.

Throughout this I believed I made a difference in their attitudes toward gays and in the hearts of people in the closet. I think I still believe that.

February 22, 1983

I was sitting in the VO-TECH building and the guy at the table next to me asked why my earring was in my right lobe. I told him it was just an earring and didn't mean anything. He *told me* it was because I am a fag. I asked him what he thought about gay people and he told me that in his opinion gays were sick. We debated for a few minutes and we agreed that it was within his rights to believe that.

February 24, 1983

The principal wouldn't allow me to post Gay and Lesbian Hotline stickers, but he accepted seven of them for the counselors.

February 25, 1983

Today in my sixth period Science class, after the rumor that I liked the looks of one of my classmates got around and the snickering was getting numbing, I loudly proclaimed my liking for his looks. The class got kind of rowdy and I ranted for a minute about my knowledge of their conversations on the matter beforehand. Then they got quiet.

March 9, 1983

Walking from first to second period a group of six or seven guys were walking behind me and jeering. I stopped and turned to them and asked them my patented "What's wrong with gay people? I don't understand." "WEIRD!" They shouted as they kept walking, making threats while staring at the floor. A short blond one looked me in the eye and called me "queer-fag."

At nutrition break the blond who called me "queer-fag" said it again. I stopped and asked him questions. He told me to get out of the school, out of Roseburg and said I need my nuts cut off or my head bashed in. Scary stuff!

And the voices around me keep on shouting. QUEER, FAG, etc. as I make my way between classes, in the smoke line and at lunch.

March 10, 1983

I've lost only one friend and only one person has moved from sitting next to me in class.

In the smoke line at nutrition break a guy made a comment about my "queerness" and its relation to the butterflies on my jacket. I went up to him and he started to get all flared up. I asked him why my being gay affected him so. He asked me why I didn't leave Roseburg and move to L.A. or Frisco where all the other queers are, or better yet where the INSANE ASYLUM was. A teacher tried to calm him down then took him away. By this time the crowd was talking amongst themselves or cheering the guy. After the conflict one of the jocks went up to the guy and asked him why he got so freaked out. He (the jock) told him that its OK to be different. Then about three girls came over and gave support and expressed their anger at their ignorance. They told me I had a lot of people on my side. As I left the smoke line the "jock" told me "Don't be afraid to come to the line."

March 11, 1983

In between first and second period I was pushed into the bathroom in the "Humanities" building. Four or five guys were there, one hovered over me. One stood at the urinal. The one at the urinal turned around and zipped up, it was the blond. The theatrics of the situation were impressed on me and . . . whatever. Anyway the blond said some things to me and the group by the door said some things and the blond kept kicking me in the groin, luckily no dead hits. He also punched me on the jaw. I fell back and hit my head on the sink (which raised a small lump!), kicked me some more, then left. I went to the principal and he expressed "professional" concern for my welfare in and around school.

The voices continued shouting, QUEER, FAG, etc. as I sauntered between classes, in the smoke line and at lunch.

March 14, 1983

Between first and second the guy who pushed me into the bathroom punched me in the jaw twice. Again I tried to talk, but it didn't affect him. The blond was edging him on. Occasionally my girl friends will walk by me to protect me or to put themselves in my place for a few minutes.

I've been advised by my family and the school faculty to "lay low" until the school quiets down.

At lunch today a group of guys were sitting at the table next to me. They were making cracks to each other and giggling alot. They asked me a dumb sex-oriented question and when I ignored them one of them expressed his anger (in a low voice) at being ignored. I quietly informed them that I was at a loss to understand why they were so negative to someone they didn't know, simply because he was gay. One of them told me it was because I played "head games." The "head games" were pertinent questions about their feelings about themselves when it came to homosexuality. At the table to my other side sat a girl and a guy commenting on the group's childishness and lack of compassion for someone in my position. Then a guy walking past the group asked them if they liked me because they're always hanging around and bugging me.

March 15, 1983

Today the blond who kicked me in the bathroom and the one who punched me in the jaw were suspended for about a week. The blond's stepbrother commented to his friends that the blond was mean and out for revenge.

March 16, 1983

Left school after sixth out of fear.

March 17, 1983

On my way to school the green jeep that passes me every morning carrying a pair of namecallers pulled up into the gas station I was passing. They called out "Queer, cocksucker," then threw tomatoes or apples and I heard a bottle crash. I really can't be too sure of what the crash was, I was too afraid to turn around. At school a group of about nine started jeering me, I took the hint. And considering it was the last day before spring break. I left.

Haiti: A Memory Journey

by Assotto Saint

I was born on October 2, 1957, one week after Francois Duvalier ("Papa Doc") was elected President. He had been a brilliant doctor and a writer of great verve from the Griots (negritude) movement. Until that time, the accepted images of beauty in Haiti, the images of "civilization" tended to the European. Fair skin and straight hair were better than dark and kinky. Duvalier was black pride. Unlike the previous dictators who had ruled the country continuously since its independence from the French in 1804, Duvalier was not and did not surround himself with mulattoes, a mixed-race group which controlled the economy. Duvalier brought voodoo to the forefront of our culture and later in his reign, used it to tyrannize the people.

I grew up in Les Cayes, a sleepy port city of 20,000 in southwest Haiti, where nothing much happened. Straight As, couldn't play soccer, ran like a girl, cute powdered face, silky eyebrows—I was the kind of child folks saw and thought quick something didn't click. I knew very early on that I was "different" and I was often reminded of the fact by schoolmates. "Massici" (faggot), they'd tease me. That word to this day sends shivers down my spine but, being the town's best behaved child, a smile, a kind word were my winning numbers.

We—mother (a registered nurse anesthetist), grandfather (a lawyer who held at one time or another, each of the town's top official posts, from mayor on down), grandmother and I—lived in a big beautiful house facing the Cathedral. The Catholic Mass, especially High Mass on Sundays and holy days, with its colorful pageantry, trance-inducing liturgy and theatrical ceremony, spellbound me. That incense took me heaven-high each time. I was addicted and I attended Mass every day. Besides, I had other reasons. I had developed a mad crush on the parish priest, a handsome Belgian who sang like a bird.

I must have been seven when I realized my attraction to men. Right before first communion, confused and not making sense I confessed to this priest. Whether he understood me or not, he gave me absolution and told me to say a dozen Hail Marys. Oh Lord, did I pray! Still, girls did nothing for me. Most of my classmates had girlfriends to whom they sent passionate love poems and sugar candies and whom they took to movies on Sunday afternoons. All I wanted to do with girls was skip rope, put makeup on their faces and comb their hair. I was peculiar.

Knowing that I probably would never marry, I decided that I wanted to be a priest when I grew up. For one, priests are celibate. Two, I had noticed that many were effeminate. Some even lisped like me. I built a little altar in my bedroom with some saints' pictures, plastic lillies and colored candles. Dressed in my mother's petticoat and nurse's uniform, I said Mass every night. The Archbishop of Haiti, Francois W.Ligonde, a childhood friend of my mother, even saw my little church when he visited my family. I was so proud. Everybody felt that I'd be the perfrect priest except my mother, whom I later found out wanted me to become a doctor like my father—who I never met, never saw pictures of, never heard mention of and accepted as a non-entity in my life.

I used to believe that I was born by Immaculate Conception until one day, I was ridiculed in school by my science teacher who had asked me for my father's name. When I told him of my belief, he laughed and got the entire class to laugh along. Until then, I had never questioned the fact that my last name was the same as that of my mother who was not married. It was then that I smelled foul play and suspected that I was the result of sexual relations between my mother and grandfather. I didn't dare ask.

In the early 1960s, Papa Doc declared himself President-for-Life and things got worse. I remember hearing of anti-Duvalier suspects being arrested. I remember hearing of families being rounded up, even babies killed. I remember the mysterious disappearances at night, the mutilated corpses found by roads and rivers the next day. I remember the public slayings. Adults sending my cousins and me to another room so they could whisper. Rumors of invasions by exiled Haitians abounded. Some of these invasions were quickly stopped by government forces. The *tons tons macoutes* (bogeymen) were everywhere, with their rifles slung over their shoulders and their eyes of madness and cruelty.

Poverty was all around me and in my child's mind I had accepted this. Some had, some had not. Fate. Cyclones, hurricanes, floods came and went. Carnival was always a happy time though. Dressed in costumes, I along with thousands took to the streets each year with our favorite calypso and meringue bands. Grandmother died of a kidney infection during Mardi Gras '65. I cried for weeks and kept a daily journal to her. Soon after, mother left for Switzerland. I moved in with Aunt Marcelle and her husband.

In 1968, my aunt had her first and only child. Was I jealous! I had been quite comfortable and so spoiled for three years that when she gave birth to Alin, it was difficult for me to accept that I was not her real child, a fact I'd at times forgotten. That year she gave me a beautiful birthday party. My schoolmates were making fun of me more than ever. I still wanted to become a priest. I said a Mass for Martin Luther King and Bobby Kennedy when each got murdered. Duvalier declared himself the flag of the nation and became more ruthless. I took long walks on the beach by myself. It was a year of discovery.

One afternoon, as I walked on the beach, I saw Pierre swimming alone. He called me to join him. I was surprised. Although we went to the same school and had spoken to each other once or twice, we were not buddies. Three or four years older, tall and muscular Pierre was a member of the volleyball team. I didn't have a swimsuit so I swam naked. I remember the uneasiness each time our eyes met; the tension between us; my hard-on. We kept smelling each other out. He grabbed me by the waist. I felt his hard dick pressing against my belly. Taut smiles. I held it in my hand and it quivered. I had never touched another boy's dick before. I asked him if he had done this with other boys. He said only with girls. Waves.

He turned me around and pushed his dick in my ass. Shock. I remember the pain. Hours later, the elation I felt, knowing that another person who was like me existed. In Les Cayes, there had been rumors about three or four men who supposedly were homosexual, but they had all been married. Some had no less than seven children. Knowing Pierre was a turning point for me. The loneliness of thinking that I was the only one with homosexual tendencies subsided.

In 1969, man walked on the moon, I was so happy. Pierre and I met each other three or four times (once in my grandfather's study and he almost caught us). I didn't say anything about this to anyone. Not even in confession. I didn't pray as much. I passed my certificat which is like graduating from Junior High School in the U.S. Mother moved from Geneva to New York City where I visited her in the summer of 1970.

New York to me was the Empire State Building, the Statue of Liberty, hot dogs and hamburgers, white people everywhere, museums, rock music, 24-hour television, stores, stores, stores and subways.

I remember the day I decided to stay in the U.S. A week before I was to go back to Haiti, my mother and I were taking a trip to Coney Island. Two effeminate guys in outrageous shorts walked onto the train and sat in front of us. Noticing that I had kept looking at them, my mother said to me that this was the way it was here. People could say and do whatever they wanted; a few weeks earlier, thousands of homosexuals had marched for their rights.

Thousands! I was stunned. I kept thinking what it would be like to meet some of them. I kept thinking that there was a homosexual world I knew nothing of. I remember looking up in amazement when we walked beneath the elevated train then telling my mother I didn't want to go back to Haiti. She warned me of snow, muggers, homesickness, racism, alien cards and that I would have to learn to speak English. She warned me that our lives wouldn't be a vacation. She would have to go back to work as a night nurse in a week and I'd have to assume many responsibilities. After all, she was a single mother.

That week, I asked her about my father and found out that they had been engaged for four years while she was in nursing school and he in medical school. She got pregnant and he wanted her to abort. A baby would have been a burden so early in their careers, especially since they planned to move to New York after they got married. Mother wouldn't abort. She couldn't. Though the two families tried to avoid a scandal and patch things up, accusations were made, feelings hurt. Each one's decision final, they became enemies for life.

Arranging a meeting with my father was not as difficult as I had thought it would be. Leaving myself wide open with a phone call, I spoke to him for the first time and informed him that I would soon be flying to Haiti to meet him. He'd expected this all my life. I remember the pauses, the uneasiness as he addressed me as "Mr." while I called him "Doctor Mercier."

My friends were happy for me, especially Counsel who was dying of AIDS and felt that in this age of health crisis, I needed to complete my relationship with my father while I still had time. "One never knows," he used to say. Jan, my significant other, promised to fly down with me. He had always complained that my father was everywhere in my poems, my performance pieces, my plays, yet invisible in my life.

Mother was not pleased and warned me as usual that my father was a "low-down pig." Still on June 1, 1983, I went to Haiti. I went so I could stop living in so many questions. I went to discover some meaning and understanding of myself, my mother, him. I went out of hunger and wonder. I went to break new ground.

He drove to Villa Creole where Jan and I were staying, ten minutes after I called. He brought along my half-sister and half-brother (either he was scared or they genuinely wanted to meet me, like he said). I was surprised that they had known about me. I'll never forget the first time I saw my father standing in the hotel lobby, the first time we looked at each other, the first time we shook hands. Jan claims I was dazed. I remember I kept thinking that our resemblance was striking: same lips; same height; same complexion; same body posture. Carbon copy. I look much more like him than did either my half-brother or my half-sister. I also remember their suspicious eyes when I introduced Jan as a close friend—the formality of that first brief encounter, the coolness.

Wishing to discuss further certain matters, we made an appointment for the next day. When he didn't show up 45 minutes after the time we had agreed on, I called him. He stated that he had never made such an agreement. I reminded him that three other people had been witnesses and that I'd come to Haiti to meet him and clarify certain things. He still denied it. Jan took the phone and cursed him out. My last comment before I hung up was that I expected him at the hotel within the hour.

He arrived in a rage. Insults were exchanged; he told Jan to butt out. Jan shouted that he cared about me and that I didn't deserve to be treated in such a way. A fight ensued between them. I sat on the bed watching this mad scene. This was not my vision. This was not the reunion of my plans. I separated them and desperate to mend matters, sent Jan out of the room, then apologized to my father.

He went on in his tirade about how foreigners should stay out of Haiti, how Americans had ruined the country and given it a bad name. Those remarks didn't register until later. I let him vent his spleen until he ticked my last nerve. He told me with friends like Jan, he wondered what kind of person I was. I literally picked him up, threw him out of the room and slammed the door.

Jan came back soon after to find out what had happened. He had seen my father in the hotel lobby. I distinctly remember pinching myself, to make sure it was not a nightmare. I remember the diarrhea. I couldn't breathe. I was choking. I told Jan I wanted to get a gun. I wished my father dead. Jan wanted to call American Airlines and get us out of Haiti as soon as possible.

Half an hour later, the phone rang. Jan answered. It was my father. Jan asked me if I wished to speak to him. I said no. Jan advised me to hear what he had to say. Against my better judgment, I did. He apologized and asked if he could come back to the room. We had waited 26 years and couldn't start then end like this.

When he knocked, Jan held me, kissed me then went out for a swim. Father and I shook hands and sat at opposite ends of the room—silent, testing each other, waiting, not knowing where to begin. Then the questions poured out of me, fast and furious. There were outright lies, vague answers, semi-confessions for each which gave me a clear awful picture of him. Fine. At least I asked.

One hour into our conversation, I noticed that he had kept looking at my hands. He grabbed them and held them next to him. Similar size...similar shape...similar hairs. It was then that he asked me to apologize to my mother for 26 years of denial—for a scandal she had survived. It was then that we touched—flesh and blood. It was then, for the first and only time, that to me, he became real...loving...father.

I forget how the conversation turned to AIDS, but he asked why I was so interested. I told him that my best friend had been diagnosed and that I wanted to know what the situation was in Haiti. He asked if my friend was Haitian. I said no but that he was gay. I remember his pause. I knew what he was thinking and told him that I, too, am gay. I told him of my fear, when in 1981 the first reported AIDS cases hit the news, that out of the four "high-risk" groups then cited, I fit into half.

Pandemonium. Tears flowed. Mother always said that he was a damned good actor, and perform he did. He said that my gayness was God's punishment upon him. I became gay because I didn't have a father figure. He had to do something about it. I told him I was quite comfortable with my gayness; I had written on the subject and I didn't need to change. Mother and her whole side of the family had accepted it, welcomed Jan, and treated us as a couple. He calmed down somewhat then asked why I had really come to Haiti. Thinking he meant money, I told him that I was quite capable of taking care of myself, and did not expect anything from him.

I thanked him for his time and answers, then escorted him to the hotel lobby. We shook hands as formally as when we had first met. No promises made. No embrace. Shattered dreams on both sides.

Jan and I stayed in Haiti for three more days. We drove to my hometown.

The roads were in better shape but the mentality hadn't changed much. Pierre didn't live where he used to. I wondered what had become of him. Had he married? Had he had children? Had he come to the States? Was he gay? Did he remember me? The majority of my classmates I found out, had either moved to Port-au-Prince or abroad. If anybody had told me 20 years ago that most of us wouldn't continue living in Les Cayes, I would have thought it was a bad joke.

My aunt and uncle were happy to see us. Alin their son was big for 15. My grandfather, young and vigorous at 88, was now Chief Justice of the Court. The Cathedral stood as majestic as ever. Four or five new restaurants had opened, as well as three or four small hotels, yet there were few tourists. Faces had no visions. Hands reached out for anything. The *tons tons macoutes* with their uzis sped through the streets in open Jeeps. Jean-Claude Duvalier ("Baby Doc"), whose father had passed him the presidency before he died in 1971, had not done much. The 90° heat hit us hard.

The morning of our departure for New York, I discussed with Jan my need for closeness, ties and happiness between my father and me. Maybe a phone call with nothing to lose could create that possibility. I spoke to my half-brother who was rather curt, and asked him to tell my father to please call me before noon; that I'd be at the hotel all morning. While we were eating breakfast, the waiter delivered a handwritten note which the desk clerk had taken. It said: "It was good that we finally met. Long overdue. Good luck. Bon voyage. Doctor Mercier. P.S. Be healthy." I crushed that note in my hand and imagined it was his heart.

Rape: A Personal Account

by David Sunseri

Dear Brothers,

I am enclosing an account of an experience I had many years ago, almost eighteen to be exact. It was by far the most traumatic experience of my life, and I have a real need to share it with you all at this particular time. I guess it has to do with "coming out" as a person who has been raped, which I feared to do for so long. I'm not afraid any more and need to express that.

I love M. and feel a closeness with the men who write and share their wonderful (and also difficult) experiences, ideas and feelings. I'm thankful that M. exists and that there are men who support women in their struggle, and who also support other men like me trying to change.

Much love and peace,

David Sunseri
Santa Cruz, CA

I was raped in late February, 1967, at the old Avalon Ballroom in San Francisco. I was with a group of friends at a rock concert headlining Quicksilver Messenger Service and B.B. King. I was young not only in age but in experience. I didn't realize then that a man could be raped.

That evening we had all "dropped" mescaline and were feeling very close to one another. When we entered the ballroom, I remember the warmth and openness that pervaded the evening. We were so beautiful then; we were the messengers of peace. That night we were high and wanted to go higher. It was 1967—the summer of love was ahead of us.

The young women and men I lived with decided to hang out down in front of the stage. My lover, Elaine, and I wanted to check out the crowd to see who we knew. We were separated in the crush of bodies. I was very stoned and feeling an incredible openness to everyone we saw. I loved the world that night. Three men asked me if I wanted to share a joint. I went with them downstairs behind the stage to a small room.

We stepped inside. They had huge smiles on their faces and their eyes were wide and wild. Before I was aware of anything being wrong, two of the men grabbed me and pushed me down. The other pulled at my long hair and spit in my face. I struggled, although I felt I had no strength. Also the drugs were somehow inhibiting my action. I felt totally vulnerable and begged them not to hurt me. They laughed. I heard my father's voice in the back of my mind, "I'm a lover not a fighter." I was my father's son.

The men kept calling me cutie and sweetie, names guys use when they're trying to seduce women. They tore off my Levi's and ripped off my T-shirt. I was beneath them, naked and fighting. They were large men. I was wiry and not strong enough to get away. At that moment, I thought I was going to die. I began to shake uncontrollably, and that seemed to egg them on. Then they each raped me. I had never, nor have since, felt such pain, such complete raw pain. Two held me down while the third forced himself against me. They changed positions. Took turns. When they were done, I lay bleeding and whimpering on the dirty floor. I remember them saying as they left, "fucking dirty hippie." This was the dawning of the age of Aquarius, and the sun was in that sign.

I put my Levi's back on and sat in the corner of the room. I was still shaking, looking at my bare feet which were cut and bleeding. My whole body hurt, and there were scratches and marks on my chest, stomach, arms and legs. My back felt bruised, and I was bleeding from my ass. I was petrified and hysterical, not understanding what had happened. I made my way back to the concert. Two women noticed me and helped me find my friends. When my housemates saw me they were shocked. I wasn't able to talk; I shook uncontrollably and was crying. They reported what had happened to a cop; the police questioned me in the offices of the Avalon. I made little sense and was barely able to speak. Then I blacked out.

I regained consciousness in the emergency room of St. Mary's Hospital where I received treatment. My friends stayed close to me through the whole ordeal, holding me and reassuring me that I would be alright. Their love kept me sane. That night we returned to our house, and my lover, Elaine, and my closest male friend, Tony, slept with me, one on each side. I slept little that night, but they were there for me, keeping me safe from harm and from the memory of the attack.

Soon I was in therapy and dealing with all the feelings that had surfaced. It took years for me to regain my self-esteem. The era of the flower children may have ended in 1968; for me, it ended a year earlier, on a cold night in February.

I know about rape. I know the complete emptiness of spirit that is the initial response to rape, the intense fear of people, of men, of closeness to anyone. I know the guilt, the self-hatred, the loss of dignity, the feeling of helplessness, of anger and frustration. I have the scars on my body, and those healed in my heart.

This is the first time I have written openly and described this terrible experience. I do it for myself, to let it go a little more. I do it for all those who have been raped or battered, so together we can exorcize this demon from our lives and expose it to all the world. No more rape. No more rape. And finally I do it to let go of the hatred I've felt for those three men who were as truly victims as I was. I hate the act but not those people any longer. For that I'm thankful.

On The Job
excerpts from a workingman's journal

by John Ceely

Sunday, January 28, 1973

The first week Shelby and I were hired—we're the two newest men—Big Hal grabbed Shelby into the air and rocked him like a baby in the void over the sewer pipe ditch. Had he let go, Shelby would have dropped 20 feet onto bedrock. Everybody laughed.

Monday, June 4, 1973

The wall they were starting was only about 10 feet from the sidewalk, and some of the bricklayers were saying "Hi!" to the pretty girls that walked past. One stunningly beautiful young student, braless, long hair and healthy, smiled shyly and chirped back, "Hi!"

The guys melted. Nobody said, "How'd ya like ta come home with me?" No one muttered, "Now ain't *she* a loose one!"

She was too close and personal.

Tuesday, January 16, 1973

Shelby and I came on the job the same day and we both got Hal's heavy kidding treatment: "Hey John, ya got a picture of yer wife naked?" "No, and if I did, you think I'd show it to you?" "Well *I* got a picture of her naked. How much ya gimme for it?"

Pretty soon I learned to be more aggressive (with a big grin on my mug). "Hey John, does yer wife bite yer cock when she blows ya?" "No, but your wife does. That's why I quit going with her. But she told me she had a guy lined up that liked to have his cock bit. Name was Hal, she said."

Hal would smile, and we'd razz-ma-tazz back and forth. When Hal gave Shelby the same treatment Shelby sulked. If he kept at it long enough, Shelby got mad. A stylized kind of mad—Hal being 6 foot 5 and solid as a crowbar.

Wednesday, January 27, 1971—Don

Fingernails fractured and purple
bruised knuckled
tanned hide to his hand
battered animal claw
     nicks and scabs.

Even stacking steel beams
     he won't wear gloves.

Monday, March 28, 1982

Two guys stand at a power buggy loaded with cement, one guy on either side,
and they race each other shoveling the concrete out of the buggy and into the
wall forms. Their shoulders start to ache, they're panting at the edge of swoon,
and the buggy's only half empty. The older guy is matching the younger guy dive
for dive, but he wants to yell, "Jesus, we're on the same side! Aren't we? Why the
fuck don't we shovel this stuff out at a reasonable speed?" But the kid's 25 and
worried about getting laid off, and the older guy is 45 and even more worried.
They try to kill each other.

Tuesday, September 12, 1972

At 8:00 A.M. I get to the house where we're going to work. We're going to
pour the basement and garage this morning. The cement truck's here, but the
driver's looking at the motor. He walks over to where we're standing in a group.
"The fuel pump's busted. I'm gonna put a call to the mechanic."

There's nothing we can do till the mechanic comes, so Ted, Bob, Fred, Doug,
and I stand or squat near our cars and shoot the shit.

Bob's talking about his pickup, "I never knew a Ford transmission to fuck up
the way this one does. I seen plenty o' lousy International transmissions but this is
the first Ford I ever seen it happen."

"Oh, you get lemons in every brand."

Bob again: "Remember that Chevy Tom Berger used to drive to work?
Ja-*hee*-zus! The goddamned stick for the stick shift broke off one day, so he
takes my vise-grips out o' my tool box and clamps *them* things on there. *For
three goddamned months* we had to shift that thing with them vise-grips. By
Jesus, the day I quit I took them vise-grips home with me. I dunno how the fuck
he drove his truck home. I didn't *give* a fuck, neither."

Quiet, warm rattle of talk. Getting to know one another. It's okay, it's okay.
Each in effect is saying to the others, "I feel pretty okay being here working with
you guys."

Tuesday, January 30, 1973

Everybody snapping at everybody else. Fred our foreman was Snapper
Number One. We didn't see who was snapping down on *him*, probably

somebody in the office. Fred made it seem like we were doing everything wrong, and us flunkies below tried to shift the blame onto each other's head.

Snapping is uncontrollable jitters wanting out. You walk around with a shovel in your hand wondering what you're spposed to do, and Fred barks at you, "Get the goddamned cable around the pipe, so I can at least get it into the air." (Whereas yesterday he told us be sure and have the rings and gaskets on before you raise 'em up.) You wonder if maybe Fred thinks you're a dumb cluck and ought to get fired at the first layoff; after all, manholes aren't all that special a situation, and probably Fred feels you ought to *know* the pipe's got to be raised up first when it's going into a manhole; so you're worried the rest of the morning that you'll make the fatal false move, some *really* dumb, absent-minded move. So when you and Shelby are driving over to pick up cement block and Shelby makes a wrong turn in full view of the whole crew you yell at the dumb son of a bitch because Fred might be watching and think it's *your* fault.

Snapping at your co-workers comes from fear. It's usually not premeditated or malicious. I try to let snaps wash off my back. No need to add another link in the chain. After getting snapped at (except by Fred) I find it best to answer the person, tell him plainly why I did what I did. Let him know I am accepting no blame for petty human fallibility.

Tuesday, June 24, 1971

Mel's a big, swaggering student, a 220 pounder. Blue eyes, blond short hair. He's a zoology major, has a wife and kid. His hips are wide like a chopping block, his torso sits above them like a barrel. He's not muscular, he's beefy. A corn-fed Wisconsin boy. Works construction every summer to get through the University.

On the job Mel undergoes a transformation. Every other word becomes "fuckin." He throws himself into the work, rushes for what he takes to be the manliest jobs—cement hose operator, power buggy operator—anything involving phallic locomotive machinery.

Comes a lull in the work, Mel begins his reminiscences. Flat-footed, arched back, belly sticking out: *"Jee-sus kee-riist!* You shudda seen that dumb cock sucker. Why, the sonovabitch couldn't even get the fuckin Bobcat started."* His assumed stud voice is an oily singsong, almost a whine. He speaks through tightly pursed lips, and if he pauses he leaves his upper teeth showing, as he absently gazes at other workers in distant corners of the job site. Then he'll start again, not loud, that same oily singsong (restrained, modest); he's a big man taking his break, a nice guy who likes to talk with the boys and can back up all his claims.

Friday, December 5, 1981

Hank is 60, the oldest guy on the job. I worked with him all day. He looks straight at me out of clear blue eyes. His face is round and firm, with deep creases but no wrinkles. His hair is thin, but still dark, dark brown, and crew cut. Hank is burly, and he walks stoop-shouldered, hunched a little forward. Long, loping strides with plenty of armswing.

"I'm a Irish Swede. How do ya like that? My mother was Irish and my dad was a Swede . . .

"I never got much schoolin', really, I learned figures, though. Nobody can bluff me at figurin'. Readin'? Not so good. I can read, but I'm slow. I like it better when somebody reads *to* me . . .

"I quit school when I was fourteen, went to work in a loggin' camp. It was on the bluffs, north of the Wisconsin River. That was the Depression, you know. I *had* ta work. The truck come and got us Sunday night and took us to the camp. We provided our own blankets. We slept, worked, and et up there. We worked Saturday, too. We worked six days a week in them days. Then the truck would take us home Saturday night . . . .

"I worked on a two-man crosscut saw. They didn't start usin' chainsaws, really, 'til after the war. She was 6 foot long. You didn't push on 'er, you pulled. You didn't bear on 'er, neither. The guy I was teamed up with was about forty. Nice fella. You end up settin' on your knees and sawin' in the snow. Now do you understand why we was wet all the time? And coldern a sonovabitch! We never took no clothes off to sleep.

"All winter long we worked. At night we'd sit around in the sleepin' shack filin' our saws—we had a pot bellied stove in there—and some a the men would tell stories. We was too pooped to do much else . . .

"Summers, I worked around, on farms mostly. 'Til the war come . . .

"Yep, I was in the service. North Africa. Then they shipped me home. Then they shipped me to the Pacific. All them islands: Iwo Jima, Okinawa . . . I was back in the infantry. Even today, I see a Jap and my back goes up. After all that time . . .

"When I got outa the service I joined the union. Oh, I was farmin', too, for awhile. But that's awful fuckin' tough, tryin' ta run a farm *and* go to a job every day. I finally give up farmin' . . . .

"I been a foreman for a couple outfits. If they let me work 'longside the men, it wasn't so bad, but when they'd tell me I can't work, I just gotta watch the men, that's when I'd get tired . . . Shit, yes, I get tired now! After 4 o'clock if I stop movin', I fall right ta sleep. But it was worse when I was foreman and just watchin' the men. I ain't shittin' ya!"

Wednesday, May 19, 1976

Mark sent Toby and me out to the boneyard this morning. We were piling 4 by 4s all day. Thank God. I could never have faced those beams.

I can't write my way out of this impasse. Somehow I've got to walk my way out—on the beams.

Yesterday as I stood 25 feet under Spike and watched him hopping along the 5-inch wide beams overhead. I began to understand. The big-mouthed practioners of yoga, the young businessmen, all the poets and squabbling professors: they are physical and spiritual babies compared to this high school dropout, this unliterate loner who has learned to live with the fear of death.

It's a mistake to imagine Spike is "insensitive" to fear. When he was going up the freight elevator with me for lunch-break last Friday, Spike told me, "I fell last year. I cracked 3 ribs and cut my neck. I missed a month and a half of work. I landed on a 4 by 4, that's the trouble, otherwise I probably wouldn't have cracked by ribs. For two fucking weeks I had to sleep sitting up. It hurt every time I breathed. When I got back to work I wouldn't go up on the beams for five weeks. Even now I don't like to do it. If somebody else'll go up, I always work on the ground. I go up when Mark tells me to, but otherwise..."

Spike admits to feeling fear. And yet, as I watched him up there yesterday I was awed by his slow, unwobbling precision. No trembling, no grabbing, no fast moves.

Monday, August 27, 1973

I used to dread being around when a mason yells, "OK boys, it's about time to raise us up." I used to tighten up, secrete adrenalin, and invariably end up confused and overpowered by their 16-foot feeder plank. Yesterday Smitty helped me raise their plank.

"It works easier if you stand on the outrigger and just lift the plank straight up."

"Stand on the outrigger! Christ. That ain't much holding you. I'll try it." We were working 25 feet about the ground, and I was shaky.

Smitty was right. It puts your feet higher so you get that extra 16 inches of lift.

Now, whenever the call comes to raise the plank, I know I can do it. I move deliberately.

Friday, May 28, 1976

Orange disk in the sky. Sun just before setting. Long, slanting distance of atmosphere filters out the injurious, high-energy rays so I can look directly at the huge exploding ball. It sits 2 inches above our horizon. Every movement on earth; every warm, lubricated, re-combination of sliding molecules; every growth; every expenditure or transfer of energy: the power for all this movement comes from that exploding, burning, shearing, fusing sun.

A guy with a paunch walks down the sidewalk trailing his little black dog on a leash. Evening piss. Those two creatures, their energy, their consciousness, the metabolic smokestacks that their bodies are—all of this was and is from the sun.

The sun gives Sara and I our flash when we make love.

What about gravity? I was scared to the point of shame today up on the beams. Bernie did the plank-carrying work that was clarly mine, and he did it because I was too slow, too hesitant.

If I were to slip on the wet gypsum that coated some of those beams I'd flash 12 feet down to hard concrete floor. It would more than just "hurt."

The mass of earth below was yanking at me to come down. Like I was meant to walk on ground, not balancing on sticks of steel 12 feet above concrete floor which itself was 100 feet above earth's dirt. This whole building is cold, hard, heartless greed and calculation, and we build it at our peril.

Wasting our sun-loaned energy erecting this rigid stack of pennies. Sun and earth have *already* established their natural balance. Sun's gravity pulls earth around and around and never lets go. Earth forever facing and softening to the light.

What am I doing up on slippery steel beams? I should be home with Sara.

Singing Off The Beat

by Tom Wilson Weinberg

My fascination with muscial theatre developed at about the age of six. Though I was no prodigy, I *felt* muscial. I memorized songs and sang for myself. My younger brother and I staged Broadway musicals in puppet-scale productions. My older brother was a self-taught guitar-playing rock-and-roller.

The primary muscial influence on me was my mother. When I was a child she was a talented pianist. She hasn't played for years but I still remember her sound, her technique, her terrific sight reading. My mother's interest in music probably came from her mother who was a proud and fearless amateur opera singer. My Grandmother Rosetta had a little training and a lot of tremolo; I still remember her for having a beautiful voice.

In fourth grade I decided to take up clarinet. I really wanted to play flute but it seemed that only girls chose this delicate instrument. My father bought me a clarinet. I took lessons, joined the band and marched all the way to college. At age 12, I added piano, taking lessons for a year and fighting it all the way. As soon as my mother let me quit I started playing for a few hours every night after dinner. I played the Broadway tunes, I improvised, I created orchestras in my head.

In junior high school I entered and won a competition for composing a new school song. The chorus I was afraid to audition for sang my song and I took a bow afterwards. I sang in the shower but not for another person. In most ways I was not a shy kid, but I was afraid to sing. I hadn't yet learned what I know now: everyone can sing.

I was in college in the Sixties. It was a Big Decade in which to become an adult, to learn some hard political realities, to begin the process of coming to terms with my gayness, to mourn in despair for John Kennedy and Bobby and Martin Luther King. My major was English literature but my main acitivity was musical theatre. I wrote music for, and performed in, an annual musical revue. I danced and even sang in a chorus line. We rehearsed for months, had a six week run and then went on tour over Spring break. In the summers I wrote and directed camp shows. For whatever reasons, my growing sense of politics, my participation in demonstrations against the war in Vietnam, my work in ghetto schools in Philadelphia and my emerging gay self never entered my songs.

In the Seventies I became a full-time, dedicated gay liberationist. I co-founded Giovanni's Room, a lesbian/gay/feminist bookstore in Philadelphia, I was a member of the Gay Activist Alliance, I was active in the Eromin Center, a gay counseling agency, I was a member of the Governor's Council on Sexual Minorities, the first such committee in the country, I founded and edited a weekly gay newsletter, the Philadelphia Gayzette, and I was a member of a gay/lesbian speaker's bureau. I took my politics seriously and seemed to have no time for music. I did no writing and rarely played the piano.

Now I see that this was OK. My writing and my creativity were directed toward gay politics. Through political organizing and speaking and testifying and writing articles, I had an outlet for my politics and theatre and humor. I learned that the politician and the performer derive their energy from a close source.

When the music began to happen for me again, my source of inspiration wasn't Rogers and Hart or Cole Porter, it was the gay liberation movement. First I wrote the predictable spoofs on standard songs and played them at parties and for friends. They were clever and gay in a wry, affirmative way. But I hadn't found my own voice.

My first public performance, my world debut, was at the Philadelphia Gay Coffeehouse in February 1977. I played a few original songs and filled out the set with some Noel Coward and odd ditties that somehow expressed a gay consciousness. The response was good, especially to my own material

I remember my audition for that first performance. Afterwards a classical pianist who had also auditioned drove me home. "Your songs are funny and touching", he said, "but I felt embarassed by them". As unsure as I was of myself that day, I heard his comment and took it as a reason to write more gay songs.

But there has been support, enough to sustain me and sometimes much, much more. An enthusiastic review, a serious article, warm applause and a call for an encore, letters from people who have discovered one of the albums, invitations to return and perform again in the same place, someone citing the particular meaning a song has for him or her—this is what reminds me how lucky I am to have a talent, the drive to put it out, and an audience to hear me.

Now, in addition to my solo performing, my interest is turning to musical theatre. I'm still intrigued, as I was at age six, by songs that evoke a particular characterization or tell a story. Now I'm writing for ensemble performance and finding a special thrill in hearing the songs sung by others.

The writing is lonely and always a struggle. Is it valuable? Am I saying this the way I want to say it? Can I sing these notes? Do I deserve the platform for my stories, my messages, my songs? Will the meager financial reward sustain me? So far it's all enough but not enough. I want a larger audience, I want to write more and better songs and have more albums in larger numbers. But I've already received the major payoff, learning in my deepest self that I can sing to another person.

Mad As Hell

by Craig G. Harris

Discrimination in the workplace should come as no surprise. Caught in an economic web dominated by heterosexual white males, we know that our being black, or female, or gay is viewed as a demographic mutation, if not a handicap. We are unconsciously conditioned to equate success with an alabaster phallus and go to self-abasing extremes to attain that success. Blacks are reared to set super nigger goals for themselves—"to get over, you gotta be twice as good as the white man." Fashion consultants tell women executives that tailored pinstripes will aid their success in a man's world. Second-rate career counselor/interior designers advise gays to conform to the status quo by constructing revolving doors for our closets.

When we make the choice to follow these instructions, we are in effect slashing our own wrists and dressing our wounds with Band Aids—praising the American dream in acceptance of our alleged inferiority. Ostensibly, our navigation through alien waters into a pseudo-Aryan, gender specific, male supremacist territory is testimony to our crossover appeal. In reality, it is this type of assimilation that feeds a malignant self-hatred which we use to oppress ourselves and undermine our own efforts toward achieving our individual and collective civil rights.

Subconsciously, we all know this. But we go on role playing, eating crow, accepting our bi-weekly momentary insults until something, some last-straw incident, triggers a response like that heard in the movie *Network:* "I'm mad as hell, and I ain't gonna take it no more!"

For me the breaking point came last summer, when I entered my office clad in a blue button-down oxford, white linen tie, baggy seersucker trousers with multiple pleating and a tiny turquoise stud. Within the hour, the management consulting firm's business manager had deemed my sartorial presentation inappropriate, demanding: "Don't wear an earring into this office again." When I questioned the logic behind the order, she responded, "Don't push it, the pants are questionable as well."

Following her into her office to continue the conversation, I was told that my immediate supervisor, an avowed racist and sexist, had problems working with a black male assistant. He had also intimated that several clients had difficulty with the pitch of my telephone voice. The business manager's response: "Craig, you gotta sound more butch on the phone."

I was hot, but I also had bills and no other source of income. I talked and thought about it over the weekend, searching for a reason to tolerate the condition. Against the advice of family and friends, I phoned in my resignation on Monday morning.

This situation is typical and more often than not goes unreported. So many believe there is nothing that can be done, no way of fighting the system. Others fear "coming out" in an emotionally wrenching court case and risking maltreatment from a homophobic legal system, or of gambling away large sums of money and time in a precarious pursuit of justice. Few are willing to make the necesary waves to propel the advancement of civil rights in our society.

It doesn't take much time, or money for that matter, and, considering the stakes—self-respect, esteem, and possibly a favorable judgment ($$$)—the challenge is worth it. And all it takes is a little research, careful preparation, and some follow-up.

I took the advice of a co-worker, who had noticed the harassment I was continually subjected to, and met with her sister, an attorney for the Puerto Rican Legal Defense and Education Fund. She instructed me to file for unemployment insurance claiming "constructive discharge" (meaning an employee is essentially forced by harassment to quit), and to contact Lambda Legal Defense and Education Fund for further information.

According to a Lambda board member, my best course of action was to file a complaint with the Equal Employment Opportunities Commission charging discrimination on the basis of race and sex. The private firm which I had worked for had no contracts with the City of New York and so was exempt from the provisions outlined in Mayor Koch's Executive Order 50, prohibiting discrimination on the basis of "sexual orientation or affectional preference."

There is no filing fee for registering a claim with any of the three government agencies (EEOC, the State Division of Human Rights, and the NYC Bureau of Labor Services), and there is no need to retain a lawyer. The initial complaint is filed by an intake officer, who also explains the process—to the point of settlement, or if necessary, litigation.

Blatant discrimination is a rarity—no sane employer will call you a "nigger faggot" in the presence of witnesses. Subtle discrimination is not so easy to prove, and the burden of proof lies with the complainant. Documentation is essential and can come in the form of employee profiles, performance evaluations, detailed accounts of discriminatory incidents, and witnesses. Build a strong case and the opposition will be hardpressed to produce a convincing denial.

An out-of-court settlement is the desirable solution for all parties involved. From the respondant's viewpoint, the legal fees incurred during a lengthy trial can cost more than a cash settlement. The complainant benefits by having equal power in negotiating the terms of a cash settlement. The entire process, from start to finish, can last as long as two years. As in my case, steady telephone follow-up can bring about an agreeable settlement within six months.

Employment is only one example of discrimination which can be addressed legally. Third world gays face all types of discrimination within both the gay and straight communities. Once my case was settled. I began to repay my debt to the various attorneys who counseled me by becoming a member of Lambda's Public Education Committee. With help from members of the staff and board of directors, I planned a conference to facilitate an exchange of information and to ensure that the legal needs of third world gays and lesbians were heard. As a result, Lambda is currently making program alterations based on the feedback from this initial meeting.

In order to achieve civil rights, get gay rights legislation passed, and assert our legitimacy, we must first accept that legitimacy as a given. It is time that we take a closer look at the political/legal implications of our position as gay people of color. By doing so, our intolerance of prejudices and role expectations will become second nature. Only then will we evolve into more self-loving, liberated individuals.

Thriving As An Outsider, Even As An Outcast, In Smalltown America

by Louie Crew

From 1973 to 1979, my spouse and I lived in Fort Valley, a town of 12,000 people, the seat of Peach County, sixty miles northeast of Plains, right in the geographic center of Georgia. I taught English at a local black college and my spouse was variously a nurse, hairdresser, choreographer for the college majorettes, caterer, and fashion designer.

The two of us have often been asked how we survived as a gay, racially integrated couple living openly in that small town. We are still perhaps too close to the Georgia experience and very much caught up in our similar struggles in central Wisconsin to offer a definite explanation, but our tentative conjectures should interest anyone who values the role of the dissident in our democracy.

Survive we did. We even throve before our departure. Professionally, my colleagues and the Regents of the University System of Georgia awarded me tenure, and the Chamber of Commerce awarded my spouse a career medal in cosmetology. Socially, we had friends from the full range of the economic classes in the community. We had attended six farewell parties in our honor before we called a halt to further fetes, especially several planned at too great a sacrifice by some of the poorest folks in the town. Furthermore, I had been away only four months when the college brought me back to address an assembly of Georgia judges, mayors, police chiefs, and wardens. We are still called two to three times a week by scores of people seeking my spouse's advice on fashion, cooking, or the like.

It was not always so. In 1974 my spouse and I were denied housing which we had "secured" earlier before the realtor saw my spouse's color. HUD documented that the realtor thought that "the black man looked like a criminal." Once, the town was up in arms when a bishop accused the two of us of causing a tornado which had hit the town early in 1975, an accusation which appeared on the front page of the newspaper. "This is the voice of God. The town of Fort Valley is harboring Sodomists. Would one expect God to keep silent when homosexuals are tolerated? We remember what He did to Sodom and Gomorrah" (*The Macon Herald,* March 20, 1975: 1). A year later my Episcopal vestry asked me to leave the parish, and my own bishop summoned me for discipline for releasing to the national press correspondence related to the vestry's back-room maneuvers. Prompted in part by such officials, the local citizens for years routinely heckled us in public, sometimes threw rocks at our apartment, trained their children to spit on us from their bicycles if we dared to jog, and badgered us with hate calls on an average of six to eight times a week.

One such episode offers a partial clue to the cause of our survival. It was late summer, 1975 or 1976. I was on my motorcycle to post mail at the street-side box just before the one daily pickup at 6:00 P.M. About fifty yards away, fully audible to about seventy pedestrians milling about the court house and other public buildings, a group of police officers, all men, began shouting at me from the steps of their headquarters: "Louise! Faggot! Queer!"

Anyone who has ever tried to ease a motorcycle from a still position without revving the engine knows that the feat is impossible: try as I did to avoid the suggestion, I sounded as if I were riding off in a huff. About half-way up the street, I thought to myself, "I'd rather rot in jail than feel the way I do now." I turned around, drove back—the policemen still shouting and laughing—and parked in the lot of the station. When I walked to the steps, only the lone black policeman remained.

"Did you speak to me?" I asked him.

"No, sir," he replied emphatically.

Inside I badgered the desk sergeant to tell her chief to call me as soon as she could locate him, and I indicated that I would press charges if necessary to prevent a recurrence. I explained that the police misconduct was an open invitation to more violent hoodlums to act out the officers' fantasies with impunity in the dark. Later, I persuaded a black city commissioner and a white one, the latter our grocer and the former our mortician, to threaten the culprits with suspension if ever such misconduct occurred again.

Over a year later, late one Friday after his payday, a black friend of my spouse knocked at our door to offer a share of his Scotch to celebrate his raise—or so he said. Thus primed, he asked me, "You don't recognize me, do you?"

"No," I admitted.

"I'm the lone black policeman that day you were heckled. I came by really because I thought you two might want to know what happened inside when Louie stormed up to the sergeant."

"Yes," we said.

"Well, all the guys were crouching behind the partition to keep you from seeing that they were listening. Their eyes bulged when you threatened to bring in the F.B.I. and such. Then when you left, one spoke for all when he said, 'But sissies aren't supposed to do things like that!' "

Ironically, I believe that a major reason for our thriving on our own terms of candor about our relationship has been our commitment to resist the intimidation heaped upon us. For too long lesbians and gay males have unwillingly encouraged abuses against ourselves by serving advance notice to any bullies, be they the barnyard-playground variety, or the Bible-wielding pulpiteers, that we would whimper or run into hiding when confronted with even the threat of exposure. It is easy to confuse sensible nonviolence with cowardly nonresistance.

In my view, violent resistance would be counter-productive, especially for lesbians and gays who are outnumbered 10 to 1 by heterosexuals, according to Kinsey's statistics. Yet our personal experience suggests that special kinds of creative nonviolent resistance are a major source of hope if lesbians and gay males are going to reverse the physical and mental intimidation which is our daily portion in this culture.

Resistance to oppression can be random and spontaneous, as in part was my decision to return to confront the police hecklers, or organized and sustained, as more typically has been the resistance by which my spouse and I have survived. I believe that only organized and sustained resistance offers much hope for long-range change in any community. The random act is too soon forgotten or too easily romanticized.

Once we had committed ourselves to one another, my spouse and I never gave much thought for ourselves to the traditional device most gays have used for survival, the notorious "closet" in which one hides one's identity from all but a select group of friends. In the first place, a black man and a white man integrating a Georgia small town simply cannot be inconspicuous. More importantly, the joint checking account and other equitable economies fundamental to the quality of our marriage are public, not private acts. Our denial of the obvious would have secured closet space only for our suffocation; we would have lied, "We are ashamed and live in secret."

All of our resistance stems from our sense of our own worth, our conviction that we and our kind do not deserve the suffering which heterosexuals continue to encourage or condone for sexual outcasts. Dr. Martin Luther King used to say, "Those who go to the back of the bus, deserve the back of the bus."

Our survival on our own terms has depended very much on our knowing and respecting many of the rules of the system which we resist. We are not simply dissenters, but conscientious ones.

For example, we are both very hard workers. As a controversial person, I know that my professionalism comes under far more scrutiny than that of others. I learned early in my career that I could secure space for my differences by handling routine matters carefully. If one stays on good terms with secretaries, meets all deadlines, and willingly does one's fair share of the busy work of institutions, one is usually already well on the way towards earning collegial space, if not collegial support. In Georgia, I routinely volunteered to be secretary for most committees on which I served, thereby having enormous influence in the final form of the groups' deliberations without monopolizing the forum as most other molders of policy do. My spouse's many talents and sensibilities made him an invaluable advisor and confidante to scores of people in the community. Of course, living as we did in a hairdresser's salon, we knew a great deal more about the rest of the public than that public knew about us.

My spouse and I are fortunate in the fact that we like the enormous amount of work which we do. We are not mere opportunists working hard only as a gimmick to exploit the public for lesbian and gay issues. Both of us worked intensely at our professional assignments long before we were acknowledged dissidents with new excessive pressures to excel. We feel that now we must, however unfairly, be twice as effective as our competitors just to remain employed at all.

Our survival has also depended very much on our thorough knowledge of the system, often knowledge more thorough than that of those who would use the system against us. For example, when my bishop summoned me for discipline, I was able to show him that his own canons give him no authority to discipline a lay person except by ex-communication. In fact, so hierarchical have the canons of his diocese become, that the only laity who exist worthy of their mention are the few lay persons on vestries.

Especially helpful has been our knowledge of communication procedures. For example, when an area minister attacked lesbians and gays on a TV talk show, I requested equal time; so well received was my response that for two more years I was a regular panelist on the talk show, thereby reaching most residents of the entire middle Georgia area as a known gay person, yet one speaking not just to sexual issues, but to a full range of religious and social topics.

When I was occasionally denied access to media, as in the parish or diocese or as on campus when gossip flared, I knew the value of candid explanations thoughtfully prepared, xeroxed, and circulated to enough folks to assure that the gossips would have access to the truthful version. For example, the vestry, which acted in secret, was caught by surprise when I sent copies of their hateful letter to most other parishioners, together with a copy of a psalm which I wrote protesting their turning the House of Prayer into a Court House. I also was able to explain that I continued to attend, not in defiance of their withdrawn invitation, but in obedience to the much higher invitation issued to us all by the real head of the Church. In January, 1979, in the first open meeting of the parish since the vestry's letter of unwelcome three years earlier, the entire parish voted to censure the vestry for that action and to extend to me the full welcome which the vestry had tried to deny. Only three voted against censure, all three of them a minority of the vestry being censured.

My spouse and I have been very conscious of the risks of our convictions. We have viewed our credentials—my doctorate and his professional licenses—not as badges of comfortable respectability, but as assets to be invested in social change. Dr. King did not sit crying in the Albany jail, "Why don't these folks respect me? How did this happen? What am I doing here?" When my spouse and I have been denied jobs for which we were the most qualified applicants, we have not naively asked how such things could be, nor have we dwelt overly long on self-pity, for we have known in advance the prices we might have to pay, even if to lose our lives. Our realism about danger and risk has helped us to preserve our sanity when everyone about us has seemed insane. I remember the joy which my spouse shared with me over the fact that he had just been fired for his efforts to organize other black nurses to protest their being treated as orderlies by the white managers of a local hospital.

Never, however, have we affirmed the injustices. Finally, we simply cannot be surprised by any evil and are thus less likely to be intimidated by it. Hence, we find ourselves heirs to a special hybrid of courage, a form of courage too often ignored by the heterosexual majority, but widely manifest among sexual outcasts, not the courage of bravado on battlegrounds or sportsfields, but the delicate courage of the lone person who patiently waits out the stupidity of the herd, the cagey courage that has operated many an underground railway station.

Our survival in smalltown America has been helped least, I suspect, by our annoying insistence that potential friends receive us not only in our own right, but also as members of the larger lesbian/gay and black communities of which we are a part. Too many whites and heterosexuals are prepared to single us out as "good queers" or "good niggers," offering us thereby the "rewards" of their friendship only at too great a cost to our integrity. My priest did not whip up the vestry against me the first year we lived openly together. He was perfectly happy to have one of his "clever queers" to dress his wife's hair and the other to help him write his annual report. We became scandalous only when the two of us began to organize the national group of lesbian and gay-male Episcopalians, known as INTEGRITY; then we were no longer just quaint. We threatened his image of himself as the arbiter of community morality, especially as he faced scores of queries from brother priests elsewhere.

Many lesbians and gay males are tamed by dependencies upon carefully selected heterosexual friends with whom they have shared their secret, often never realizing that in themselves alone, they could provide far more affirmation and discover far more strength than is being cultivated by the terms of these "friendships." Lesbians and gay males have always been taught to survive on the heterosexuals' terms, rarely on one's own terms, and almost never on the terms of a community shared with other lesbians and gay males.

Heterosexuals are often thus the losers. The heterosexual acquaintances close to us early on when we were less visible who dropped us later as our notoriety spread were in most cases folks of demonstrably much less character strength than those heterosexuals who remained our friends even as we asserted our difference with thoughtful independence.

My spouse and I have never been exclusive nor aspired to move to any ghetto. In December, 1978, on the night the Macon rabbi and I had successfully organized the area's Jews and gays to protest a concert by Anita Bryant, I returned home to watch the videotape of the march on the late news in the company of eight house guests invited by my spouse for a surprise party, not one of them gay (for some strange reason nine out of ten folks are not), not one of them obligated to be at the earlier march, and not one of them uneasy, as most of our acquaintances would have been a few years earlier before we had undertaken this reeducation together.

Folks who work for social change need to be very careful to allow room for it to happen, not to allow realistic appraisals of risks to prevent their cultivation of the very change which they germinate.

Our survival has been helped in no small way by our candor and clarity in response to rumor and gossip, which are among our biggest enemies. On my campus in Georgia, I voluntarily spoke about sexual issues to an average of 50 classes per year outside my discipline. Initially, those encounters sharpened my wits for tougher national forums, but long after I no longer needed these occasions personally for rehearsal, I continued to accept the invitations, thereby reaching a vast majority of the citizens of the small town where we continued to live. I used to enjoy the humor of sharing with such groups facts which would make my day-to-day life more pleasant. For example, I routinely noted that when a male student is shocked at my simple public, "Hello," he would look both ways to see who might have seen him being friendly with the gay professor. By doing this he is telling me and all other knowledgeable folks far more new information about his own body chemistry than he is finding out about mine. More informed male students would reply, "Hello" when greeted. With this method I disarmed the hatefulness of one of their more debilitating weapons of ostracism.

All personal references in public discussions inevitably invade one's privacy, but I have usually found the invasion a small price to pay for the opportunity to educate the public to the fact that the issues which most concern sexual outcasts are not genital, as the casters-out have so lewdly imagined, but issues of justice and simple fairness.

Resistance is ultimately an art which no one masters to perfection. Early in my struggles, I said to a gay colleague living openly in rural Nebraska, "We must stamp on every snake." Wisely he counseled, "Only if you want to get foot poisoning." I often wish I had more of the wisdom mentioned in *Ecclesiastes,* the ability to judge accurately, "The time to speak and the time to refrain from speaking." Much of the time I think it wise to pass public hecklers without acknowledging their taunts, especially when they are cowardly hiding in a crowd. When I have faced bullies head-on, I have tried to do so patiently, disarming them by my own control of the situation. Of course, I am not guaranteed that their violence can thus be aborted every time.

Two major sources of our survival are essentially very private—one, the intense care and love my spouse and I share, and the other, our strong faith in God as Unbounding Love. To these we prefer to make our secular witness, more by what we do than by what we say.

I am not a masochist. I would never choose the hard lot of the sexual outcast in smalltown America. Had I the choice to change myself but not the world, I would return as a white male heterosexual city-slicker millionaire, not because whites, males, heterosexuals, city-slickers, and millionaires are better, but because they have it easier.

Yet everyone faces a different choice: accept the world the way you find it, or change it. For year after year I dissented, right in my own neighborhood.

America preserves an ideal of freedom, although it denies freedom in scores of instances. My eighth-grade civics teacher in Alabama did not mention the price I would have to pay for the freedom of speech she taught me to value. I know now that the docile and ignorant dislike you fiercely when you speak truth they prefer not to hear. But I had a good civics class, one that showed me how to change our government. I rejoice.

Sometimes I think a society's critics must appreciate the society far more than others, for the critics typically take very seriously the society's idle promises and forgotten dreams. When I occasionally see them, I certainly don't find many of my heterosexual eighth-grade classmates probing much farther than the issues of our common Form 1040 headaches and the issues as delivered by the evening news. Their lives seem often far duller than ours and the main adventures in pioneering they experience come vicariously, through television, the movies, and for a few, through books. In defining me as a criminal, my society may well have hidden a major blessing in its curse by forcing me out of lethargy into an on-going, rigorous questioning of the entire process. Not only do I teach *The Adventures of Huckleberry Finn,* my spouse and I have in an important sense had the chance to be Huck and Jim fleeing a different form of slavery and injustice in a very real present.

Loving Dance

by Carl Wittman

I mutter silently: do the Dusty Miller's go behind or in front of the Shasta Daisies . . . . Alyssum, alyssum . . . lissome . . . lissome. I wonder what they look like. I wonder if this soil is rich enough. And as I press the tiny bedding plants into their new ground, my thoughts drift: it's awfully nice of them to give us all these plants, especially when selling plants is their livelihood; I wonder what I could give them in return. I'm feeling just an edge of guilt; perhaps I should offer to pay them for these flowers-to-be. I pause, wondering what I could do for them. And then it strikes me; I already do something for them when I involve them in country dancing. I am a dance teacher. I am a dance teacher. Mmmm, that sounds good. I do something that is worthwhile, as worthwhile as growing a plant or working for an employer. I feel good and go back to setting out the seedlings. Alyssum, lissome . . . shasta daisies . . . .

*   *   *   *   *

Many people come to my dance class full of anxiety. Their bodies are not lithe, but rigid. The men, particularly. Occasionally an athlete will come: he will be terribly awkward. He has learned to move gracefully on the basketball floor, but his grace is cultivated only for that tiny spectrum of acceptable masculinity. Otherwise he is alienated from his body. The other men, too, are alienated from their bodies. There are more of them, the awkward ones: men, and women too. They have had a dreadful time, probably all their lives. The misfits, the weirdos, the klutzes, the queers.

I used to wonder why they are the ones attracted to folk dancing, to country dancing. I realize now that many many more people are misfits than we commonly believe. The body that likes itself, that even acknowledges itself, is probably the exception, not the rule. But there is a sixth sense they have. They know on some unconscious level that I will not threaten them, I will not degrade them.

And they are right. For I am among them. I got chosen last (or, thank God, next to last, leaving the final indignity to someone I despised even more) when teams "chose up" at high school gym class. I slouched and leaned, trying to make this big awkward body as small as possible, so my classmates wouldn't be reminded how useless it was in the things which counted: athletics and school dances. When I kept being asked why I held myself as if I had a stomach ache, I might have said; obviously, to cover up my shamelessly queer genitals.

And when I teach, it is instinctively that I reach out to the clumsiest. Encouraging the graceful ones to develop style and skill is gratifying, but the very very special moments are when joy spreads over the face of a body experiencing flight for the first time. A combination of a relaxed situation, the compelling airs of country dance music, and my encouraging teaching has managed to pierce the defensive fat, the armored muscles, the limp apathy.

I am not primarily a therapist. I hate therapeutic exercises, they remind me of my limitations. I am an enthusiast of Scottish and English country dancing, and I have begun to discover that through these eccentric and esoteric dance forms, I have a gift of opening up to both neighbors and strangers the joy and ecstasy that I feel when I dance.

*   *   *   *   *

On a rainy winter morning I pore over Arthur Evans' articles about witchcraft and the existence of an old religion of Europe which was democratic, affirmative of (homo)sexuality, women, and nature. I don't much care if it really happened, this culture he describes; I care only that what Arthur has read has helped him to envision a better scheme of things. I notice the picture, a ring of fairies dancing in a circle. A few weeks later I am scribbling furiously, delving into figures that I have danced for 15 years now: circles, reels, crosses. I am creating a mock-ethnology of Celtic dances. Surely these wonderful dances must have had their origin in some pre-Christian era. Without sources, without footnotes, without doubt I realize that the figures are celebrations of how the ancient people loved each other. Sex is one kind of celebration of that, dance is another. That, of course, is why the dancing feels so good: the unspoken tradition of loving has been passed on to us, intact.

*   *   *   *   *

Months later, I read in the latest *Fag Rag* that this academic and that are taking exception to the notion of an Old Religion. I surely hope that faggot historians will find evidence of our antecedents but I do not want to depend on it. Simultaneously, a friend tells me he thinks my Celtic dance-ethnology is on thin ice. I realize that what I see in the dance figures is important; whether my ancestors in the British Isles saw the same meanings or not is only interesting.

*   *   *   *   *

One afternoon in our living room, a half dozen of us revel in the delightful tune on an old 78 phonograph record, the Dorset Ring. We evolve the figures of the country dances, starting from the very beginning. Holding on tight, we all lean back, making a taut circle. Each person is cooperating, and each one is vital. By slowly relaxing the tension or increasing it, the circle stretches and contracts, breathing. This surely is the simplest way to express the oneness of us all, the love of the community and how vital we are to each other. To the music, we move around one way and back the other, keeping that delicate tension which makes the circle perfect.

Occasionally, perhaps, a group finds itself cooperating in that way spontaneously, and that is a rare and wonderful experience. Through the ritualization of the figure (the music determines the rhythm, and the duration), we can conjure up that joy any time at all. Magic, surely.

* * * * *

An evening party in that same room, shortly after my excursion into dance-ethnology. Dance parties here reflect our community: many lesbians, fewer faggots. It is friendly territory for exploring the social implications of country dancing. Over a year ago we decided to junk the tradition of heterosexual couples, the men on one side, the women on the other. The removal of that one convention freed us from much of the sexism in country dancing. Tonight, we are exploring further. The old Playford dance *Gathering Peascods* takes on new meaning. The dance begins with a circle for everyone, slipping to the left and back to the right, punctuated by "turn single" (each person turns around in place). I suggest that we think of it as a celebration of each self within the group—a balance of collectivity and individuality. The dance continues with a men's circle and a women's circle: a wonderful enactment of our brand of "separatism". The dance continues with the ingenious geometrical democracy of country dancing: if the men circle before the women the first time through, then the women's circle preceeds the men's the second time. These are not new concepts politically among us. It is our dream. Fairness, enjoying our little valley as one group, and times and places for fostering what is special among lesbians, and what is special among faggots. The non-dancers smile indulgently at my offering; the regular dancers glow with an understanding of the simple, deep meaning therein.

* * * * *

My companion and I are dancing together at a formal Scottish Ball in the Bay Area. Two men dancing together is a major breach of etiquette. I am not aware until after the ball how much anxiety I feel. We have danced together before, at such events, but tonight the excitement and novelty of it have worn thin, and I understand that the nearly universal reaction among the other dancers is hostility. I am sickened by the rudeness extended us; the coldness from "friends" who have heretofore seemed open to my homosexuality. There is a party game for which each person is given a tag, and is to dance with someone carrying the companion tag: Troilus and Cressida, Romeo and Juliet, Abelard and Heloise. The four of us from Wolf Creek nervously laugh about Lord Douglas and Oscar Wilde, Gertrude Stein and Alice B Toklas. I am angered by the realization that I am a second class citizen here despite my dancing skill. I think of the rage that would erupt if only 10% of the nametags included *homo*sexual couples; and I realize how hard it would be to explain the indignity of it all to my straight friends here. And there are always the women sitting out on the sidelines, waiting for men to ask them to dance. I have witnessed this insult to them for a decade. The irony of it, that some of these women are resenting us because when we dance together that diminishes their chances of being asked to dance. Nellie bluntly suggests that they ask each other to dance: it is sad to realize that many of them find dancing with another woman a less vital experience, a makeshift second-best. Much later, I find out that some women are discovering new and good things dancing with other women: relaxation, and a less competitive spirit. But at the time, the feelings well up into my throat and eyes after the Ball is over, when one young woman comes up and expresses her support for the changes which we are initiating. Will things improve when more of the dancers desire these changes? Or will there be outright war?

*   *   *   *   *

Back at home, even at the weekly class I teach at the local community college, things are better. After one class, a visiting brother from the city comments on how much of a faggot I am when I teach. I glow with pride, glad that the schizophrenic years are over. A week later as I relate this to a neighbor who also dances, she laughs and praises me further: how rare, she says, that a male teacher would try to conjure up the idea of smoothness by referring to creaming butter for a cake. And she tells me that a friend of hers remarked that ours was the first dance class she'd ever been to that was free of sexism. I am ecstatic.

Part of the ease in the dancing hereabouts is that as a teacher in an isolated area, I am free to introduce this material as I choose. I do not find it upsetting any longer if a class is composed largely of women; and consequently, they do not find it upsetting either. I ask them to form into groups of eight, rather than couple up first. Not knowing what a taboo it is for women to dance with women, men with men, they are quite satisfied with the arrangement. And it avoids the uncomfortable shuffling around that usually happens—the embarassing problem of who will dance on the "wrong" side. (One evening, after a session with six of us—all men—one newcomer indicated surprise when he heard that women, too, did this dancing!) And perhaps best of all, it creates an atmosphere where everyone assumes she or he will dance; no one sits out and waits to be asked. And from my perspective as a gay person, it removes the one major barrier to enjoying fully the dance form. For the dancing is sensual, physical experience with others—and as such it is not devoid of sexuality. To dance always in heterosexual couples is like always reading novels or watching movies of only heterosexual love. For the straight people in my classes, this is an opportunity for them to see gay people dancing together in a loving and relaxed situation; for us, it is an avenue to expressing the full meaning of the dances.

*   *   *   *   *

While we have felt it necessary to "abolish" the men's and women's designations in social dancing, some of us are beginning to explore these deeper meanings to the traditional sexual divisions, not as roles between men and women but as statements about how men and women are unique, as part of a whole.

While the exact emotional content of pre-historic Celtic dancing may elude us, some of the recent history of the dance form is clear. The heterosexual dictatorship since the Middle Ages took these simple circles, reels and other figures and choreographed them to fit their own assumptions. One prime assumption was that homosexuality was taboo—and all of the figures were forced into a heterosexual mode, thereby losing whatever meaning they might have had among people of the same sex. The many forms of loving: between men, among men, between women, among women, among large groups—all were suppressed. The simple figures were stripped of much of their social meaning and forced into a sterile obligatory heterosexuality. The result was a proliferation of extremely intricate ballroom dances, appealing only to the idle rich or the very clever. And while I enjoy immensely the complexity and technical difficulty of these dances, I am coming to see them as only one of the joys of the country dance experience. Certainly it is a testament to the vitality of the simpler dances, and particularly to the music, which remained intact, that country dancing survived this abuse.

And now, when re-connected to the loves which they seem so lucidly to celebrate, they again shine in their simplicity (And while my prime concern is not finding ways for heterosexually-oriented people to relate better, it seems clear to me that our "innovations" permit a more authentic and voluntary mode of expression even among a man and a woman.)

*   *   *   *   *

There is some risk in saying that dance forms "celebrate" or "represent" something else, anything else. The dancing is intact and self-sufficient—and all the struggling to find proper meaning is only necessary because we have been so brainwashed by our social and sexual conditioning. I believe that these dances are not sacred in some symbolic way—they are not representational of some greater truth. They *are* that truth, pure and simple. When I dance a reel of three with two of my friends, that act can *bring* us closer to some state of equality and mutual love, as much as any consciouness raising group or manifesto. And when our community dances in a large circle together, we are what we dance.

Men Together In Group Therapy

by Louis W. McLeod and Bruce K. Pemberton

The decision to lead an all-male therapy group was a logical extension of our friendship. We met at a party and spent several hours talking about ourselves, our mutual friends, and our beginning practices of psychotherapy. We learned that both of us had recently experienced an increase in the number of men we were seeing in therapy and speculated about the reasons. Sitting together, we began to realize we had met in each other a man with whom we could share, trust, and risk.

After such an intense sharing, we were ready to play. Entering a room where people were dancing, we discovered everyone in pairs, including some women. With a little bit of wine and feeling quite safe, we began to fast-dance together. We were laughing, enjoying ourselves, and thinking ourselves quite smart when suddenly the record changed to a slow song by Johnny Mathis. Looking at each other we knew it was a moment of truth. Finally one of us said, "What the hell!" After some awkwardness over who would lead, we slow-danced for the first time with another man. One of us closed his eyes, put his head on the other's shoulder, and followed his lead. The experience of slow-dancing with each other became very important in our relationship and later in our work with men. It was a great relief to dance with someone our own size, to lean on and be supported by a partner, and to share the responsibility for leading and constantly being alert. Slow-dancing with another man symbolizes many issues confronting men today: following as well as leading, being receptive as well as active, letting go as well as being in control, facing homophobia as well as our attraction to other men, and acknowledging competitiveness as well as cooperative efforts. Our developing relationship with each other led us to speculate about the many men who yearn for a qualitatively different relationship with other men. As a result, we helped form a peer-support system for men called the Atlanta Men's Experience.

For two years, we were in a weekly male peer-support group. We learned the value of peer support in which men socialized and helped each other outside the group. That experience challenged many of our notions of the traditional coed therapy group. At the same time the limitations of a leaderless men's group led us to imagine what a men's therapy group might be like. An increasing number of men were calling us about the Men's Experience and male support groups. As we talked to these men we began to understand that some were looking for therapy and we regretted not having a men's therapy group to offer.

In the fall of 1978 we decided to begin a men's therapy group. Our first step was to conduct individual interviews. We explored with each man the appropriateness of his being in a men's therapy group. With our own clients, we explored the transference issues that would emerge from seeing one's therapist in an intimate relationship with other men. We also explained the basic structure of the group. Particularly helpful was our insistence that the men know each other by first name only. We discouraged contact outside the group so the men could relate as "intimate strangers." We asked for a 4-month minimum commitment. We knew that many men had difficulty with commitments involving intense emotions and intimacy. Holding participants to this commitment was a crucial factor in helping a number of men through the initial stages of the group. We find men are less likely to drop out early in a group if women are present to provide basic support and nurturance. Another requirement was returning for a minimum of four times to say good-bye after deciding to leave the group. Many men do not end relationships well. Staying to say good-bye afforded each man the opportunity to acknowledge and experience his sadness in leaving, express any unresolved anger, and share his warmth and caring for the other men.

We held the first group in January, 1979, and continued meeting weekly until the fall of 1984. The average length of group membership was two years. In the first meeting we asked men to choose a partner, talk about their fathers and then introduce each other by sharing impressions of the other man's father. Our goal was to create an early bonding experience through talking about fathers; and connecting with one another provided many men with a "buddy" during the group's initial growing pains.

To enhance our effectiveness as leaders we met an hour before the group for supper and 30 minutes afterwards to debrief. During the debriefing we took turns writing our responses to three questions:
1. What is the state of our relationship and how are we doing as co-therapists?
2. What are we learning about a men's therapy group and where do we see this group in its development?
3. What is the development of each individual man and what needs to happen for him next week?

Prior to each group, we took five minutes to read the previous week's notes. This allowed us to move from the social experience during supper to preparing for the group.

What We Learned About Ourselves As Co-therapists

Doing a men's therapy group has been a very nourishing experience. We nourished each other in our pregroup connection while eating together. Experiencing men exploring their relationships with each other deepened our own relationship. During the last five years we have consistently regarded Monday nights as the most personaliy rewarding part of our practice.

Our relationship became a model for the group of how two men could relate. Over the years, we became comfortable in sharing our own relationship dynamics and began to disagree and fight openly in the group. Several men talked of how important it was to see us resolve our differences. For men who were mostly locked in competitive stances with the other men in their lives, we demonstrated how men can love, disagree, and reconnect.

In any intimacy, regardless of gender, male/female roles will exist. As the group evolved, members would assign maternal/paternal, feeling/action and female/male roles to us as co-therapists. Very early the group assigned these roles and talked quite directly of experiencing one of us (Bruce) as initiating, talking more, interrupting, leading, and so forth ("You seem like the father"); and the other (Louis) as supportive, reflecting, summarizing, listening, and so forth ("You seem like the mother"). We suspect that initiative and integrative functions have evolved from primitive or archetypical images of the masculine and feminine. In our groups not only did these roles get assigned to the two male leaders but they also shifted between us over the years depending upon how we functioned in the group.

In our own relationship we were working hard to become more equal and were beginning to integrate our individual masucline/feminine aspects. Bruce, who had been most active in the group, was working at being more receptive. Louis, who had provided the more supportive function, was working at being more confrontive. The relationship of trust and friendship resulted in our ability to experiment with new behaviors and to risk making mistakes in the group. Early in the group Bruce confronted one group member even to the point of becoming careless. While Louis reported later an internal sense of discomfort, he neither protected the client nor confronted Bruce. We both agreed that we eventually lost that client from the group in spite of his generally having had a good experience. However as Louis became more confrontive with Bruce and as Bruce listened and accommodated to Louis, the group experienced a shift in the roles, viewing Louis "as the father" and Bruce "as the mother." Four years after the early confrontation, Bruce faced a group member with some anger that surprised even him. Louis was prepared to intervene if there was a need. The client, who was quite shocked, later reported how Louis' manifest presence gave him protection and enabled him to stay in a powerful connection with Bruce during and after the confrontation.

Finally, both of us worked through many residuals of homophobia in our relationship. In this society, any two men being intimate will have to confront the issue of attraction and homophobia at some point in their relationship if they are to deepen the trust and caring. We found that our relationship affirmed our heterosexuality rather than threatened it. Modeling our comfort with intimacy and acknowledging the sexual aspect of any loving relationship allowed group memebers to explore their own fears and questions concerning their masculinity and sexuality. This issue is perhaps the most difficult for a men's therapy group to confront and explore. It is not surprising therefore, that it took a number of years for this to become a focal issue in the group.

Steve sought therapy after an unsatisfactory six months with another male therapist, "I thought if I told him enough information about myself, then he would tell me what to do. I also did not feel close to him." Steve's initial goals included resolving issues about his sexual orientation, being less judgmental about himself, and becoming more intimate with other people. He was involved in a relationship with a woman, had had platonic and sexual relationships with women before, but was afraid he might be homosexual because of his attraction to other men and early feelings of being "different sexually." After 1½ years of individual therapy, he joined the men's therapy group. Steve found that the group enabled him to explore his relationships with other men at a deeper level.

Initially he focused on his troubled relationships with women and explored openly his attempts to be sexual *and intimate* with the same woman. It was only after much trust had developed in the group that Steve risked talking about his sexuality and his concerns about his attraction to men.

He wondered openly, "Am I gay?" His initiative sparked other men to look at doubts about their own sexual orientation and attraction to men as well as to explore previous homosexual experiences. The support Steve received from the group allowed him to experiment sexually with men outside the group. His sexual relationships with women were also enhanced. A key element in his experimentation was the support for exploration that came from other men.

What We Learned About Therapy Groups For Men

1. When women are present in a group, men automatically "play" to the women. When men and women are together, men focus on the relationship: How am I doing? Am I scoring? What does she think of me? In the men's therapy group the men first explored their intrapersonal dynamics and later their interpersonal relationships. Without women present, competitiveness was diminished.

2. In a coed group males tend to turn to women for nourishment. In the men's therapy group we modeled nourishment and intimacy between two men as well as with each individual man. As a result, the men in the group began to see each other as sources for support and nourishment. Often men in the group

began to establish intimate relationships with other men outside the group. With women present, men seldom identify another man as a primary source of nourishment and support.

> *Men often see themselves bonded in intimacy with women and bonded in competition with men. Therefore, men most often turn to women for support when in pain and most often self-disclose with women about their vulnerability. Two problems arise from this practice. First, women are much more skilled at self-disclosure and yearn for a partner who can be open and vulnerable. More and more, women are openly admitting their withdrawal from men who are unable to share feelings, emotions, and secret fears. Yet as the man "breaks down" and becomes more open, the woman experiences a bind, since she has been taught to seek a strong partner who will provide for her. This dilemma means she will often stop the very process of his being more vulnerable that she encourages in the man.[1]*

In a men's therapy group men do not need to compare themselves nor compete with women, who are often more experienced at identifying and expressing feelings. As men begin to identify and express feelings at their own pace, a camaraderie and excitement grows into a self-perpetuating process.

3. Male/male intimacy is also one step in understanding and deepening male/female relationships. Intimate sharing and sexuality often become confused when men establish relationships with their women.

> *There is nothing inherently wrong with support and sexuality being mixed in the same relationship; but, for most men, warm, close feelings call for a sexual advance. Few men have learned that sexual feelings can be enjoyed, acknowledged, and not acted upon, in the service of intimacy. Being vulnerable, open, experiencing pain, joy, closeness, and comfort with a woman often becomes sexualized by men. Thus, the man is moved to initiate (sexually) just when he could get most from being receptive (support, nurturance).[1]*

In a men's therapy group men come to appreciate a non-sexualized intimate relationship with other males. This provides the experience and idea that intimacy can be separated from sexuality with women. In the group men often expressed their relief and enjoyment in establishing non-sexual friendships with women for the first time. At the same time, many men experienced a more integrated intimacy with their *sexual* partners.

4. In many circles it is the prevailing notion that men are more comfortable with their anger and rage than they are with their sadness and tears. Our experience is that anger, rage, sadness, and tears are equally difficult for men. Men tend to express a form of intellectualized anger whenever they begin to feel helpless. Most men in this society are inadequate in expressing anger and rage in the service of intimacy. It is interesting to note that the treatment of choice for

physically abusive males is the all-male support group in which they explore how they use anger to control, dominate, and avoid issues of intimacy, helplessness, fear, and potency.

Often men display their intellectualized anger through sarcasm, put downs, temper tantrums, demands for perfection and so forth. These men are terrified of their anger. They fear any strong expression of anger might lead them to be the abusive, murderous, out-of-control male stereotype.

Anger and rage evolve predictably as an issue in a men's therapy group. For the man who is initially afraid his anger will become uncontrollable and consume him, a men's therapy group provides an immediate reassurance that he cannot overpower the group. In the group it is easy to provide limit-setting structures where the man can fully experience his rage in a safe setting.

We still live in a society in which most men have an internal prohibition against feeling, expressing, and getting support for their sadness. That prohibition has been perpetuated and continues to be enforced by males in this society (fathers, bosses, politicians). In the men's therapy group, men slowly begin to explore ways they block their expression of tears. It is a unique experience for men to receive support, holding and acceptance of their sadness from other men.

5. Leading a men's therapy group is fun. We have led this group for over five years. The personal learnings and enjoyment of working with men have become a high point in the week for each of us. Prior to this experience, neither of us could imagine a men's therapy group being as personally stimulating as a coed group. We now feel that a men's therapy group has a uniqueness, power, and potency for the male therapist that cannot be replicated in any other group. Being with men as they grow and relate intimately to each other is unique and invigorating.

NOTE:

[1] McLeod, L. & Pemberton, B. (1982) Men and mental health. In F. Crawford (Ed.), *Exploring mental health parameters* (Vol. 3) p. 267. Atlanta: Emory University.

Retired

by Jim Warters

There seems to be a tendency on the part of men, their families, friends, and society to view their future retirement in narrow, simplistic ways. It is going to be either some fantasy event (24 hour per day of fishing, golfing or traveling) or else a sign of imminent death. The reality of retirement is far more complex.

I retired in 1983 at age 55 when my company eliminated the job I had had for the past 30 years. My personal response to retirement was a mixture of confusion and relief at the opportunity to escape a bad work situation. Other men's circumstances are different. Some leave work knowing their health is gone and they are dying. Others know they are no longer wanted and are allowed to save face by retiring. Still others stick it out until 65 (or 67 or 70), take their pension, party and gifts—just as it is supposed to happen.

Although the circumstances surrounding retirement are unique to each person's work situation, there are developmental stages during retirement that I believe are common to many men. Retirement is the beginning or intensification of a major life passage that a good many men are totally unprepared for by their training, experience, or their male roles. Because men are socialized to define themselves in relation to their work, most are ill-prepared for this major life event and its effects on their self-concept, their emotions, and their primary relationships.

The Retirement Process

The process of adjusting to my retirement turned out to be a series of emotionally charged steps. The initial phase of *separation* consisted of three parts, the first being imagining myself back at work. I would wonder what's going on at work (they'll never manage without me) and what I'd be doing at a particular time of day (fighting rush hour traffic in the ice and snow). A second, more active response to retirement involved trying to hang on to elements of work life. It consisted of visiting work or calling co-workers or fellow retirees, nosing around for consulting jobs, having lunch, trading gossip, trying to still assert influence, etc. The third aspect of the separating process was more subtle, and concerned unresolved emotional issues I experienced during my last days at work. For example, I had to deal with the anger, hurt, and sadness at what was said or not said at the last meeting with my boss, the farewell party I never got, all the promised "carrots" I never received. It also included in some way my attempt to rewrite my work history. At some point during the process of separation, I became aware of, and had to begin coping with, a loss of identity. For the first time in 55 years, no program was laid out for me by others. I could no longer slot myself easily into society by means of my job title, company, or work history. Gone were the familiar benchmarks, rules, and structure that work had provided me. Without the distractions of a daily business/work life, I became aware of how guilt had become a substitute for joy in much of my life. I became more aware of a fear of vulnerability to and closeness with others. I also became aware of unfinished business with my father, scare and confusion about money, and some of the empty places in my life.

Then, at some point, I gradually experienced a critical new phase of grief and grieving. An important part of my life had ended and I could never experience (or change) it again. Fortunately, I let myself fully grieve this loss, and experienced the now familiar stages of denial and isolation, anger, bargaining, depression, and finally acceptance described by Elizabeth Kubler-Ross.

Where I find myself today is, I hope, the final phase, consisting of acceptance of self, as well as a search for a new identity. It is manifesting itself in how I live day to day and how I think about and plan for the future. There is overlapping in the above phases, and the work done in coping with retirement is not always neat and clean. It often involves getting stuck at a certain point in the process, overcoming the obstacle and moving on to the next stage. Some men deny that they need to readjust to retirement. For myself, I have come to trust the process, and trust myself.

Setting retirement aside for a moment, a maturing male faces other passages such as growing old and facing his own mortality. He begins preparing for death and may grieve for his lost youth and unfulfilled ambitions. Couple this with retirement, and each of these stages can be intensified to a painful level.

Side Effects

Retirement and the retirement process have a strong impact not only on the retiree but also on mates, family, friends, and the community. The first side effect that many people think of is the effect on the retiree's spouse or partner. Time structures get rearranged. His Time, Her Time, and Their Time becomes mostly His Time and Their Time. Many couples are unprepared for and fear this shift. Also, the increased proximity often intesifies latent or avoided relationship problems. Family roles are threatened and/or changed. The partners can sometimes have conflicting fantasies about what retirement will be like. Unless these issues are consciously tackled, often the prevailing feeling is one of being scared: afraid that family members will change or have to change, or afraid that the whole process is out of their control. In addition, money concerns evoke many practical and emotional responses, and are often accompanied by confusion and power struggles.

Changes in the family go beyond effects on the retiree's partner to include children and other dependent members. Changes include family time structures, roles, expectations—family dynamics in general. Children seem to experience fear and anger around the pressure for them to adapt to their father's retirement. They are often unsure how to react to the perceived vulnerability on the part of the former breadwinner. Also, children suddenly get some vivid first-hand experience of what it means to retire which may cause them to rethink their assumptions about their jobs and their own fantasies of retirement.

Friends and the community are also affected by the retirement process. Friends can be lost due to the retiree's lowered economic status, by his withdrawal from his social circle, or by his moving to a retirement area. Because retirees aren't identified with their work roles, they can often become invisible in their community.

The process of my retirement involved pains of loss, pains of transition, pains of self-acceptance, and the shared pain of others in similar circumstances or those affected by my life. I can't, for the most part, label them "bad" pains. They were (and are) more like birth pains—a birth into a new life. Some of the pains I am currently labeling as "bad" are pains associated with learned guilt. Guilt is unnecessary pain, and at the moment I seem to be stuck with it.

The male roles of doer, provider, tough guy, game player, and controller gives a particularly male flavor to the problems of retirement. Some major difficulties seem to come from men's fear of being vulnerable and the male conditioning not to feel, give up, or admit defeat. When men stop viewing normal life changes as defeats, they will open themselves to the power they can continue to have in their lives. Retirement can be a life-enhancing opportunity rather than a life-killing problem.

Retirement has led me to seek out other men in a new way. I've discovered the Pittsburgh Men's Collective and I'm actively making new male friends. With the artificiality of the business world out of the way, I can experience men as supportive, vulnerable, and of interest in their own right. I am surely still cautious in my opening to them. I've lost the structure of the work world and find I miss it. But I also know I'm better off without that structure. I've found new men willing to assist me to overcome my need to control, men who support my attempts to establish a new, healthier structure.

Wandering The Woods
In A Season Of Death

by Allan Troxler

March 26

Dear Leo,

Went to the woods the other afternoon. Thought you might like a report on your man on assignment in the Eastern hardwood forest.

Taking the wide path off Whitefield Road, first thing you pass leggy jack pines tangled with honeysuckle. Within memory, this was cornfields and tobacco. No old growth, to speak of.

Over the last few years since I came back, I've pondered the state of the Piedmont woodlands some. It's been a process of unlearning a Sierra Club book version of nature. One sweaty afternoon late last spring I stretched on the cool clay bank of Cane Creek, watched the light glowing through the dense vines, breathed the dark creek smell and half listened to several friends from Vermont nattering about the poison ivy and the bugs. I studied the opalescent interior of a freshwater clam shell, and just smiled.

I went walking out in Duke Forest in the spring, my eyes and ears informed by the dying of a friend. I discovered, in the order of things there, intimations of my own death and of yours—the tree trunk resting on the slope, the water's timeless sounds. There was reassurance to this wandering through the woods' changes and through seasons. For some, however, there is the forest fire, or the hunter.

I caught myself pushing on past the honeysuckle and scrub pine the other day, and I wanted to find things to report to you, and partly because of the old prejudices. Then I got to thinking of the honeysuckle's beneficent smell—in my North Carolina grand cru along with the wood shrush's song, lightning bugs, thunderstorms, muscadines, rabbit tobacco and winter sunsets. I slowed down. What right have I, a left handed Southern queer, to snub a fellow weed? So, pausing to respect the honeysuckle, I wish to report that its exuberant vines were spangled with tiny new leaves.

In the blowing snow the next day I saw a pear tree in full bloom and couldn't tell where the flowers ended and the snow began.

Leo and I came to share our love for the woods of childhood—his in Alabama and Virginia, mine in North Carolina—when we were in college together. Years later our paths converged in the rough mountains of southern Oregon. He had heard of Wolf Creek, where Carl and I and our friends lived, and he sought us out.

Leo was wrestling, such as he ever did anything head on, with the problem of being gay and being a doctor. He had recently finished med school and was just beginning to come out. In Oregon we walked under the madrones and Doug firs, and out on the slopes where the ceanothus bloomed deep sky blue, and talked.

He told me of his doctor mother and his lawyer father; of how all along he had met their expectations, more or less; of the placid course of his life until recently.

Generally when Leo approached passion over anything, the lower half of his face would get amused, the upper half mildly distressed, his voice would crack and give out and, directly, the intensity would pass. But in Wolf Creek this time his anguish lingered. He stayed with us for several months, fretting.

Looking down on a buckeye sapling I was powerfully taken by the geometry of the ruddy new leaves, stems going off at right angles, then leafing out in fives, deeply ribbed, ready to unfurl and spread.

Why is the order in nature so exciting? Crystals, skeletons, shells—why this hankering for symmetry? I assume it's not an exclusively human tropism. Recently I noticed a wasp nest in a sourwood tree. Surely the wasps would not have settled for less-regular cells. Honeybees refuse machine-made comb base when the hexagons are off the least bit. And the Greenpeace people report that whales and dolphins will follow along for miles listening rapt to Mozart. There you have it, whatever it is.

Finally Leo decided to move to San Francisco, where he found work with a group of gay doctors. I remember climbing the hills of Buena Vista park with him, up behind his office, and comparing the rhododendrons there with those back East. For all the wonders of the Northwest coast, we both longed for the woods back home. "Eastern hardwood forest" became code between us, a metaphor for Home, for which we were in exile, trying to become ourselves.

In the dwindling light down by the creek a pale cocoon hung from a twig. I'll keep an eye on it. The steely water shone against the dark hills. Upstream the rocks rattled against each other.

In 1979 I moved back to North Carolina to hazard being openly gay in a place I loved after a fashion, and which I understood. (Oregon is closer to Japan than to Europe and the dogwoods there have five petals.) On my last trip down to San Francisco there were posters everywhere protesting the fate of Joann Little and the Wilmington 10. I needed to get on home.

Years passed, Leo and I lost touch, and then I heard through a college friend that Leo had AIDS. The opportunistic infection was severe meningitis. He could neither talk nor see. He had a reservoir for drugs implanted in his skull.

I wanted to communicate somehow, yet I didn't want to taunt him with the details of my daily life. I decided on a journal, of sorts, from our Eastern hardwood forest. Hickory and trout lily could be our vocabulary. Possum and star.

April 18

Dear Leo,

Since I last wrote, late winter has turned to high spring, practically. Bare branch to leaf, bud to seed pod. Rest, stir, swell, split, sprout, rise, spread, bloom, fruit, seed, droop, shed, rot, rest. It all keeps changing; except for water, light and air, which are pretty constant, aren't they. Or rather they don't change like organisms change, I guess.

In a way though, the vast spectrum of events attendant upon the coming and going of light every day is like an organism: still dark, first stirring, sap rising, breath quickening, chirping, humming, speaking, light to sugar, air to CO_2, land warming, wind shifting, and so on. And isn't a pond or creek a body in some animate sense? Breathing, generating, waking, sleeping.

Oh, Leo. Such medieval animism. My mind has gone to seed.

Well, to begin. The sun is still up and the light which suffuses the intricate infinity of pale grey trunks and branches tempts me to rise and float among them creekward. Sometimes I float in my dreams. Aside from feeling lifted up by my heart and my lungs I especially enjoy the state of being untouched—free of floor, chair, bed, table—moving among things unencumbered. Floating outdoors, however, is another matter. Uncontained, I rise higher and faster and invariably, when landscapes have dwindled to tiny patterns, I lose it and hurtle earthward. But in the pellucid woods this afternoon, with a ceiling of branches, floating is safe. I believe tonight will be the full moon.

On my walks I got to thinking about what we choose to perceive, and how. It's such a temptation, to which I often succumb, to celebrate the perky signs of life without paying attention to quieter, more extended processes. When the lavender crested irises spangle the slope by the creek, who notices the fallen beech leaves there, pale and curved, damp, darkening, and then letting go into earth? And when one does take the time to study those subtler events (the returning, from the going forth), where are the words to describe them positively, or at least with neutrality? Our words are prejudiced by our fear of dying.

As I watched and listened for things that spoke to Leo's waning, to his coming stillness, I reckon I was loosening my own fatuous grip on immortality a little.

One afternoon, an air raid siren tore through the quietness. "So this is it. He's gone and done it." Half seriously I thought to lie down in the leaves and wait for destruction to sweep through the trees. The only regret I could imagine was not being with those I love most. Otherwise, my own death seemed brother to the empty wasp nest, the bleached box turtle shell, the lichen on the rocks, and the soughing water.

Then I remembered the volunteer fire department nearby.

In the dusk, two small white clouds hang over the creek; a long bleached bone lies on the bank. A shad tree in bloom; a cedar skeleton.

Tennis shoes on sand, clay. No more crashing down the hill through the leaves. Such elating closeness with earth, suddenly. Roots/veins/sinews stretch across the path. I stop to stroke a muscular ironwood trunk. A comely young man lopes up the path out of the dark "H'lo" "H'lo"—and passes. My ears pound.

Then I hurry downstream to find the cocoon. I can barely see. Have I gone too far? I backtrack. No. Must be further on. Downstream again. Where the creek foams noisily, it is hanging out over the water, suspended on a thin ligature from its branch. Ovid, rough. Waiting.

I hadn't expected Leo to respond, I guess, but as the woods became opaque green and the heat settled in, I got out there for walks less and less, and eventually with no word from San Francisco, I stopped writing.

Early one morning before the air got feverish, I walked downstream to check on the cocoon. There was no sign of it ever having been there.

With fall and then winter, the epidemic moved in over our daily lives, with its low clouds and its chill. A friend in Durham was diagnosed. An acquaintance in Chapel Hill died. Several friends organized the N.C. Lesbian and Gay Health Project and as part of that I began visiting a man over at the V.A. Hospital who had moved back from San Francisco to be near his family out in Marion.

Talk didn't come readily for Michael and me. Often he would keep staring at the IV, so I took to massaging his skinny legs and swollen feet, and then his rigid shoulders and his bruised face. "Brings me flowers and rubs my legs," he explained to a new nurse in his soft mountain voice.

I didn't know if Leo was alive or dead. The reports of his meningitis had been so severe, I figured he was gone. Then word came that he was in DC. He had rallied unexpectedly, as is the case with AIDS sometimes, and had come back East to see his folks. Things were fine and then suddenly they weren't and now he was in a fancy hospital up there.

May 1

Dear Carl (my partner/friend Carl had just gone off for the summer),

The time with Leo was pretty good. Like Michael he's starved for touching. Says about the only contact he has now is with cold medical instruments and hypodermic needles. He's gaunt and weak, but a good deal chattier than M. has become. Nothing much profound to our talk, but still it seems important.

Being around his mother, a gracious woman who brings lilacs, bleeding hearts and lily of the valley from their place in McLean, puts me in mind of "The Garden of the Finzi-Continis," except these Jews are Southern.

Michael died on May the 16th. With Gail, his generous, feisty little sister, I watched his crusted lips opening and closing, slower, slower and his unseeing eyes. "You stubborn bastard! You just won't die, will you?" she cried and laughed at the same time. The gaping mouth slacked and, finally, was still. Something in me felt like a bass getting ripped from a pond.

We held on to each other and wept.

May 19, DC

Dear Carl,

Leo sleeps now, drugged for the injection into the reservoir in his skull, coming shortly, that will make him extremely nauseated. Before he dozed off he told the nurse he was afraid.

I see now why Whitman embraced the chance to nurse Civil War soldiers. Surely the democracy of death confirmed all the egalitarian effusion of Leaves of Grass. *Here the waiting, the pain, the wasting away are familiar from Michael's ordeal at the V.A. The fuss about petty things, the erosion of civility. Although Leo still says "Thank you" after I massage his legs—a vestage of his rearing—mostly such differences fade and he and Michael, who clogged for nickels at the bus station as a boy, become brothers.*

Last time I was up he talked of how exciting the gay scene in SF was at first. A chance for him to be close to men he had been protected from growing up in the patrician burbs.

Now the doctor is injecting the drug into his head that will incite vomiting.

Next day, Sunday

Bedside again. Leo's sleeping. With long hawkbeak nose and sunken cheeks he looks like an unwrapped mummy, or the Danish bog man. Today there's a new IV hooked up, this time into his foot. Blood and sodium solution.

Yesterday his mother, who in spite of breeding is rattled by her son's ignominious demise, insisted that we drive out to McLean to visit. Now, looking at Leo, I see a good bit more than before. Their place is all vast lawns with grand plantings of azalea and boxwood. Huge oaks. Leo's mother was just coming up from the pool, in her bathrobe and espadrilles. I had thought her invitation might be a muted call for help, but as she led us from flower bed to flower bed she seemed put upon and distracted. Here were rare azaleas. Here the enormous rhododendrons Leo planted as a boy.

Leo's father stalked around in pajamas, growling at the Salvadoran yardboy who had scattered the tools. No time, just a few gruff words for his son's faggot friends. No wonder Leo always seemed paralyzed—partly from waiting for the next silver platter to come around, and partly from the terror of a bitter, disappointed father.

So here I am, back watching the ruined scion sleep, crumpled among engulfing sheets and gown. A week ago his Puerto Rican lover, Ramon, visited. He's young, working class. Glad I wasn't a fly on the mansion wall for that.

Monday, May 21, Durham

Once Leo woke up yesterday, I helped him with his lunch and we talked a little. I asked him how he would rather have had all this proceed and immediately he said he wished he were back in California with his lover and friends.

I'm tempted to call the gay clinic in DC and inquire about folks to visit Leo. In the hall as I was leaving I asked one of the nurses if she knew of anybody visiting AIDS cases—they have five or six there. She looked confused and a tetch nonplussed and said she hadn't run into anyone. It made me value our Health Project work here more, and to appreciate the warmth of some of the V.A. staff. I reckon those country club hospitals tend to be high tech and low empathy sometimes.

And so I part ways with Leo L. Back in college, when he would bake shortbread in the biology lab oven during off-night study jags, or when we luxuriated among the camellias in the snow-covered greenhouse, or wore our whites for dancing "Spring Garden" and "Step Stately," I would never have guessed that 20 years later I would mop up the diarrhea in which he lay, or stroke his stubbly, waxen face as he dozed in a drugged stupor.

July 20

Dear Carl,

Late Thursday night I got a call from Ramon Santos, Leo's lover in SF. Leo Died June 21. His family buried him quickly and notified none of his gay friends. For the last month Leo couldn't or wouldn't talk. Ramon would call and talk to a silent void. He was going through Leo's papers and found some letters I wrote last spring. Funny to have such a forthright, emotional conversation in the middle of the night with a man I've never met.

It will be years and years before we understand the magnitude of this AIDS experience. I wonder that it might prove to be one of the major events of late 20th century culture. The minstrels become Greek chorus.

I was too shook up when we were done to go back to bed. I fetched ballpoint and pad, put on my sneakers and drove out to the woods, to retrace the route I used to take. The moon was full and the lightning bugs were out, but as I walked I got all turned around and scared and could only think about trying to find my way out. A storm was coming on. For a while the lightning helped, the rain set in and I got soaked.

Finding a path in leaves, on earth, is one thing in the dark. Groping along jagged rocks is another. I thought about how death is graceless—getting lost on terrain that was once familiar and then suddenly is strange and hostile. A few hours later I ended up on Whitfield Road, somehow, standing shirtless in the rain, staring up at the sky, breathing deep.

September 12

Now Warren, Glen and Philip have died, too.

In the woods the thin, high songs of crickets merge with the wind in the trees, like a distant river. I process through this world of leaves waving a dogwood branch to fend off spider webs and beggars' lice.

I pass the shiny orange berries of the hearts a-bustin', hanging from their deep pink hulls; then the stiff brown seedheads of self-heal, or heal-all. After weeks of terrible heat the morning is cool and grey. Down by the creek a spike of cardinal flower glows blood red.

III ISSUES

Myself in the Image of the King of the Wood

by Mutsuo Takahashi
(Translated by Hiroaki Sato)

I have no voice. The owl living on a high oak branch has my voice.
I have no shadow. The rustling reeds behind the oak wood have my
    shadow.
I have no gestures. Instead of me, the world beyond the reed lake
has my gestures, swaying.
I have no face. Instead of me, the only person to visit me
will have my unmistakable face.
On a night of a beautiful full moon, from the world beyond the lake,
    he will come.
Rustling the reeds he will cross the lake and dash toward me as I
    stand in the wood to welcome him.
A sword will flash, and voiceless, I will lie fallen by his feet.
That moment I will become him, I will for the first time have a face,
    the face of the one who visits me.
He will become me. He will have become the one to continue to wait
    in the wood,
without a face, without gestures, without a shadow.

Oh My Loving Brother

by Clinton Joyce Jesser

Judging from the discomfort and pain I produce for myself, I sometimes feel the times in which we live are all wrong for me—a white, middle-aged married male with two teen-aged children. Then, on a higher level, I sense that these times may be almost perfect, for my life has been about encounter in marriage, parenthood, feminism, and especially my male sex role and who I really am.

My transformation seems to have begun with a jolt about eight years ago (after I had already achieved some "success" in my career) while waiting by my father's bed for 78 hours until he died, and while my wife was becoming independent, clear, and assertive. My personal experience of this change mingles inexorably with my scholarship and teaching in the sociology of sex (gender) roles at my university.

The problems and struggles of women are surely important, but I am not writing about these. I want to talk about men and men's lives. Although men are diverse in their stamina in life and in economic and racial-ethnic background, I sense a new awareness common to all of us.

In my opinion, "sexism," with its popular association with political and economic discrimination and with the double standard in sexuality, does not accurately describe the disabilities and growing concerns of many men of this time. Many of our lives began with subtleties of upbringing that are only now being exposed by research: boys more than girls are treated with less direct affection, security, and nurturance. This is not to say that boys are grossly neglected, but translated it means research findings such as these:

1) by six months of age boys receive less physical and verbal contact[1];

2) fewer are breast-fed[2];

3) when held, boys are more often positioned outward, away from the holder[3];

4) boys more often get spanked[4]; and

5) they feel that their mothers desire them less than girls[5] (in spite of the fact that couples' preference for a first child is more often for a boy).

"Snips and snails and puppy-dog tails" is not far from the truth, if these findings are correct. Male socialization seems to be directed toward instilling achievement need and anxiety through some amount of rejection by adult socializers. Although experts disagree, I don't think genes, hormones, or "skin to skin" messages have much to do with this. As one of my wise women friends put it: "It seems that mothers (or fathers) send little boys away (from the nest) *unfulfilled* because this guarantees that they'll have to come back."

The picture that emerges is not one of a tough, independent man, but one who must *earn* identity *via* achievements—win (and keep winning), a good job, a high salary, and a supportive woman. It is surprising—in the midst of the myth about male independence—that the very symbols for manliness are actually so precarious; they can vanish at any time! Perhaps men's need to control wives, situations, job security, etc., emerges from these unhealthy and unacknowledged dependencies.

Again, in school boys are encouraged and choose to assume the "over-dog" role in which, from the outset, a better performance is expected of them in most tasks than from girls just because they are males. At the same time, learning disabilities, stuttering, and other handicaps abound many times over for boys, making the over-dog expectation less and less tenable.

Role stereotypes for boys' and mens' personal lives are rigid and limiting. (More men than women want to change their sex—a complicated solution, indeed.) This includes not just the constriction with regard to emotional expression—discouragement to men crying, for example—but in many other ways, such as manner of speaking, choice of subjects, and dress. When I once asked a young man in one of my classes what his girlfriend/wife would do if he wanted to use and used some eyebrow/lid coloring and painted his nails, he replied that she would drop him! It may be that "where we are" is in the double-message situation: Men are often starved for affection but afraid (or unable) to ask for it for fear of loss of expected dominance or of being inappropriate. They may even feel they are unworthy of love because they haven't earned (achieved) it.

Men's emotional tie to women—an admittedly complex and controversial topic—is noted in the higher incidence of suicide of men in the breakup of relationships with women and in the very inability of widowers to survive. There is even a theory floating around that says men keep "going for" women partly out of tradition and training, but also because of the sense of self inadequacy, incompleteness, anxiety, and male limitations in personal life. Men can only vicariously experience through women (THE Woman) some of their own denied femininity. Many men have only their wives to talk to on an intimate basis and even this may be difficult because of the economic obligation that often surrounds that role relationship. One feminist writer has suggested that women have a richer heritage and folklore for sharing and empathizing with one another through the everyday vicissitudes and the critical seasons or passages of our lives. One begins to understand what women are talking about when they set up conferences (as one told me recently) around the apprehension that in moving into a "man's world" they will lose this personal enrichment and affinity to others.

The impact of socialization and social structure on men is again attested to in crime rates. (I won't even talk about some of the stupid sexual scripts we consume as boys.) Why can't men genuinely ask for help with frustrations, inner fears, and problems instead of acting them out violently or in other big power games that contribute to the fact that over 90 percent of convicted felons are men? Another related issue involves the way men handle anger. Anger is often mixed with fear of failing or it is easily provoked when our vulnerabilities and pretenses as men are exposed or when our tacit dependency bargains with women we support break down.

I'd like to see more love, nurturance, warmth, and protection shown to boys and men (skid row is about 99 percent men!). I'd like to see real social supports which will encourage men to love themselves. I'd like to see men loving other men (not just sexually), commiserating with each other, and integrating genuinely recreational play activity with their work (not hunting or drinking "sports"). Maybe I'm different, but I'd like to see two men plan ahead for breakfast with each other when no "shop talk" is scheduled or when no instrumental problem to be solved seems to be the occasion for their getting together.

Recently during a conference on human growth, I had the exhilarating experience of sharing intimately in a men's group for a series of "rap sessions" over a two-day period—a first for me. Men *can* talk with one another and share the inner self.

There will be those who will read this and say, "All that's true for women, too," or that "Women have it worse." OK. Some might say that I sound "whiny," that men already have all the privileges. Perhaps so, but I am not talking about privilege. I know that, although as a class men may oppress women, only a *few* men (working in a system to which we often consent) have significant social and economic power. I suspect that more and more men are going to confront some difficult change in their lives involving themselves and their male sex role. At this point, the "new awareness" may be nothing more than anticipation of that among men.

I predict the men's revolution is coming and it may not look anything like the women's, since our issues are not easily politicizable. I am, nevertheless, convinced that they are highly important.

NOTES:

[1] Michael Lewis, "Culture and Gender Role: There's No Unisex in the Nursery," *Psychology Today,* Vol. 5 (May, 1972), pp. 54-57.

[2] Warren Farrell, *The Liberated Man,* New York; Bantam Books, 1975, p. 31.

[3] Michael Lewis, "State as an Infant-Environment interaction: An Analysis of Mother-Infant Interaction as a Function of Sex," *Merrill-Palmer Quarterly of Behavior and Development,* Vol. 18 (1972), pp. 95-121.

[4] Kay M. Tooley, "Johnny I Hardly Knew Ye," *American Journal of Orthopsychiatry,* Vol. 47, (April, 1977), pp. 184-195.

[5] Ruth E. Hartely, "Sex Role Pressures and the Socialization of the Male Child." in Joseph A. Pleck and Jack Sawyer, ed., *Men and Masculinity,* Englewood Cliffs, N.J., Prentice-Hall, (1974), pp. 6-13.

Men and Their Health—
A Strained Alliance

by Sam Julty

Among the powerful messages in the tradition male role are: Do *unto* others; do *for* others; deny thyself; you are your tasks. The product of these imperatives is the alienation of men from others and from self. Consequently, men are not taking care of business concerning their own health and well-being.

This problem is not fully explained by calling men slaves to the macho role, suicidal, or jerks who don't know what's good for them. My work in the area of men's health has helped me make some observations which might explain why fewer men than women are found in doctor's offices, clinics, health fairs, and workshops.

First, the absence of biological reminders. Nature has made women aware of their normal bodily processes and stages of life in more profound ways than it has made men. Menstruation, maternity, and menopause are but three vivid examples. Sometimes these processes require intervention by practitioners with knowledge and experience in these areas. Hence, for most women the medical profession, healer or mentor is an acceptable attendant to her life's processes. For most men the highlights of our natural processes of passage are few and less dramatic. If I had to choose three my vote would go to: our first cognitive erection, first shave, and first grey hair—none of which require any 2nd-party intervention. In the course of the average man's lifetime they somehow lose their significance almost as quickly as their onset.

The second reason for the low health consciousness among men deals with the social rules of our present culture which assign most life's tasks on the basis of gender. Despite the fact that half of the nation's wage earners are women, the operative ideology for most of our population puts the responsibility for family healthcare in the hands of its female members. Regardless who needs the medical attention—parent, child, husband, or the woman herself—our prevailing social order gives women the task of nurturing, nursing, healing, or bringing in the healer. Of course, many men and women have reorganized their lives so family duties are not gender-specific. But, while the prevailing ideology says men are expected to be the providers and women the nurterers, it becomes easy for men to view healthcare as something others need; others take care of; it doesn't apply to them.

A third reason deals with estrangement of men and healers. Right here, it is vital that we drop the myth that all men patients enjoy special or preferential treatment from doctors because medicine is a male-dominated institution. My studies, my personal experience, and recent medical literature suggest that men have no decided advantage over women as patients (especially in surgery). The super-professional, super-cool, and supercilious physician with the bedside manner of a cobra does not suddenly become Dr. Niceguy when he has a man stretched out on his examining table. The sensitive and supportive doctor will be so to all his patients.

Men have no surrogate similar to the women's health movement to represent them in cases of patient abuse. So, they do what men often do when faced with what appears to be an impossible situation—they vote with their feet, cuss out everyone involved and stay away from any type of healthcare provider.

These are but three factors which shape attitudes about health and healing among the general population of men. I have no doubts that they, in alliance with the traditional learned roles (and lies) we are taught about our so-called invulnerability, contribute largely to the 10-year gap in longevity which now exists between men and women.

A Political Issue

I believe that as men who claim to have an elevated awareness of the social order around us we must get behind the concept that men's healthcare is a viable political/social issue. By commission or omission we must no longer support the concept of the medical establishment that healthcare is a personal/private matter. Our work and studies must begin to demonstrate the many connections between a man's lifestyle and attitudes and his own health.

Work. On the job men generally reveal three behaviors: a) They drive themselves hard. b) Many are not strict about the use of safety equipment or procedures. c) Their diets are often secondary to the obligations of the job.

As we develop the issues which would change these behaviors we have to be able to deal with a strong belief system held by many men: A man's value of himself is closely connected to his primary means of income. For a great many, his job isn't the only thing in his life—it's everything. It represents solvency; the fulfillment of his role as provider; the product of his training; the realization of his ambitions. Somehow we have to make connections between the type of job a man has, how he performs, and how they relate to his general health.

Physical Wellbeing. The average man knows very little about his body, what makes it work, and why it sometimes doesn't. As a boy he learned that how he behaved, reacted, and achieved as a male was more important than how he took care of his heatlh. Physical fitness was little more than a support to excellence in mastering his masculine training. As an adult he often displays two distinct attitudes about his health. On the one hand he usually takes it for granted. If it has been good up to now, it will be good forever. On the other hand, when something does go wrong he goes into a tailspin. Some men do not like being reminded that they are mortal and vulnerable. Some see sickness as an intrusion into their orderly structure. Others fear disability and loss of income.

Emotional Wellbeing. Certainly men are aware of the stresses imposed on them, but few make the connections between traditional masculinity and those pressures. They say, "Sure it's a tough road, but what choices do I have? I have to eat; I have to provide for my family." It is for us to come up with real answers to these questions, rather than knee-jerk responses.

Today, the effect of those emotional stresses on the overall health of men are just beginning to be understood. We, I feel, have the task of taking this problem beyond the medical model and showing how closely connected these stresses are to the impositions of the traditional masculine role. And while we perform the task we have to focus on the alienating aspect of traditional masculinity, and drop the assumption that all men are taken care of by an "Old-Boys Network," or covered by the so-called concept of "male bonding."

What We Can Do

The alliance of men and their health is indeed strained. What will we do to reduce that strain? Doctors can wait until pain and debilitation forces men to their offices. Hospitals can wait until accidents and homicides drive men to their ERs and morgues. We simply cannot wait until stardust falls on men's heads and raises their consciousness about their health and wellbeing. If we are serious about our concerns for the carnage wrought by the present male role we cannot exclude the many ways that role separates men from their own wellbeing.

Where do we start? In my view the first task is for us to develop a consciousness of our own about men's health and the social/political issues connected with it. Sexism induces stress; traditional roles induce heart attacks; insecticides induce infertility; work pressures induce maimed bodies; economic pressures induce maimed minds; wars induce death—in men. There isn't a single political issue that doesn't adversely affect the health of the men involved in it.

Next, I feel we should do what we can to promote the dissemination of more data on men's health. This may come as a shock but information specific to men's health is sparse for both professional and consumer. Even statistics on how many men suffer this or that, or how many men are dying of what, is available to only the most diligent researcher.

If we ignore the connections between men's lives and their health and if we accept the idea that it is OK to keep data on men's health buried we give credence to the idea that men are just expendable bodies in service of a higher order.

Circumcision: A Conspiracy of Silence

by James Whipple

No male on this earth begins life without a covered penis but then rituals and ignorance take over and many lose their foreskins. Wouldn't it be more meaningful for each male to decide his own fate as an adult?

My interest in this subject began when I first realized I was different from my father. Since that introduction I have had my knowledge expanded by those who are against this surgery, and I have matured enough to share the feelings I and others have experienced concerning the second most frequently performed operation in this country—one that is not talked about openly except in Lamaze or LeBoyer classes even though its results are visible to every man.

I was born during WW II when the practice of circumcision was being strongly promoted for all newborns. Luckily (?) I was premature and not mutilated at birth. I don't remember when I was aware that my penis and my father's were different. I'm sure it was not a verbal awakening, as he has always been extremely uptight sexually. The only verbal information he ever gave me was that I had to retract the foreskin and wash the glans, or it would be irritated. I didn't do this faithfully, as the warm bath water erotically tickled the exposed skin, and so I did experience some slight problems. However, he never mentioned the word "circumcision," attempted to tell me why or how I was different from him, or expressed his feelings about the operation.

At the age of five, I suffered the shocking reality of being "natural." Like many others, I was taken to the doctor for a pre-tonsillectomy exam and ended up naked on the table with my genitals and abdomen being covered with antiseptic. I assume (even to this day, I continue to block out the details) that I was told that he was going to cut off the skin covering the apex of my masculinity so it would always be healthy. I recall crying and yelling and being physically drained before my mother took me home. I was still intact.

After that experience I constantly thought about my penis. I began my fanatical efforts to look at any nude man, which proved to be a highly frustrating assignment. The real, but unwelcomed, opportunity came when I was in the seventh grade and had to swim *au naturel* in swim class. I happened to live in a medium-sized city in the Midwest where most of the boys were circumcised and just a few non-WASP and disadvantaged ones were uncut. During those three miserable years, I observed possibly twenty others who were normal in this school of six hundred. I was a SKINHEAD and every time I heard either of those words I prayed someone would offer to cut it off or that I would find a way to permanently get out of PE for the rest of my life. I just couldn't understand why I was so inferior. The two swim teachers made each of us pass a shower inspection "to keep the pool clean" (it was chlorinated). Unfortunately we three in Period 5 had to retract our foreskins in the shower while one of the men watched. I either got a roaring hard on or was shivering so violently that my genitals shrank to invisibility.

These traumas gave me a complete set of negative self images. I was sure that I was not circumcised because I was somehow deficient. My "big" father was clipped, the great majority of my peers were mutilated, so what was so wrong with me that I was different? A good answer evaded me for too many years! The only good memory is my discovery of masturbation. I learned to enjoy that wonderful sensual feeling of the air making my glans tingle when I pulled the skin back, the excitement of a cock that became marvelously long, not to mention the thrill of coming. Now I was "sexually mature" but hurt and humbled by being different.

I began haunting the public library praying that I could be allowed to read the sexually explicit books of the 1950s. I read anything noted under *Circumcision* in the index. Unhappily, what I read was not comforting. I learned that the amputation stopped masturbation, VD, insanity, and other horrible physical and mental problems I never knew existed. I was really done in! I was probably going to experience all those consequences. And my self-loving was evil incarnate—and I was enjoying it every day! The reason for my being non-athletic in build and interests was evident: I was not circumcised. I felt completely alone. I didn't feel my friends would understand me, and I knew no way to learn if any adult was thinking positively about foreskins. I kept looking for and seeing a scant number of covered penises, but I continued to be obsessed with finding positive written statements about a male in my condition.

We moved to a rural area, and I was going to a sports-centered high school. All that summer I worked on making my penis look "normal". I retracted the skin above the corona. After fourteen years this was not easily done, but I had made the commitment that I was going to fit in with the majority. To anyone watching me, it must have been an excellent summer theater program, as I continually had my hand in my pants because the prepuce was always sliding down to its normal position; my glans was so sensitive that every time I moved I felt like one big raw nerve ending; the erections were impossible to hide and I spent many solitary hours. I had learned that circumcised guys jacked off using their spit or slippery liquids. Since I was to be like them, I had to act that way. I was not successful, I couldn't keep myself from using my skin, I didn't want to work that hard. Even today I have never come without using my skin.

The first day of PE at the new school came. I was ready and so proud to show off my new look. "I was a *real* looking man!" (Un)fortunately this group of teenagers had not gotten into the mainstream. Most of the male athletes were natural with impressive genitals. I couldn't win! I was glad that I only had passing fantasies about being cut, and I began to think that self stimulation enjoyments were more important than looks. Anyway, these guys did look masculine. I wasn't satisfied. My search for positive written information continued. I would have settled for just one positive sentence indicating that "natural" was OK.

In college I read several articles that hinted that a majority of mankind considered that a penis had a moveable part, but I couldn't figure out why American men didn't need everything. Slowly I became at peace with my body, deciding that it was time to return to normal. Six months of stretching and taping finally got it back, and within two or three years the sensitivity returned to the glans.

Soon I was able to spend time in a large medical library. I read about the interesting medical failures and successes with prepuces but still nothing about the American reasons for the amputation. My most welcomed experience concerning the value of a complete set of genitals came from readings in military medicine. A soldier's eyelids were burned off, but since he was intact, reconstruction was possible. His foreskin could provide the only skin that would do the job. Almost simultaneously several veteran friends told me that the uncut men didn't stay that way in the American military establishment. Just as I was fighting with my Draft Board!

I also gained knowledge of a few "off the wall" persons in medicine who were talking negatively about circumcision, but my profs insisted that the surgery was necessary for the male's health and that was what medicine was for. More than ever, when I heard the word "circumcision" I felt my face turn deep red and felt my penis shrinking into oblivion with the words: "Please, don't discover I'm not circumcised" shooting through my mind. Only later did I hear mutilated men say they felt and experienced the same sensations about themselves.

In the 1970s I began working with childbirthing classes. There were no films or slides available then concerning the procedures used in this operation. It was only quickly mentioned or an educator had to rely on drawings and personal comments concerning the pain involved. I then started posing the question of letting the baby decide his own penis' fate, but resistance was high. Only the mothers wanted to hear about the subject. Eventually men started debating the issue of conformity with me, and I was hearing such comments as: "Aren't all men circumcised?"; "Isn't it the law?"; "I remember uncircumcised guys being operated on in the Service; they were embarrassed then"; "My wife thinks it looks better that way". "I want my son to be like me."

With the movement toward more natural living and childbirth, the circumcision questions began to be openly examined by individuals like Bud Berkely, Tony Lesce, Jim Peron, Roger Saquet, Russell Zangger, Rosemary Romberg Wiener, Jeff Woods and Paul Zimmer. Today there are several excellent resource books on the subject and even the medical community is publishing articles asking for a review of its attitudes concerning the operation.

I started being surprised by the number of men who were not pleased with their cut state and were willing to discuss their feelings with me. That allowed me to reject much of my negative self image. In time I began corresponding with a man who shared his story of foreskin restoration because he wanted to be "completely male." That friendship got me to the point of being actually proud of all my body.

A sampling of statements made by cut males would probably include: "I was mutilated without my consent"; "I was always afraid that after getting me circumcised at age five, my mother would have some other part of me cut off"; "I wish I'd said 'No' when the medic had me sign the circumcision authorization; I lost a lot, but I didn't want to be dishonorably discharged." The one comment I'll always remember is: "I envy my dog."

Where Now? Only a few of us will have the money, desire and determination to submit to penile surgery but a few have done so. Those who want adult circumcisions have few problems finding a physician. Like I once felt, these men consider getting to that state their most masculine priority and most feel positive afterwards. I have heard comments such as: "I always felt ashamed of being different; now I'm circumcised and happy"; "I'm proud to be circumcised; now I'm a real man"; "I never thought that any real American male was not circumcised."; "I kept my foreskin for about twenty-five years . . . so when the opportunity presented itself, I had the damn thing removed . . . it was the best thing I ever did."

On the other side, change is not so easy. While foreskin restoration has probably been with us since the first man's penis was forceably altered, today's American medical professionals will test your masculinity, your personality, sanity and your financial resources before agreeing that you really want a pseudo-foreskin. The scrotal implant technique is most common for those who have no excess tissue to work on. If one has extra skin, the stretching method is widely promoted since the only cost is time and privacy, and a man can set his own pace. I know of men who have used these methods, and there are other ways known to medical history. The individuals tell me that they are comfortable with having recovered part of what they had taken from them. Although their anger remains, they are philosophical about their replacement being better than nothing.

If your interest and compassion have been stirred, I would ask that you learn more and openly support those of us who have been or are currently troubled by "such a little piece of tissue" so that some day our society will allow adult men to make their own choice.

Bringing War Home:
Vets Who Batter

by Rick Ritter

When he sees jets or hears planes he still ducks and tries to get away—he gets real paranoid. Then he'll start talking about dead bodies that he used to see.... There are times when he loses control, but it is never with the children.... I would rather let him take out his hate (the war) on me.... He doesn't always know when he's hit me.... I ask myself, 'Why am I still hanging around for this?'.... Sometimes I confront him with God, and he just gets real quiet and stops—those are the times he is more aware. Our daughter is five and she tells him that he shouldn't hit mommy and then he feels guilty for awhile ....

Things seemed to be getting straightened out when I met my ex-husband at a friend's party and he proceeded to hit me in the stomach, the head, the legs and slap me. This alarmed me and awakened me to the fact that even though we are not married anymore, I must physically put distance between us because he seemed to want to kill me this last time. It appeared to be too premeditated to suit me.....

My boyfriend is a Nam vet, and several months ago he experienced a flashback to Nam in which he perceived my son and myself as VC prisoners and he proceeded to batter both of us. He was on narcotics in Nam and it is difficult for me to sort out where exactly his behavior emanates from when he gets in an angry/vengeful mood. On another occasion he tortured me as though I was a prisoner by heating a dry saucepan on the stove and then holding it on me causing some very severe burns. His problems since coming back from Nam have been exacerbated by alcohol and drug addiction problems. He has felt that [alcohol and drugs]... help him deal with his Nam ghosts....

Excerpts from case histories of women
battered by Vietnam war veterans.

Battering is a problem for a large number of Vietnam era veterans who come to the Ft. Wayne Vet Center seeking assistance in dealing with the Vietnam experience. The Nam vet is similar to other men in society in the sense that he has a very difficult time confronting the fact that he may have battered a significant other. This denial is accompanied by guilt and shame. One difference between the vet and the non-vet batterer is that the vet may also be dealing with guilt and shame from his combat experience in Nam. He is more likely to react to stress with the use of physical violence, and those veterans trained to be ground troops are even more prone to react this way.

Counseling vets at the Center focuses on "readjustment counseling," an umbrella term that includes counseling for delayed combat stress, physcial and mental disabilities, bad paper, family problems, herbicide poisoning, employment problems, drug addictions, and anything else that is a "problem" for the Nam vets. The majority of the vets at the Center are also struggling with their definitions of what is male. Socially imposed machismo gets in the way of their being human and of relating effectively to the people they are close to. They want so badly to regain this portion of their identity that was lost in Nam and to be successful and productive human beings again—but not necessarily the way this society defines either success or productiveness. The problem of battering does not come to the forefront in some counseling sessions until the vet gains some insight into the healing process and also develops a trust in the counseling staff. The majority of the vets are ashamed about what they have done. They believe that we will judge/reject them because of what they have done to a woman or a child. (Approximately one-third of the 600 vets presently at the Center have been involved in battering women or children.) Though vets have come to the Center specifically to get better control of themselves so they will not continue as batterers, in some cases we deal with the victims of battering, because the vet may not come in.

It is tempting in beginning counseling to allow the vet to use tangential issues to legitimize his battering. However, I cannot, in all honesty, tell a vet that he batters because he was drinking, or because his wife or girlfriend deserves it, or any other false reason for having initiated abusive action against another human being. I can empathize about his being a batterer, but I cannot and will not condone it under any circumstance.

I prefer to focus primarily on the revivification of the military training and the vet's combat experience. This can be uncomfortable, and the counselor must be prepared to help the vet dig to the very bottom of the material that he has so effectively suppressed over the last ten years. There have been many instances of battering situations where the root of the problem has been a flashback/ nightmare, yet it seems that in most cases the psychiatric community and the legal system have turned deaf ears to what has actually occurred. Instead of trying to listen and understand they have crucified these vets for flashback nightmares that they have little or no control over. These occurrences cause the vet to perceive that he is back in combat and feels that his life is in danger, and he acts out survival strategies. During a flashback/nightmare, he is not conscious of his actions or his surroundings. If the vet feels as though he is in any type of physical danger, real or imagined, then he will act out the survival mode of his previously learned behavior patterns. This phenomenon is seemingly difficult for many women's counselors to accept. The reaction that I have gotten from many counselors is that this is a cop-out we are using to excuse the vets' behavior. Let me stress that we are not making excuses for Nam vets but rather encouraging people to understand a generally ignored problem. The existing literature in the field of delayed stress would seem to indicate that through the revivification of the Nam experience, a vet can begin, even if only rudimentarily, to more successfully process that experience and again be a whole person.

After these experiences have been relived, then it is our job to see that those experiences are properly identified and correlated to the vet's behavior and attitudes as they exist today. This is crucial if the vet is going to have the basic tools to heal himself. Those vets in particular who were trained to be the ground troops in Nam were given the type of training that made them killers. They were taught to react to certain types of stimuli in a physically aggressive manner. What seems to unnerve the people of this land is that the same Nam vet is fully capable of using those same destructive skills against the general population. These dehumanized troops never had the opportunity to be deprogrammed from the aberrant methods of that war. They are simply sent home to deal with the Vietnam experience in the best way that they can.

The Nam vet is a survivor because of his conformity to such destructive patterns of behavior. A vet has faced death experiences and has survived. Because he has survived he will not deviate from those behavioral patterns that served him so well in the military setting. Most combat vets react to everyday stress situations in similar ways, no matter how seemingly insignificant the stimulus may be. The survivor syndrome is one that must be dealt with if a vet is to gain insight into his battering behavior. Once the vet begins to understand that it's OK to show emotion and to communicate those suppressed feelings about Nam, he can begin to understand what it is to be a male in the most complete sense. Once the vet begins to feel capable of caring for, and nurturing other human beings, the attitude that "a woman should be beat daily whether she needs it or not" will not be acceptable any longer. This process also requires that the vets have role models other than John Wayne, Wyatt Earp, the Rifleman, George Patton, or survival expert Lt. Colonel (Ret.) Anthony Herbert.

Many Nam vets feel they lost a portion of their humanness over there. Isn't it high time that they be allowed and assisted in regaining some of what they lost? Isn't it time that some gentle...men appear on the societal scene in much greater numbers.

Rape Prevention and Masculinity

by Kendall Segel-Evans

Most articles on preventing rape and other forms of sexual assault are addressed to women and other potential victims. They present suggestions for self-protection ranging from ideas about effective caution to methods for aggressive counter-attack. As necessary as these ideas are, they are necessarily temporary solutions. Potential victims cannot prevent sexual assault. This article is addressed to men. Men rape. Men can stop rape.

As a man, I find this difficult to accept. I would rather believe society's myths about rape: that women enjoy rape; that women "ask for it" by teasing men sexually; and that rapists are disturbed people very different from myself. Such myths are comfortable, but untrue.

Rape victims do not "ask for it." Victims can be attractive or ugly, rich or poor, very young or old, married or single, female or male, or anything at all. In fact, rape is not primarily sexual. To the victim, it is an attack. To the rapist, it is an expression of anger or a need to dominate. In addition, rape is not uncommon, or committed only by disturbed men. Up to one in three women in Los Angeles will be sexually assaulted in her lifetime. For that to be true, an incredible number of men, ordinary men, are committing sexual assault. Forensic evaluators have consistently found that convicted rapists are no more disturbed as a group than other criminals. They are more angry.

Furthermore, when I talk with women about their treatment by men, I find that rape is just an extreme form of what men do to women every day of a woman's life. Rape conveys the message that the victim is only a sexual thing to be used, and has no right to physical or emotional safety, comfort, integrity, or even dignity. The same message is given by comments from strangers on the street and by treatment from male acquaintances on the job and socially that demonstrate to women that to these men, a woman is a vagina first and a person second, if at all. Every woman I have talked to has had the experience of being pressured to have intercourse through a variety of tactics, including pleading, bribery, lies, blackmail, drugs, and threats.

In other areas of life, such as on the job, doing business, or talking about topics like politics, women often feel men do not take them seriously. Men ignore, interrupt, and condescend to women when they talk together. In addition, women (and men) are constantly exposed to advertising that emphasizes women's sexual availability ("if you buy X"...), and magazines, movies, and record covers that show naked women wanting sex, dying for even violent, sadistic sex. Every one of these experiences is an emotional rape. Women know that to be safe, each woman has to be on guard at all times and with every man. Men rape.

These are differences between a man who rapes in the literal, legal sense and the rest of us men. The major difference is that most of us stop with lower levels of coercion and violence. But it is necessary for us to know and acknowledge that all of us, growing up male, have learned the attitudes towards ourselves and women that make rape a reality. Only then can we begin to see that we are all victims of rape; we must all stop rape.

We men are not basically evil, mean creatures. Most of us are well-meaning people. Even rapists are generally people who want to see themselves as decent, humane people who do not mistreat others. (Because of this, it is easier to blame our victims than to face the reality of what we do.) We men are just doing the best to be the men that society taught us to be.

Tough, confident, self-reliant, aggressive, daring, dominant, successful, competent, sexually potent, emotionally controlled, and masculine in every way—that is, not feminine in any way. As boys we learned to avoid being called a "sissy," "cry-baby," or "queer". Our heroes were supermen like John Wayne, James Bond, or Humphrey Bogart. We learned that "winning is everything."

However, we knew we were not super. We sometimes felt like crying, felt weak and stupid, made mistakes, and often did not "measure up." We learned to hide those human feelings and ignore those human needs. We men learned to pretend, to lie, to brag, and to make do. We learned not to cry, not to show weakness or need, and not to be emotional. We learned whom we could dominate, where we could succeed, how we could appear to be as close to the impossible ideal as we could manage. Most of us have had some measure of success, and feel O.K. about our manhood—sort of. But we have all paid a price.

We gave up part of being human. We gave up meeting our needs for loving, caring, and mutual relationship. We have given up asking for support, comfort, affectionate cuddling, and permission to feel sad, weak and needy. We learned, instead, that only success, sex, and respect (or fear) were important or possible. That's all "real men" are supposed to want or get. We learned to make do with these substitutes for our true human needs, so that we could be "masculine" men.

Our quest for masculinity is expensive. Nothing is left undamaged, not our relationships, not our friends and family, not even our own health. Men have a high level of stress-related diseases and deaths, a high level of injury and death from unnecessary accidents and war, and high levels of alcohol and drug abuse. The intensity of general dissatisfaction with life among men is matched only by our resistance to seeking help. We men also show a high rate of violence and coercion toward each other as well as women and children. In many instances, we hurt others without realizing it, or believing we could do it any other way. We feel alienated from others, and bewildered by our difficult and unsatisfying relationships.

Part of the price of being a "real man" is difficulty in knowing women as they really are—people like ourselves. As boys we learned to avoid anything "feminine." Although our mothers were important to us as infants, we soon learned not to be a "mama's boy." For a while we learned not even to be associated with girls. (Remember at ten—girls, yecch!) Then we learned that female = sex, success, and respect for any male that "possessed" one. Women became the stuff of our nightmares and dreams, our enemy and prey. We learned that it was necessary to do anything to succeed with women. Women always want "it," but say no to test and tease—a challenge men must win over. These are attitudes that divide men and women and make rape possible.

Most of us learned to relate to women as real people some of the time, in spite of these ideas. But we all have had to struggle against the fantasies we have about women. The beliefs that sex will make us feel like men; that women are the source of everything that makes a man feel good—and vice versa; that women exist only for sex and service; that women are primarily sexual beings who use their sex to manipulate men; and that a "real man" dominates women. These and related attitudes interfere with and sometimes destroy our relationships with women. They also lead us to blame women, and to forget our own responsibility for our own sexuality and behavior.

We often feel a need to blame someone. We frequently do not feel in control of our lives. The feelings we try to hide force their way into our actions, and we do things even we do not understand. Success and respect are never really ours for more than a moment; we are either accepting half-best or constantly concerned about losing what we have to someone more competent or aggressive. Women seem frustrating, confusing, mysterious, and dangerous. Insulting them as weaker and less logical is often a protection against such fears. We are afraid of getting close even to male friends for fear of being seen as "homosexual," and we do not know how to handle our need to be close. Ironically, homosexuals also suffer from this fear of other men, and are also trapped in the pursuit of masculinity. Our lives are out of our control. We are trapped in our impossible quest for masculinity. The quest damages us, and in it, we damage others. Often that damage is in the form of rape.

Rape. The extreme essence of male rage at being trapped, and the ultimate expression of the trap in action. Rape occurs when a man no longer sees the victim as a real human being, but instead sees an "object" through which to become a "real man"—sexually powerful, successfully irresistible, and feared if not respected. It would be pathetic, if it were not so damaging to so many victims.

It is also pathetic that rape continues, and is so much a part of society. Society supports the attitudes about being a "real man" that result in rape and less severe forms of sexual assault and harassment. Society cooperates in portraying women as being primarily useful for sex and service—and victims as being to blame for their own victimization.

There have been some changes. At least in law a rape victim in California no longer has to prove her/his own innocence in court. Legally, a woman cannot be considered unsuitable for a job simply because she is female. Nevertheless, the old stereotypes still affect our lives powerfully. The trap, and rape, continue.

We men, together, can stop all this. We can stop sexual assault and other male violence against women, if we change ourselves and our culture. We must change our larger culture, including both customs and laws, to reflect the life-supporting belief that women and men are equal. We have similar needs, feelings, abilities and rights. We must also change our personal culture, the nature and quality of our relationships with other men and women.

We must escape the trap of impossible masculinity. It will not be easy; we have spent most of our lives learning the damaging rules. However, we can unlearn and relearn whatever we were taught, or taught ourselves. We can learn to feel openly, to cry, to be silly, and to ask for comfort and caring. We can learn to negotiate instead of forcing our will. We can learn to have relationships built on mutuality instead of dominance and servitude.

This relearning will require major changes in attitudes and assumptions about life and people. It definitely requires questioning everything we ever thought we believed about ourselves and our motivations.

Above all, it requires learning to listen—to one's lover, to one's friends, to strangers, and to one's own gut feelings. Not as a debater listens, not preparing our counter argument; but listening to understand. We men often do not listen to others, or even to ourselves. It is no wonder we often fail to understand, and find women, and our own and other's feelings, to be mysterious. The self-discipline of listening can be difficult, painful, irritating, and frustrating. It is also necessary, and by itself can cause major changes. Effective listening creates understanding.

It is harder to hurt someone when you are accurately listening to their feelings. If we learn how women feel, including the fear and pressure that the reality of rape causes its victims, we will stop laughing at jokes that trivialize women and the seriousness of sexual assault. We will stop using sex and threats of male force to intimidate the women we deal with. Fortunately, the work of listening is rewarded by the tremendous improvement it can bring to our relationships. Traditional men often feel isolated and estranged. Truly listening can bring us closer to others and more in tune with ourselves.

Another major change for men will be giving up all pretense of male privilege. It is flattering to one's ego to assume a protective stance with women. It is comforting to believe that it is natural to be dominant over women. Male privilege is only an illusion, however. The average male feels powerless and not in control of his own life; and that is real for them. No matter how much power one has over others, if a person is alienated from their own self and unable to meet their own needs, that person is powerless in the area of life that counts the most. The reward for giving up our belief in our superiority over women will be that we men can reclaim our full (and equal) humanity. We can reclaim our right to our own lives and needs, our own most precious power, by giving up all pretense of power over others.

Winning is not the only thing: living is.

Other Men

by John Stoltenberg

Some of us are the other men that some of us are very wary of. Some of us are the other men that some of us don't trust. Yet some of us are the other men that some of us want to be close to and hang out with. Some of us are the other men that some of us long to embrace.

The world of other men is a world in which we live behind a barrier—because we need to for safety, because we understand there is something about other men that we know we have to protect ourselves from. The world of other men is also a world in which we know we are sized up by other men and judged by other men and sometimes threatened by other men. The world of other men can be, we know, a scary and dangerous place.

I have been obsessed with other men for a long, long time. I have lived years of my life agonizing about how different I felt from other men. I have wanted more than anything to be more like other men than I could ever hope to be. At the same time I have harbored a terror of other men: afraid that they would see through my attempts to act like a man, afraid that I would not measure up, not fit in, not be right. Many of the men I talk with are also in various ways obsessed with other men. We don't talk about it readily; we don't really have the vocabulary for it. But always the issue is there, within us and between us—the issue of how one identifies oneself in relation to other men, the kinds of accommodations and compensations one makes depending on how one rates oneself on some imaginary scale of masculinity: If you think you rate relatively high, or if you think you rate relatively low, you make certain choices in your life, you choose the best deal you can get with the quantity of maleness you feel you can muster. And always other men are the measure of the man you try to be.

As individuals and as a movement, we need to understand what this issue is—why the issue is what it is—and how to think about the issue so that we can do something about it in our lives.

What the Issue Is

One of the reasons I started to care about radical feminism as much as I did was because it seemed to resolve for me a certain dilemma about myself in relation to other men. I had always felt irremediably different—even when no one else noticed, I knew; I knew I wasn't really one of them. When I first began to come in contact with the ideas of radical feminism, those ideas seemed to put to rest that certain trouble. Radical feminism helped me imagine a gender-just future, a notion of a possibility that men need not be brutish and loutish, that women need not be cutesy and coy. It was a vision that energized me. It helped me view the whole male-supremacist structure of gender as a social construction, not as a final judgment on our natures—and not as a final judgment on mine. Radical feminism helped me honor in myself the differences that I felt between myself and other men; radical feminism helped me know my connections to the lives of women, with whom I had not imagined I would ever find a model for who I could be. And it's also true—and not easy to admit—that radical feminism helped provide me with a form in which to express my anger at other men—an anger that in men can run very deep, as many of us know. I think that for many men who have become antisexists over the past several years, their antisexism has had meaning to them for similar reasons. In various ways, feminism has blown like a gust of fresh air through a lifetime spent agonizing and anguishing about the place of other men in our lives. For a few of us, feminism has helped us breathe a bit easier.

But it would be a mistake to suggest that a man's antisexism puts to rest his ambivalence toward other men. I think that an antisexist consciousness actually makes the conflict more acute. Such a man perceives even more clearly the behaviors and attitudes in other men that he rejects, and he understands more about what those behaviors and attitudes mean, and in a sense they are the behaviors and attitudes in himself that he wants to be rid of, and somehow other men can remind him of the parts of himself that have not changed very much at all, and whereas he briefly felt good about being different from other men, a part of him no longer feels quite different enough; so his anger at other men intensifies, as a means of keeping clear to himself that he's an exception. Meanwhile he misses the company of other men—their ease, their companionship, the good feelings he remembers having had in their presence.

For many men, the issue of other men is a classic conflict of approach and avoidance. For a man whose life increasingly has to do with antisexism, the conflict cuts to the bone. He struggles with what it means to be a man—and whether he feels ashamed or proud.

For antisexist men who are gay, this conflict has an explicitly sexual aspect. The more sensitive a man becomes to the sexism in other men's attitudes and behaviors, the more it matters to him that his sexual partners be men who share his world view, and the less able he is to accept sexist small talk and jokes as a token of the kind of comradeship that he seeks. As the sexual-political character of his sexual partners begins to matter, he is increasingly faced with a choice between abandoning his principles and abandoning his sex life. A man of good character is hard to find, as anyone who has looked can tell you.

But whether or not a man longs for a companionship with other men that wants to be sexual, he is confronted with a seemingly insoluble dilemma: He has his ideas, his beliefs, his vision, his commitments, about a just future in which gender would not divide us; and he has a longing for the company and validation of other men—men who, more often than not, do not share his antisexism.

Many of us have lost male friends over our antisexist politics—for the simple and terribly complex reason that we just could not abide a friend's sexism anymore. There seem to be two untenable options: affiliation and assimilation with men, just falling in with men on men's terms; or separation and estrangement, self-defined isolation. Neither option seems to hold out any long-term promise or possibility; at least to my knowledge, neither really works. You can't hang out all the time with men who are not working at being antisexist and feel good about yourself—it just doesn't work. And you can't feel good about yourself cutting yourself off from other men; that kind of separation becomes what you do and all that you do; who you are becomes a person who is estranged from other men to no purpose. No wonder so many of us are drawn to a notion of a brotherhood that is oblivious to women—a brotherhood that would make it easier to enjoy being a man because you wouldn't ever have to take women's lives seriously—you wouldn't ever have to take seriously what men have done to women because you would live in a world entirely circumscribed by other men, who are all that really matter. That is, after all, what most men seem to enjoy most about being men: They're not women, and they know they don't ever have to really pay any attention to women's lives.

Many of us have come to expect so much isolation from other men that even the prospect of cooperating and organizing with other antisexist men for change can make us really wonder, "How do I know these men are any different? How do I know their values are not just the same as other men's? And how do I know, once I fall in with them, that I'll be any different?" For many of us our feminism is virtually synonymous with isolation from other men. And our isolation becomes so debilitating that it stops us from doing anything about our antisexist beliefs. One example: In the past few years there have been a few men—very few, but some here and there in this country and others—who have recognized in most pornography the very values that infuse men's social and personal power over women, a structure of eroticized male supremacy and woman-hating. The recognition has been a difficult one; and some of those men have in fact cried over it—not sentimental, self-indulgent tears but tears of terrible, dreadful grief over man's inhumanity to woman. And these few men have recognized how much pornography imitates and helps create a power relation in sex between men and women of dominance and submission. They see that what most of pornography teaches, what it shows, what it extols, is like a handbook for most men—a manual of ways to view women, ways to feel about themselves, ways to keep dominance and submission most people's basic idea of what is "sexy." The dominance-and-submission model of sex, a few men have come to see, is the dark heart of dominance and submission in the world. And what have these men done about this recognition? Well, there have been actions, pickets, letters written, support given to the movement of radical-feminist women who are slowly but surely educating people about the model of dominance and submission in pornography and how these are the very values upon which is built the whole sexist superstructure—but the fact is that this recongition comes to men too often in isolation, and the isolation itself is paralyzing.

We have a vision of a world of gender justice, and we want male friends and allies who can enter that world too. We want male friends who respect our women friends. We want male friends with whom we don't have to censor out our political commitments in order to have a conversation. We want male friends who are also helping to create that world. We want male friends who will help get us there. Yet the fact is that each of us is just one man away from selling out our antisexism. All it takes is one situation with another man—a situation that will be different for each of us—a particular man whose company and esteem and companionship we most want, and we will sell out our convictions for that connection; we won't speak our beliefs in order to bond.

Why the Issue Is What It Is

Our antisexism, it's important to remember, has its roots in feminism, which arises out of a sex-class analysis. This sex-class analysis that stands behind us is about men's domination of women and others; it's about how that structure is cultural, not biological, and why that structure can change; it's about how men are not by nature who they are in the world, yet they are in the world as those men; it's about how the sex-class system is male supremacist and why it's got to to go; it's about both the possibility and the responsibility for making the world a different place.

How do we know that change is really possible? One important answer to that question is contained in a passage from the book *Our Blood* by Andrea Dworkin, where she makes this crucial distinction between reality and truth:

> .... *Reality is social; reality is whatever people at a given time believe it to be.... Reality is always a function of politics in general and sexual politics in particular—that is, it serves the powerful by fortifying and justifying their right to domination over the powerless. Reality is whatever premises*

social and cultural institutions are built on.... Reality is enforced by those whom it serves so that it appears to be self-evident. Reality is self-perpetuating, in that the cultural and social institutions built on its premises also embody and enforce those premises.... The given reality is, of course, that there are two sexes, male and female; that these two sexes are opposite from each other, polar; that the male is inherently positive and the female inherently negative; and that the positive and negative poles of human existence unite naturally into a harmonious whole. Truth, on the other hand, is not nearly so accessible as reality.... Truth is absolute in that it does exist and.... it is the human project to find it so that reality can be based on it.... I have made this distinction between truth and reality in order to enable me to say something very simple: That while the system of gender polarity is real, it is not true. *It is not true that there are two sexes which are discrete and opposite, which are polar, which unite naturally and self-evidently into a harmonious whole.... The system based on this polar model of existence is absolutely real; but the model itself is not true. We are living imprisoned inside a pernicious delusion, a delusion on which all reality as we know it is predicated.*[1]

So here we are: men, inside a male-supremacist system, inside a male-supremacist sex class, inside it as men. What do we do about it? And why is it so difficult and so unthinkable to live as a traitor to that sex class? Why does it touch such a raw nerve to imagine ourselves having just one conversation with another man in which we declare our beliefs and say of his we don't go along when the issue at hand is male supremacy?

Individuals have been known to disavow their allegiance to other kinds of classes without suffering the same identity crisis. For instance, there have been a few children of the rich who have committed their lives to economic justice. Not everything they have done has been exactly the right thing to do, but they have understood that it is wrong that some people are poor and starving and that their own lives can matter and they can do something to make a difference. Despite the fact that their own wealthy families may have sniped at them with scorn, they went ahead and did what they needed to do to create economic justice in the world—and they didn't lose themselves doing it. As a matter of fact, I think many of them would say that they discovered through their activism a sense of themselves that's better than who they were before. In a somewhat analogous way there have been some white people who have understood that to grow up white in this country is to grow up racist, and that either you are doing something and striving through your life to be antiracist or you are racist. It is a choice, and not choosing is to choose to be a racist. Not everything these white people have done to change their own racism and the society's has been exactly the right thing to do, but they did what they did because they understood that racial hate is wrong. As individuals working for racial justice these people met with great animosity from other white people whose race-class interests were being threatened, but these people persevered without losing who they were; on the contrary they *kept* who they were, they kept the best part of who they were.

It is a measure of how much sex class determines "who we fundamentally are" that for us as men to disavow the interests of our sex class makes us feel we disappear. Tangible membership in the sex class men is our primary means to identity. It's a familiar story: You grow up to become a boy and you are terrorized into acting like a boy and you are rewarded for being a boy and you learn to dissociate from your mother by adopting a whole range of fears and hatreds of women and you learn what you need to learn to be accepted into the company of other men. Women shore up this identity; we look to women to affirm this identity. But we get the identity from other men; it is other men we look to as the arbiters of sex-class identity, the identity that gets inside of us, an identity so close to who we think we are that letting go of it scares us to death.

This sex-class construct of identity is not the only possible form in which we can know who we fundamentally are. There is another way that we sometimes do this, and it stems from a part of ourselves that wants fairness and concern and respect between people, a part of ourselves that is very close to our antisexism and our ideals of gender justice. It's that part of ourselves which recoils at sexualized hate. It's that part of ourselves which wants caring and mutuality, both in sex and in the world; it's that part of ourselves which wants to live in a gender-just future already. I'd like to give that part of ourselves a name, and what I'd like to call it is our moral identity. I don't mean moral in the sense of righteous or pure or politically correct; what I mean by moral identity is that it is the part of ourselves that knows the difference between fairness and unfairness, at least in some shadowy way. It's that part of ourselves which is capable of weighing what we see, what we do, what other people do, in terms of some sense we have of what justice should look like. It's a part of ourselves that is capable also of living beyond gender, and it sometimes does. It's also the part of ourselves that is nearest our experience when we are feeling deep remorse and pain over the suffering and injustice that we see in the world.

The sense of ourselves that we get from this moral identity, however, collides inside of us with the identity that we get from our sex class. We have learned that the suffering under male supremacy we see in the world can cause us great pain to look at it—to look at it hard; but we have also learned that blocking out of our minds the awareness of how bad things are is easier to do than making things better. So we try to put together a life view that isn't such a bummer. Yet our emergent moral identity whispers, even though its whispers sometimes pitch us into despair and denial.

Which is more real to us: our moral identity or our sex-class identity? Which makes us feel more real? Which gives us back more the feeling of who we want to be? These two constructs of identity are at war inside us. We go in and out of our moral identity, and for each of us there is a pattern of circumstances that makes us go out of it—episodes, for example, of retaliatory anger or laziness. We don't go in and out of our sex-class identity as much. We feel we measure up against it better at times and worse at other times, but in fact we stay in it and we stay in there more than we think. Our sex-class identity is a constant, and we are fundamentally loyal to it. Our moral identity is more ephemeral, and we tend to be only its fair-weather friend. Other men represent to us the crux of this dilemma—other men especially who are at ease in their sex-class identity and status. It's uncomplicated for them; it's complicated for us. We admire their ease, their masculine complacency; at the same time we're angry at them and we don't want to be like them. We experience the dilemma most acutely at those times when we are feeling in a bind between other men and feminism. For instance, an antisexist man's moral identity might respond to the feminist analysis of the sex-class system by wanting to be an exception to it, by not wanting to be like the men the analysis describes, by wanting to make sure he is living in such a way that the analysis isn't true of him in particular. But then his sex-class identity rejects any critique of men as a class, reacts either as if he is the defender of his whole sex class or as if his spectacularly exemplary life redeems it and thus refutes the analysis; his sex-class identity wants to blend in, wants alliances with other men on any terms. His moral identity, on the other hand, recognizes the truth of the sex-class analysis and believes individuals, including himself, can confront male supremacy and transform themselves and the culture; his moral identity recognizes how he is both different from his sex class and yet very much part of it. But his sex-class identity has an overriding vested interest in his identification with the class as a whole.

We can always give up our moral identity in favor of our sex-class identity. It's really quite easy, and it can happen quite without our thinking. For most of us, the issue of other men makes us actually feel an urgency to abandon our moral identity because in order to deal with other men on their terms, that's what we almost always have to do.

Understanding the Issue in Our Lives

So what can we possibly do? How can we sort through this conflicted issue in our lives? In what terms can we possibly understand it so that we might have some clarity about what to do about it both as individuals and as a movement?

First of all, we need to be clear that we're not talking about a market strategy for the men's movement; we're not talking about how to package the men's movement so that we can run it up the flagpole and all the men in America will salute. We're also not dealing superficially with some difference between conscience and camaraderie. Nor are we talking about yet another great occasion for navel-gazing—heaven knows we have enough of that.

What this issue really comes down to, I think, is an issue of who we choose to become.

In my view, the discipline of focusing on antisexist activism is really the only way that one can keep choosing to keep one's moral identity alive and awake. I don't believe one's moral identity can survive in an actionless vacuum. It can't just exist in one's mind or in one's statement of principles. It has to be expressed in action.

I don't know the answer to the question "Well, what happens to the sex-class identity we always seem to carry around with us?" But I do know there is a possibility for one's moral identity to shine through one's life more often. As a movement and as individuals, we cannot achieve clarity about our moral identity by evoking a brotherhood that is oblivious, a brotherhood for brotherhood's sake, a brotherhood whose sole purpose becomes the embrace of men simply on account of their being men—like one big sex-class club. To do so does not allow for personal transformation in the struggle to keep and grow your moral identity. The change to which we aspire has got to be predicated on a new integration of selfhood, a radical new identity, a self that knows who it is in relation to reality and who it is in relation to truth. We need a double vision: We need to keep in our mind both the reality of our being men in the sex-class system and the truth of the possiblity of a future without it. We need to know, "Yes, as men, we're part of it. And yet we are men who are trying to live differently, trying to make our lives make a difference." We need, I think, as a movement and as individuals, the discipline of action that is transformative of ourselves and society—not simply action that maintains our organization, our own social structures among ourselves. If our antisexist action in the world stops, our moral identity will go into hibernation, and the longer it sleeps, the less it resembles who we could become. As individuals and as a movement, we must not fancy ourselves redeemers of our sex class, as men who will show the world that men are not as bad as some have said—that's a trap laid by a sex-class identity determined to blend back into the comfort of unconscious masculine complacency, determined to forge out of self-congratulation some semblance of self-respect.

The pride to which we aspire is not in being *men* but in being *men who...*—men who are living their lives in a way that will make a difference.

We must be transformers of selfhood—our own and others'. If we do not, we will have betrayed women's lives utterly, and we will have lost a part of ourselves that is precious and rare on this earth.

NOTE:

[1] Andrea Dworkin (1981) from "The Root Cause" In *Our Blood: Prophecies and Discourses on Sexual Politics* pp. 109-110. New York: Perigee.

Misogyny: Gay and Straight

by John Nierenberg

The other night a close friend described a disturbing incident that occurred when she had gone to see a revival of *Gone With the Wind*. While expecting a certain amount of foolish behavior from the audience, she was upset by a group of men sitting a few rows in front of her. She explained that the particular jargon they used signaled to her that they were gay. What disturbed her, though, was the apparent vehemence of their anti-female remarks. Having relatively little exposure to the gay subculture, she asked me if such animosity was typical.

My first reaction was to grudgingly admit that misogyny is an element in the average gay male psyche. I did quickly add, however, that I was aware of a similar attitude among most heterosexual men as well. This led us to wonder what similarities and differences there are in gay and straight men's attitudes toward women.

Gender Salience and Erotic Opposition

The essential similarity in both male groups is, naturally, based on the reality of them all being raised as Men in our culture. Sandra Bem points out in her discussions of social conditioning that the first thing we notice about an individual is whether "it" is a boy or a girl. From that split-second differentiation, which Bem calls gender salience, grows a complex and sometimes unhealthy set of oppositions: Boys Do This vs. Girls Do That. And then proscriptions seem to appear naturally: Girls *shouldn't* run and jump and Boys *shouldn't* play with dolls.

In time, the Boy becomes a Man and the Girl becomes a Woman, but always with the underlying notion of the "Opposite" Sex as Other. Even with all our humanistic efforts to lessen the barriers between individuals, we retain this ingrained notion of the Other as Stranger and probable Enemy. Sadly, this atavistic fear feeds this sense of opposition, which becomes an undercurrent in all interactions between men and women.

Opposition, however, needn't always be a negative process. Like resistance or stress, it is a kind of tension between the individual and the environment that can be both necessary and productive. But nowhere is this opposition or mutual resistance more effective than in the area of sexuality.

As C.A. Tripp points out in his excellent work *The Homosexual Matrix,* there is a desire in all erotic relationships, whether heteroerotic or homoerotic, to be linked with the Other in some special way. He maintains that all sexuality is based on a more or less subtle power struggle between two individuals to achieve a certain level of mastery over the object of their attentions. Sexual attraction, then, invites a kind of combat that requires putting one's ego "on the line." Tripp also explains that the desire is often to absorb the loved one psychically or conversely to be absorbed by that person, to become truly one. And yet we hesitate to do so for one very good psychological reason: the fear of an irreversible loss of Self.

The fear of losing one's identity in the loved one can create enormous anxiety, particularly for straight men who are conditioned to expect to dominate in heterosexual relationships. Misogyny is a socially condoned way of reducing that anxiety. Anti-female attitudes are thus a convenient shield which is used mainly to defend men's self-image while tearing down the image of women. It is paradoxical that love is both the cause and the effect of this hostility. Men want to be united with Women, but also want to maintain their separate male identity.

Male Bonding

Another result of accepting the idea of Woman as Other is the establishment of male bonding. If all Women are Other, then all Men must be seen as Same. And this pressure to maintain gender identity is equally strong among gay or straight males. Men are thus socially conditioned to see one another as allies. And for straight men this bonding is traditionally experienced through domination (especially sexual domination) of Females.

But this bond is as paradoxical as the one between men and women. If one teenager sees his buddy as a "fellow hunter," he soon learns that an ally can also be a rival for a certain Female. The sense of competition *within* the group creates a different kind of tension between individual men. It is not an overwhelming problem as long as men face a common opposition: Women. In this respect, all men are indeed brothers and misogynistic behavior is used to reinforce male bonding.

Self-Victimization

The gay male is presented with a much more complicated and ambiguous psychological position. Subject to the same male indoctrination and conditioning, the gay man shares the same sense of opposition to women as a group. However, the supporting element—male bonding—is much more limited and tenuous for gays. The problem lies in the fact that a primary means of expressing identity with other men remains the sexual domination of women. This is based, logically enough, on the presumption of sexual desire. But when this link drops out, and the issue of heterosexual men fearing sexual domination by other males is added, there is an intense alienation of straight men from gay men. Gay men straddle the proverbial fence, part ally and part Other, which leaves them in a particularly uncomfortable and vulnerable position. They simultaneously identify and are accepted by other men in terms of gender role behavior, but are rejected (and sometimes reject themselves) as Men since they are confused with Women in the area of sexual preference.

Thus there is a clear and more or less overt message from straight men to gay men: "we will accept your other abilities as Fellow Men as long as you conceal or deny your true sexual/affectional orientation." There is also a more covert message: "despite these attempts to annihilate your gay identity, 'everyone knows,' on some subconscious level, that you are a Non-Man." Since there is no third gender in this system, the gay male is always identified with the Other. He becomes a Pseudo-Woman. Some gay men react to these messages by mistaking their gender and sexual identity for that applied to them by other men. These messages form the basis for homophobic behavior among straight men. Acceptance of these statements by gay men account for the special brand of misogyny that gay males exhibit.

Woman-Identification

Gay misogyny is consistently reinforced by confused self-images that result in insecurity and self-abuse. Many gay men have incorporated into their self-perception the myth that they "really want to be women." In some way, they have accepted subconsciously a loss of status because of this: they see themselves as Failed Men. These same homosexual men will identify themselves with women in the negative view only. Their misogyny thus serves as an effective expression of self-loathing. "We're just like women, and aren't they/we awful?" is the double-edged message. These same gay males tend to reject the positive characteristics of traditionally female behavior they might otherwise imitate, because they see *any* expression of "femininity" as additional evidence of being a Non-Man and a further threat to their already embattled self-image. Having abandoned the "Battle of the Sexes" in the arena of sexual dominance, they attempt to strengthen their detachment from the role of Woman on an emotional level through verbal or psychological combativeness.

Toward Non-Misogyny

In the final analysis, straight men express their misogyny and their antigay male behavior for the same underlying reason: to attack those they perceive as threats to their social and sexual supremacy. The gay male, though, has a variety of motivations for his misogyny: to reassure himself and others of his "masculinity;" to reassure *other gay* and straight misogynists of his alliance with Men; and to express his anti-heterosexual feelings by attacking at least one portion of that population.

On the other hand, both fortunately and ironically, the identification of gay men with woman can and does counter-balance the stereotype of the gay man as woman-hater. Many gay men form solid and long-lasting friendships with both lesbians and straight women precisely because they share the commonality of being oppressed by the heterosexual white male power structure. In fact, some apparently misogynistic behavior, for example, exaggeratedly "feminine" behavior, *can* be the expression of a playful solidarity. It says: "Since I'm not one of the Boys, I can enjoy being one of the Girls!" Ironically, this supports the misguided notion among dominant males that gay males want to *be* women as opposed to wanting with be *with* them. This misunderstanding is due, after all, to the notion that Real Men don't enjoy "just spending time" with women, particularly if there is no intimate or sexual relationship involved. This is in itself a basic expression of misogyny.

Identification and even analysis of the causes are not enough—they will not end misogyny. Instead, efforts must be made to remove as many of the causes as possible. The individual male's identity can be maintained through the positive expression of *individual* qualities, including traditionally "feminine" characteristics such as nurturance and emotionality. Straight men who learn to grow more comfortable with their own "feminine" sides will be able to accept *all* the qualities of themselves, their gay brothers and women. We can appreciate our differences as men and women, as homosexuals and heterosexuals, as *individuals,* without unnecessary and counterproductive fear. We can be Other without being Enemy: we can also be Friends.

The Gay Side of Manhood

by Gordon Murray

As gay men, we have had to invent ourselves, outside of approved norms for how to be men. Our stories have a common theme of self-creation. I'm not saying there's not conformity among gay men; I'm saying that there is enormous diversity and experimentation with ways of being men. Since there were no role models, since our families often ignored or even disowned our gayness, since we uprooted ourselves from our pasts to seek each other in urban centers, we were free to find and define ourselves from within.

June 1984 marks 15 years since a drag queen confronted a policeman at the Stonewall bar in New York, launching a collective self-creation which has come to be the movement for Gay Liberation. Fifteen years of profoundly changed lives.

I feel anxious: how can I summarize a movement so important to me in a way that will matter to you? And what if it doesn't? What if you, the helpers and healers, the midwives of new culture and consciousness, reject it, reject me? Coming out is always risky.

Part of the riskiness is that I would like not to be seen as totally "other," but would like you to consider your own gay side. Each man presumably has a gay side, and to acknowledge it is to be a fuller, richer person.

The Gay Man Within

Most men first experience their gay side during what Freud misleadingly called "latency," only to lose touch with it later, under the pressure of adolescence, amidst a conspiracy of silence, misinformation and misunderstanding.

Men: think back to a male friend from your pre-adolescent days, a buddy, a playmate who felt close. Feel it until you can feel the magic and joy and mystery of that bond you had, and until you can feel the pain of its breaking. For almost one man out of three, this male bonding included sex-play (Kinsey, *et al.; Sexual Behavior in the Human Male*). For others, it was an emotional closeness, a Tom Sawyer-Huck Finn partnership in adventure, a secret club, a gang. Some acted it out violently, some lovingly.

I suspect this "latency" concept still retains credibility, despite Kinsey's statistics, because there's relatively little *heterosexual* activity. In a culture which would prefer to ignore the homosexual potential of its children, such a period is comfortably dismissed.

Other cultures are not so denying. In Papua, New Guinea, boys are initiated into manhood by ritualized sexual activity with older men. In ancient Greece gay love was refined and noble. In practically every culture, homosexuality exists (Ford, C.S. and Beach, F.A.; *Patterns of Sexual Behavior*).

Our culture conspires to disguise this legacy, sometimes unwittingly. I remember well my sense of betrayal when I learned that the standard editions of Plato systematically distort homosexuality, making overtly sexual passages into sublimated scenes more palatable to Victorian morality (Tripp, C.A.; *The Homosexual Matrix*). I asked a gay friend versed in classics why there are no non-homophobic translations, and he responded, "Ah, but who wrote the Greek dictionaries? The Victorians!"

Reclaiming the Gay Self

So gay culture lies buried under multiple layers of moral judgment. The painstaking task of reclaiming our culture is a large part of the current gay renaissance.

Each individual gay man contributes to this larger task as he struggles to reclaim his own identity. Psychologists boosted the legitimacy of this quest in a major way when, in the mid-'70s, homosexuality *per se* was declassified as a mental disorder. The focus of treatment switched from changing one's homosexual preference—a path as fruitless as it was ethically dubious—to changing negative attitudes about oneself. But altering the diagnostic manual has not altered all the hearts and habits of psychotherapists, and homophobia, blatant and subtle, persists (Morin, S.F.; "Heterosexual Bias in Psychological Research...," *American Psychologist,* August 1977).

Gay therapists have suggested guidelines for a gay-affirmative therapy (Clark, D., *Loving Someone Gay,* 1977) which, at a minimum, require therapists to come to terms with their own gay side. And researchers have begun to outline the developmental process of a healthy gay male identity (Cass, V.C., "Homosexual Identity Formation," *Journal of Homosexuality,* 1979) This process typically begins with vague feelings, fantasies or even sexual experiences, moves toward a labeling of these behaviors as "gay," then to a gradual labeling of self as "gay," often with a negative charge.

Helping a client move to the next stage—a positively charged gay identity (often militantly proud at first)—is a central task of psychotherapy with gays. Ultimately, gayness tends to becomes more harmoniously integrated with other aspects of the self.

The Challenge of AIDS

The current AIDS crisis is plunging gay men into a collective identity crisis unlike anything since Stonewall. The sex-positive euphoria that was so central to the gay message to the world was played out to its logical extremes in lifestyles of multiple partners and sexual contacts.

Now, a lethal disease which appears to be sexually transmitted has wrenched into public scrutiny lives whose secrets may not be ready to be told. AIDS is forcing a public self-examination which the gay community is undergoing with remarkable skill and dignity.

Gay men are now charting a course between carefree sexual anarchy and the realities of a healthy sexuality. The crisis promises to have a maturing effect on the movement; more frankness about sexuality and safeguards, more dialogue on intimacy and relationships.

At the same time the AIDS crisis threatens to further define gay men as "other," and this is dangerous for all of us. Dangerous because the male bond which gay men manifest sensually and sexually is everywhere in our culture, in all cultures, and if we don't act it out lovingly, it may emerge in negative ways.

The male bond is a strong force in the military, in the all-male or mostly-male institutions like the Pentagon and the boards of corporate America. I suspect one reason the ERA lost is that men sense in women a threat to their accustomed ways of male bonding, and if women shared in male power-holdings, men might be forced to confront their need for male intimacy in new, more frightening ways.

The liberation of gay men touches all men, and indeed the well-being of the planet. As long as there is a bias against lovingly expressing the male bond, there will be a tendency to act it out only in contexts where traditional "masculine" values such as competitiveness, power and violence dominate.

We must dare to see the gay man not as "other" but as part of every man. We must dare to teach our male children that it's all right to care for other boys. We must dare to confront the men who aim lethal nuclear phalluses at other men, and insist they learn to make love, not war.

Men Cooperating For A Change

Keynote address to the Eighth National Conference on Men and Masculinity, Ann Arbor, Michigan; August 1983*

by John Mifsud

My first experience with the Men's Movement was in 1977 when a group of us here in Ann Arbor decided to drive to St. Louis for the Fourth National Conference on Men and Masculinity. We made it through Chicago's rush-hour traffic, a blizzard in Springfield, and then I took the wheel for the final stretch as we passed the Gateway to the West and found our way to the Registration Desk. I remember being particularly impressed with how well-organized everything seemed and, once settled in, I signed up for an ongoing workshop entitled, "Can You Be Gay and a Man at the Same Time?" The title alone was so full of promise that I realized immediately that there could have been no better way for me to spend Thanksgiving that year.

There were thirty men enrolled, and for three days we exchanged stories about how we had been alienated from our own gender (and therefore from ourselves) because we refused to identify with the rapists and war-mongers who had made the word "man" distinctly objectionable. We shared our pain, and there was a lot of it. Then we gave each other support which eased the hurt. Slowly, our emotions transformed into anger as we became aware of how cheated we had been by allowing the violence and misguided aggression of frustrated men to keep us from our birthright . . . the right to feel pride in being men. The natural step beyond pain and anger was action. We resolved to take on a new mode of thinking and try to set a new example. We began to try on for size the idea that being male was inherently beautiful and started allowing ourselves to feel a new sense of self-respect for being men trying to rid ourselves of old patterns and focusing on new ways to relate to each other and the rest of the world.

That workshop and the entire conference was a major turning point in my life. I learned that I was not alone. The fear that owning my manhood would be associated with an ever rising machismo was an anathema to all the men at the

*The author wishes to acknowledge and thank Charlie Murphy for his assistance in developing this address.

conference, gay and straight alike, and I also learned that our struggle had just begun.

And here we are today, six years later, and who amongst us isn't still encumbered with the responsibility of being a man concerned with social change in the United States of America in the 1980s. This dilemma of being male will continue to demand our attention. Still, we have travelled here from as far as Alaska and Alabama and we are here to proceed with the work of finding new ways to feel our pain and anger which will empower us to transform ourselves and our society, both culturally and politically. We are still learning to feel a sense of dignity in our personhood and our manhood, but to myself, to the brothers at that workshop in St. Louis, and to everyone here I say, "You've come a long way and aren't you glad you did!"

Who Are We?

I live in Seattle and when I told my friends that I had been invited to give a keynote address at the Eighth National Conference on Men and Masculinity they said, "What's that?" When I told them it was the backbone of the Men's Movement they said ... what's that?" Now these were everyday folks as well as longtime political activists and since even they don't know about us, it is obvious to me that we still lack national recognition.

When you think of the Men's Movement, does it carry the same weight as Women's Liberation, the Civil Rights Movement or the Anti-Nuke Movement? Our Men's Movement just isn't a household word.

What makes a national movement? Primarily, recognition from society at large, a march on Washington, strategy, goals and objectives, media coverage, faith in identified leadership, a strong cultural arm, and, even more, a common thread of oppression. The latter, more than anything, is what we lack.

We come from all walks of life, varying backgrounds and socio-economic classes but when we speak of the common oppression of mostly white men we just don't get the same response. Maybe there is such an incredible number of mind-boggling issues overwhelming our lives today that there just isn't enough space to internalize another struggle. I think that is OK because what we *do* have is a fantastic national network, strong feelings in all of our hearts, and a commitment to political action—both amongst ourselves and within all the other liberation movements today.

We are far reaching not because of media recognition but because of the way we live our everyday lives and the struggles we embrace, whatever they may be. And I think that we have made and are still making a big difference within the movements we actively participate in and especially with the people with whom we come into contact. We raise consciousness at meetings, through speeches, with songs and poetry, at the bus stop, the co-op and the computer terminal. The consciousness raising that we do on these other issues, as well as on the specific issue of sex role dynamics, is important work. We might not be on file with NBC or CBS but we all know that we are not the only ones keeping files on the work that we do. The higher ups are keeping close tabs on us and well they should. We are making special contributions in a broad-based way. Our diversity and extensive interest in a spectrum of issues has us working to further the progress of many major concerns and if what we do isn't creating a "national movement," I don't know what will.

Wellsprings of the Highest Wisdom

Years ago in Manhattan, I went to an informal concert given by an 82-year old Jewish artist. She was a classical pianist and composer and had performed a wide range of music including one of her original works. Afterwards I approached her, shook her hand and thanked her for sharing that very special part of her self. I told her that I liked the original work the best and asked her what had inspired it. I cannot recall her name, but I can still see her wizened face like it was yesterday. She looked me square in the eye and said, "Pain. There are many sources of creativity for the artist, but the most far-reaching, the most dynamic, is the creativity that comes from human suffering." I had always associated inspiration with happiness but since that concert I have learned that the more we allow pain to touch us, the clearer we experience reality and the greater our capacity for true joy. As we break down our barriers to feeling our grief we become freer to move, which can lead to anger and then action. And positive action is always inspirational.

But what do you do in a culture that brainwashes us to spend money rather than feel our natural despair, remorse and grief? It is by far much easier to go to Baskin Robbins and choose a few of the 31 flavors. It is easier to go see another movie even if it was produced by Paramount Pictures which is owned by Gulf Western. Buy more new clothes or music or some vintage French chablis or some good Hawaiian smoke. The truth is that in this shopping mall land of liberty we are all guilty of the tendency to try to buy our way out of remorse by fleeing into the world of commercialized freedom.

We are participating in being had, but why? As we try to escape our pain we financially support the conglomerate monopolies. With the power we give them, they are then able to control our lives and wreak havoc in this country and the rest of the world. Do you think they know that if we got back in touch with our despair, we might get in touch with our rage, fury and power? If we felt our grief, we might be inspired to do something about the multinationals that have us and the rest of the world dangling on strings like marionettes.

Experiencing our despair could also lead us to a new manner of thinking. The state of the world today shows us that thinking with the mind alone leaves a lot to be desired and I dare say that each of us intuitively knows that there is more to our intelligence than what comes from the brain. There is a unique intelligence that comes through our feelings. What we need to do is learn better how to know with our hearts. We have always associated the heart with emotion, sex, and sentimentality but if we allow ourselves to put our minds aside for a moment, we can experience clear visions of the heart. We are in desperate need of this extra wisdom in order to find new ways to carve paths through the mass confusion that we are engulfed by today and once we find those paths, we will be better able to stay on them and keep moving.

And what about guilt? In the past, guilt has blocked our unique intelligence and that has kept us from proceeding. We all know how passé it is to feel guilty about anything anymore and yet somehow I think we are depriving ourselves of something terrific, something vital. In an article entitled *A Flash of Living Fire,* Dorothea Matthews states, "We are a generation which, having put sin and guilt out of style, considers itself blameless, but in reality is only shameless, which is a very different thing." She goes on to say that, "We have fallen into a trap of discarding the baby with the bathwater by throwing out the entire concept of remorse along with the rubbish of a guilty conscience," and it is all too obvious how self-serving that can be. We must be accountable not only to what we do, but what we are not doing. Ms. Matthews says, "Remorse is that which cleans and purifies our inner substance and prepares it for a transformation which cannot take place otherwise; it is remorse that repairs the damages of the past and makes a future possible."

Now I am talking specifically to you when I say that I hope that as we try to deal with the issues of the world, we also recognize the tremendous despair we each carry because of them. And let's not forget that there are as many guilt-free approaches to action as there are concerns. It is unfortunate that as we let go of guilt in order to know all of ourselves we wound up depriving ourselves of experiencing something very special which was why we were trying to get rid of the guilt in the first place. As individuals, and as a nation, we need to face the task of making some crucial distinctions in our emotional dispositions.

Let's use our time together to learn from each other our various techniques for dealing with our personal grief and our anguish about what is happening in our world today. There is no patent formula for facing that void, but as men cooperating for a change, we can support each other and shatter some emotional blocks which will bring us closer to each other and encourage an even greater understanding of ourselves and what we can accomplish through collective action.

I also believe that the concept of throwing out the baby with the bathwater applies to aggression. Did we possibly let go of some of our power and initiative when we gave up the macho role? Being sensitive is *not* synonymous with being spineless. In the 1970s we identified ourselves as "gentle men", but the 1980s demand that we keep that and take one more step beyond. As poet and author Robert Bly has said, "Men today are pro-life but they aren't very life initiating." Are we still associating non-conformist action with violence? Are we still worried that all of our acts of aggression inevitably mean that someone is going to get hurt? These are fallacies I hope we can overcome as we learn to trust ourselves more and although easier said than done, as long as our action is coupled with intuitive intelligence from our hearts and a good understanding of the implications of what we are doing, we can act when we are so moved.

Building on What We've Learned

Let's allow our experience in the Men's Movement to remind us of a few things. First, there are many ways to accomplish the same task. It will take all of us working from different angles to bring down the death machine and build anew. Let's make sure that our critical feedback to each other is dignified and constructive because there isn't a one amongst us who has all the answers.

Second, although aggression has been associated with the worst side of men, it is a human attribute and we need to aggressively tap our creativity in the manner of our role models who have passed before us. Like Malcolm X, Mother Jones, Gandhi, Harriet Tubman and Martin Luther King, we need to become aggressive about the truth. Their lives are examples of creative, non-violent aggression and proof that mass movements are founded in great feelings of ferocious compassion. After all, it is forceful compassion that stops the hand of the adult about to beat a child and it will take intelligent aggression to stop the hands of greed and hypocrisy who have a death-grip on our world today.

Finally, we have to keep working hard but also recognize our limits. I hope that we can all learn what it takes to care for ourselves in order to keep our gears in motion as we follow the paths of our choice. In *Lightening East to West,* Jim Douglas says, "there is a spiritual reality for change in humankind equal in energy to the reality of nuclear devastation." So I say let's stay healthy as we continue to try to make a difference.

I want to encourage each and every one of us to continue to work for what we believe is important and I want to particularly encourage those of us who are actively doing something about the life and death struggles in this country and the world at large. Our economy has the nation grasping at straws and most everyone is challenged by the task of taking care of our own. Still, we cannot allow this war-based economy and the cutbacks to social services to get us to a point where we have no choice but to accept war as the only solution to providing for ourselves and our families. There is a better way.

Moving Into the '80s

Let's face some facts. There simply isn't enough time to not take a world perspective into account. Our strategies and goals must be timely for the '80s and the ripples of our efforts must be as far-reaching as these times demand, just as our involvement has to be to the best extent of our abilities.

I am proud of how we were there protesting the war in Vietnam. We were at those ERA rallies and now we are at meetings about military escalation in Central America, we are at the demonstrations for people's civil liberties and women's right to reproductive freedom. We work against rape and violence and we are involved in providing better care for our children. We are fighting the dumping of toxic waste and fighting for the lives of endangered species. We are active about gay rights, cultural work and improved health care. We organize meetings with union locals and the unemployed and we also organize our lives around all of these various issues.

Among us, we carry a lot of privilege as most of us are white men, and I hope that we continue using what resources we have available to us in the aid and betterment of the lives of those people denied the right to their own self determination. Our resources can become a mainstay in the progressing evolution of all liberation struggles. No, let's not feel guilty about what we have. Let's use what we've got to get what we want—the opportunity for fulfilling life for everyone.

Because while we're learning to be tender, 50 percent of the women of Puerto Rico and 50 percent of the Native American women of South Dakota have been sterilized against their will. As we get back in touch with our feelings, an American teenager attempts suicide once every 27 seconds. And as we try to let go of responsibility, homeless Americans roam the country looking for work. While we try to relax, the fascist and racist forces of apartheid are still strangling people in South Africa.

So we are forced to work on two fronts at once! We must continue to let go of being over-achievers, but let's not forget that Reagan was successful in getting the House and Senate to spend another 2.6 billion dollars of our tax monies on 21 new MX missiles. Let's get in touch with the nurturing aspect of ourselves and do something about the fact that close to 8 percent of the population of El Salvador has been murdered. Yes, let's be aggressive about justice! Let's learn and work and fight to be free men, not at the expense of other people, and let's use that freedom to get the same for those who might never see it but in their dreams.

"Goodbye John Wayne":
The Music of the Men's Movement

by Michael S. Kimmel

Popular music has always been a man's world, the music fueled by confusing sexual urges and a primitive anti-authoritarian anger, the life "on the road" providing a late 20th century edition of the adolescent myth of an Edenic homosocial world, once upon a time populated by pirates, soldiers, and sports heroes. Rock stars spin out merrily misogynist lyrics to accompany blatantly sexual rhythms; frenetically strummed electric guitars celebrated a particular vision of post-adolescent sexuality. Men sing their songs to women all right— since when do "real" men talk to each other about their feelings?—enticing them to fall in love, telling them to get lost, or wallowing in self-pity at their own rejection.

And the muscial mainstream remains resolutely sexist. The Rolling Stones, for example, derive an ominously sexual R&B by mixing a sinister misogyny with a driving rock sound. Heavy metal bands proclaim a macho hedonism for white working class teenagers, even if the band's dress is more suitable for a high-tech leather bar than an auto body shop. Newer musical trends—punk, reggae, new wave, and rockabilly—bring us no closer to a liberatory sexual ethic than their forbears.

Yet there are signs of change. Traditional definitions of masculinity are everywhere in flux, and the range of acceptable images open to men is expanding dramatically: from Dirty Harry and Rambo to Kramer and Bill Cosby, from Archie Bunker to Hawkeye and Phil Donahue, from Van Halen to Boy George. Bruce Springsteen writes open declarations of love to his former guitar player, and celebrates male intimacy in his concerts, just as Paul Simon wrote a series of love songs to Art Garfunkel on *Bridge Over Troubled Water,* as his friend left to pursue an acting career. Billy Joel exhorted his male listeners to "tell her about it," Graham Parker chides men for being "way out of touch," and Joe Jackson admits that these days we "don't know how to be a man." Even Michael Jackson, that elfine androgyne, sings "don't be a macho man." And while these men push against old boundaries of the mass culture mainstream, other men, far less celebrated, are quietly going about developing a music that challenges traditional definitions of masculinity as it builds new ways for men to relate to themselves as men, to women, and to each other. Like women's music, that diverse collection of feminist performers, writers, composers, and producers who have been inspiring and healing the feminist community for over ten years, "men's music" speaks softly and gently of the male experience—open to emotion, vulnerable, softly pushing for a change as it soothes and unifies men trying to escape the prison of gender paradigms.

In many ways, men's music resembles women's music in its earliest days. The music springs from similar sources, in this case three separate and tentatively allied places. One source is the anti-sexist men's movement itself, a loose network of local and regional men's organizations devoted to struggling against sexism by breaking men's silence about violence against women, pornography, and reproductive rights, while they simultaneously strive to develop new ways to relate as nurturing fathers, lovers, and workers. Another strain of men's music derives from the gay movement; performers reflect the cultural and political diversity of the movement as a whole and express the struggle and joy of loving someone of one's own gender. Finally, a small number of politically progressive cultural activists have understood that their synthesis of the personal and the political requires dismantling both traditional sex roles and agencies of political repression, aware of the close connection between bellicose nuclear politics and macho flexing.

The purveyors of men's music are, like their feminist counterparts, deeply embedded in the cultural institutions of this fledgling movement. Most are members of the National Organization for Changing Men, a national coalition of straight and gay men who are devoted to supporting feminist and gay struggles while they promote new and healthy ways for men to relate. Their song lyrics are frequently published in *Changing Men,* a national anti-sexist men's magazine. They perform at local and regional organizing conferences, political, feminist and gay coffeehouses, and are the featured performers at the annual conferences on Men and Masculinity sponsored by NOCM.

Like women's music, men's movement songs are voyages of self-discovery that reinterpret childhood, adolescence, and maturation—learning the rules and subsequently unlearning the roles—in ways that make the listener laugh and cry, soothing and comforting while they raise consciousness through song. And men's movement music suffers from some of the same problems that have beset women's music. The music itself is sometimes boringly bland, since the music is only a vehicle to carry the lyrical message. By ignoring the potential power of the music itself, the listener is forced into a discomforting passivity; you have to listen so carefully to the words that you can't possibly dance. (Of course, an unadulterated folk idiom doesn't exactly prompt the liberation of the body from the chair.) There is a sneaky irony here: as the music urges men to shed their obsessive preoccupation with control, to let loose, the musical package maintains that control, keeping us in our seats. Of course, the sound itself can prove vital and liberating; jazz, for example, never needed lyrics to explode the vapid asexuality of big band music and "put the sin in syncopation."

This irony is compounded by what is, perhaps, the most serious problem of the genre. Men's music is, if nothing else, an exhortation to men to express their emotions, to learn new ways to relate, to become vulnerable. And yet the musical delivery is often without emotion, without risk of exposure. Emotions are discussed, not felt. As in men's consciousness raising groups, in which men calmly and rationally discussed those emotions that defy rationality, men's music presents neatly tied, complete emotional packages, complete with resolution, so that no one has to do any emotional work. It's as if saying that you are in pain is the same thing as being in pain. Performers talk about emotions but do not have them—at least not there, on record or on stage, in front of all those people.

Compare this to some of the gutsier rock, pop, and soul performers. Like Bruce Springsteen, who celebrates the everyday heroism of people trying to find meaning in a world that deprives them of dignity, a world they neither understand nor control. He sadly resigns himself, or he'll writhe in pain, screaming that "sometimes I feel so weak I just want to explode." Or like Graham Parker, who seethes with rage over asexual politics that leave everyone without protection, and whose angry biting lyrics are delivered with a ferocious three-guitar intensity that rips at your insides while he's dissecting his own. Or take Joe Jackson, whose quirky lyrical brilliance about the dilemmas of modern romance (in songs like "Is She Really Going Out with Him?" and "It's Different for Girls" and "Real Men") complements his eccentric jive-jazz inspired melodies. The weight of Jackson's confusion about what it means to be a real man or woman is shared equally by his words and his music. Or, to switch to women's music, consider the different between a pleasant tune by Meg Christian and Aretha Franklin, tearing at her guts in "Respect." Aretha's pain and anguish become an angry plea; just in case you don't get the message, she even spells it for you. Her feminism is visceral, not cognitive, but that composition has probably raised more consciousnesses than any other single song.

This mixture of politics and art may be so difficult also because of the content of the politics and the backgrounds of the artists. All but one are white and from relatively affluent backgrounds. Raised to assume positions of power, they are more adept at self-control than self-revelation. And the political thrust of the men's movement—to become "gentle men"—further smothers its potential for expressing moral outrage. If a soft politeness remains the goal of a political movement, one can scarcely expect an outlet for raw emotion.

Despite these weaknesses, though, a number of men are singing about issues that we once blithely ignored. The best introduction to the genre is *Walls to Roses: Songs of Changing Men,* a compilation album assembled and produced by Cambridge-based Willie Sordill. The first recording by men actively dedicated to supporting the women's movement, these original compositions make it evident that men's music is not made by a bunch of anguished and guilt-ridden liberals bemoaning their fate as oppressors. Many of these musicians have released solo albums, a few have several to their credit. Some are produced on independent labels, and a few are available only on cassette, awaiting the money to press tape into vinyl. Lately, a number of major folk and progressive labels have picked up men's music performers, an indication that even if their politics are not of the mainstream, their competence within the folk idiom is recognized.

The purveyors of men's music form a vital part of the cultural wing of the men's movement. None have cracked the *Billboard* Top 100, yet taken together they evidence a growing awareness among American men that male armor is but a hollow shell, and that feminist and gay struggles offer a vision of future equality and justice as well as loving and caring. So even though their musical offerings don't pack the emotional wallop that they often promote, it is still a significant risk to stand up and sing against the prevailing macho tide. At the moment, they soothe and inspire other men who are quietly going about the daily business of dismantling the patriarchy brick by brick, from within as well as from the outside.

Annotated Discography of Men's Music

Peter Alsop: Alsop's impish humor is most suited to children's songs that demolish sex-role stereotypes; his songs for adults are clever also, but contain some disturbing messages. *Asleep at the Wheel* (Flying Fish Records, 1304 W. Schubert, Chicago, IL 60614), *Draw the Line* (Flying Fish), *Uniforms* (Flying Fish).

Blackberri: Rhythm and Blues from a Black, gay male perspective. *Finally* (Bea B. Queen Records, 1005 Market St., #207, San Francisco, CA 94103).

Gary Lapow: Lapow doesn't instruct the listener as much as share his own process of getting in touch with a more spiritual side of his feelings. Pleasant folk songs, with an often delightfully giddy presentation, he also sings songs for liberated children. *Tell it From the Heart* (Springhill Records, 4107 Lyon Ave., Oakland CA 94601), *Your Brightest Light* (cassette tape available from Lapow, Box 1317, 2000 Center St., Berkeley, CA 04704).

Geof Morgan: The most closely associated with the pro-feminist men's movement, Morgan's years as a Nashville songwriter pay off with catchy C&W flavored folk tunes that both inspire the listener to carry it on and ease the isolation by providing instant community. *It Comes with the Plumbing* (Nexus Records, Box 120875, Nashville, TN 37212), *Finally Letting it Go* (Flying Fish Records), *On the Edge* (Flying Fish).

Charlie Murphy: Resisting gay mainstreaming, Murphy extends the vision of gay liberation to other struggles, and probes gay and feminist spirituality, backed by a fully melodic band. *Catch the Fire, Canticles of Light, Fierce Love* (Outfront Music, P.O. Box 12188, Seattle, WA 98102).

Elliot Pilshaw: A soothingly melodic baritone sings sweetly of gay love, using cocktail jazz and torch songs as inspirations. Perhaps the best voice among these performers. *Feels Like Home* (Icebergg Records, 207 East Buffalo St., Suite 501, Milwaukee, WI 53202).

Romanovsky and Phillips: This daintily camping gay duo sings sarcastically about mainstream gay culture and the pain of growing up effeminate. Sometimes cutesy-poo, often on target. *I Thought You'd Be Taller, Trouble in Paradise* (Fresh Fruit Records, 2269 Market St., #301, San Francisco, CA 94114).

Fred Small: One of the nation's finest political troubadours, Small's repertoire of topical broadsides are caustic, clever, and always correct. Gender issues are assuming a larger portion of his message. *Love's Gonna Carry Us* (Aquifer Records, P.O. Box 566, Somerville, MA 02143). *Heart of the Apaloosa* (Rounder Records). *No Limit* (Rounder Records).

Willie Sordill: He produced the ground-breaking *Walls to Roses* album and two of his own, *Please Tip Your Waitress* and *Silent Highways*, all on the Folkways label.

Tom Wilson Weinberg: Weinberg is the "all American boy" who takes his sexual orientation for granted in his delightful uptempo cabaret-style love songs. *All American Boy, Ten Percent Review* (Aboveground Records, Box 497, Boston, MA 02112).

Fraternity, Equality, Liberty

by Harry Brod

"Fraternity, Equality, Liberty." Those familiar with European history will recognize this as an inversion of the slogan of the French Revolution: "Liberty, Equality, Fraternity." The ordering of these principles by the ideologists of the revolution was not coincidental, but rather reflected a certain conceptual scheme. To their minds, the first order of business was to secure liberty, by which they meant freedom from restrictions imposed upon them by others. Having won this liberty, they would then proceed to establish a society of equality. Subsequently, once men were living in this new society, feelings of fraternity for the brotherhood of man would emerge among all men. From our contemporary vantage point, we recognize that this fraternity excluded women in principle, and in practice excluded or limited the participation of a great number of men who were not of the prescribed class, race, national origin, etc.

What would happen if we were to reverse this progression? Specifically, what would happen if we were to proceed by focusing first on real fraternity, that is, real commonality of interest *as men?* Could such an approach possibly lead to equality between and among men and women, and to real liberty for all?

At first glance this approach would seem to have little hope for success. Would not any identifiable interests men have *as men* be precisely those interests which separate them from and pit them against women? How then could furthering these interests lead to any kind of universal equality and liberty? I believe, however, that these objections pose a false dichotomy. The interests men have in banding together in a fraternal way are interests in overcoming the limitations of the male sex role. And it is precisely this same male sex role which sets women and men at odds. I believe men's interests *as men* lie in overcoming sexism. I believe men have needs for separate strategies and tactics against sexism because we are coming to the project of eliminating sexism with different backgrounds, issues, and perspectives than women, but not ultimately different goals.

If one believes that men have common fraternal interests in ending sexism—a sexism that offers very real material rewards to men, but at too high a personal cost—then one has a *positive* basis upon which to work with other men. I, for example, do not regard men as "the enemy," nor do I believe I am opposing another man or violating his individual rights in moving against his sexism. When I intervene against a man's sexism, I am doing him—and myself—a favor, because trapped inside destructive and self destructive behavior is an individual who would be relieved to be rid of this mode of being if he had a free choice. If one shares my starting assumption that nurturing, intimacy, and support are real human needs, then it follows that it is essential that men establish *real* friendships with each other. Not the implicit contract of traditional male camaraderie, in which we mutually agree to keep our defenses up but not to mind it, and to keep our prejudices intact while validating each other's masculinity; rather, a shared intimacy in which feelings, including fears and joys, flow freely. Otherwise, men will continue to turn to women to fulfill these needs. And while women's abilities to nurture are clearly admirable, the necessity that they do so is equally clearly oppressive. Furthermore, such friendships with men are essential for supporting men in making and sustaining the needed long-term changes.

I would like to take the idea of finding a positive approach to working with men against sexism a significant step further. I suggest that we stop looking for the "original sin" on the basis of which men can be said to have erected patriarchy. Many aspects of male psychology are put forth as candidates for "original sin" status. We are said to have innate aggressive instincts, to have dominating sex drives, to have obsessive desires for immortality so that we force women to have our children, to have a need to create a despised "Other" in order to establish our own identities, to have a need to compensate for our "womb envy" of women's creative and regenerative powers, to either love or fear each other so much, depending on the theory, that we have institutionalized oppressive heterosexuality and so on.[1] I propose that we stop looking for the fatal flaw in male psychology which is responsible for sexism. Instead, I will make the seemingly preposterous suggestion that sexist attitudes can be understood as stemming from inherently positive aspects of male psychology, aspects which are, however, distorted by an oppressive social order.

Let me explain how I reached this position, and then go on to specify exactly what I have in mind.[2] As a general rule of social analysis, I try to give people, men specifically included, credibility for integrity and insight. Thus, when I observe a group of people acting in what seem to me irrational ways, the question I pose is not "What's wrong with them?" but rather "What are the distorted and distorting features of their situation which make these actions appear rational to them?". Until I have satisfied myself that, if I were in their shoes, their seemingly outrageous or inexplicable actions would also appear as legitimate options to me, I consider myself not to have succeeded in understanding or explaining anything. Applying this methodology to male sexist attitudes, I have obtained the following results. I believe that as we are growing up, in our early childhood years of attitude formation, we are socialized with a crucially important belief, namely the belief that in our society people get what they deserve. While this belief, in its usual interpretations, as applied to material success or social prestige, for example, is blatantly false and can be seen to be so upon reflection, it is nonetheless a principle of justice deeply inculcated in children as they are being raised. Children are also very observant. Specifically, they will observe and note that women are universally treated as less than fully human, in contrast to men. The conjunction of this principle and this observation can be expressed as a logical syllogism:

People get what they deserve.

Women are treated inhumanely.

Women are less than fully human.

I offer the above not as a historical account of the genesis of sexist attitudes and beliefs, but rather as a phenomenological description of the development of sexist beliefs and attitudes in contemporary consciousness. In this light, sexist beliefs and attitudes can be seen to result from an attempt to preserve a belief that the world is justly ordered in the face of observing the existence of gross inequality. Children are faced with a choice: either women really are less deserving than men in some fundamental way, or a basic structuring principle of their world in false, and their world loses coherence and credibility. Everything around them, as well as their own insecurities, impel children to affirm the former, sexist beliefs.

But precisely therein, I would argue, lies the hope for change. If my proposed reconstruction of the genesis of sexist consciousness is correct, then, paradoxically enough, sexist attitudes may be said to be rooted in the child's sense of justice. But as adults, we can now take the bad news that the world is indeed unjust and not reasonably ordered. That same sense of justice, the belief that people should be treated as they deserve, coupled with the belief that people really should have equal rights and freedoms regardless of such factors as the shape or color of their skin, can now be called upon to mobilize men to rectify sexist injustices.

Listen to sexist men defend their attitudes today, listen with a comprehending ear, and you will hear the pleas of someone trying to make sense of a world they never made: "There *must* be *some* reason why the world is this way," "That's just how it is," "It's always been like this, hasn't it," "You just can't change some things." This is the voice of confusion and fear, not a dominating will to power. I propose, then, that we not focus our attention on the search for an ultimate cause for sexism in the nature of the male psyche or body, but rather that we work with men in the here and now to undo the damage sexism does to all of us. While there is some need for a general explanatory theory of patriarchy so that we can properly direct our efforts for change and not pursue the wrong targets, I believe the search for such a theory is, for most of us, a misplaced emphasis.

I think we need to emphasize moving on from here, and worry less about how we got here. This is not simply a pragmatic retreat made because we happen not to have a fully satisfactory theory about the origins of patriarchy or what a future non-patriarchal utopia would look like. The search for such a blueprint for the future is miguided, an all too typically masculine attempt to impose a rigidly constructed plan upon the world. Rather, let us do the more intimately involved work of nurturing the new world to growth with our given materials. If it is true that fundamental change must be positively self-motivated and not merely reactive, then the priority must be to seek positive approaches which will enable men to make revolutionary feminist changes. The direction of these changes, as they emerge, will clearly enough show us what our new society is to look like. This is how I envisage fraternity developing. It is not simply a means to some pre-fabricated goal. To adopt a slogan from the peace movement: there is no way to fraternity, fraternity is the way.

Which brings me to the next of the three guiding concepts, equality. I believe all men are equal. Let me make that more directly relevant by making a statement that I expect some will find terribly false, and others will find trivially true. I hope to show that it is very significantly true. The statement is this: no group of men in our society is any more or less sexist than any other group of men. Gay or straight, black or white, rich or poor, we are all equal in this regard.

Let me proceed by articulating the point of view I take myself to be arguing against. It is fashionable in some circles to characterize our society as one dominated by white males. Fashionable, but inadequate, as many feminists are aware. Socialist feminists, for example, would insist that we are plagued not only by sexism and racism, but also by capitalism.[3] So the description of the dominating group has to be widened to ruling class white males. But why stop there? Our society also systematically discriminates against the old and the young, so one would need to specify the age bracket of the ruling group, and so on. By the time one was finished, one would have constructed a description which fits at most a relative handful of men, who, according to this theory, are somehow oppressing all the rest of us, usually in multiple ways. I regard such a result as untenable for a coherent social theory and practice. It is a mistake, and a serious one, to attempt to reduce the multiple systems of oppression which characterize our society into one matrix.

Let me give a personal example. Some people have attempted to commiserate with my wife, who is Greek, about how sexist Greek or Mediterranean men are. They thought they were practicing international feminist solidarity. What they were really practicing was Anglo-Saxon cultural imperialism. Mediterranean patriarchy is qualitatively different from Anglo-Saxon patriarchy. Each has distinctive features, which are more or less taken for granted within each culture and look more or less objectionable to others. To try to assess these qualitative differences on the same quantitative scale is, as the old saying has it, like trying to mix apples and oranges.[4]

It makes more sense to say that we live in a patriarchy, and under patriarchy men oppress women. Period. We also live under capitalism, the ruling class, men and women, oppresses the working class. Period. And so on with regard to racism, etc. I am aware that the situation is in reality more complex than this. Patriarchy also ordercs men into hierarchies and capitalism divides the genders. However, the fundamental point I wish to make is that just as, for example, ruling class women's gender does not excuse them from accountability for their class privileges, so too their lack of class privileges does not excuse working class men from accountability for the exercise of their male privileges. These, and all other forms of oppression, are overlapping and interrelated but distinct systems. While it is true that, because they suffer from other forms of oppression, men from oppressed groups do not reap the material rewards of patriarchy to as great an extent as men from dominant groups, one should not therefore conclude that men from oppressed groups are to be held less accountable for their sexism.

I propose therefore that we abandon all discussions and debate about whether gay men, or working class men, or Hispanic men, or any other group of men, are more or less sexist or patriarchal than any other group. I propose instead that we realize that all sexism is simply wrong and unsupportable, and that to attempt to establish some sort of graduated scale is at best meaningless and at worst oppressive in some other form. And I propose further than men go back to their respective communities and get on with the task of instituting the specific and specifically different kinds of fraternities within each community which will enable us to move towards equality and liberty for all people.

Which brings me to the concept of liberty, the last of the triumvirate. Liberty is the most expressly political of the three concepts. I believe it is essential for men to retain a perspective which is self-consciously political, and not merely personal or psychological, regarding the tasks of overcoming male role restrictions. Correspondingly, we must also expressly link our efforts to the feminist movement. Personal freedom, of whatever kind, requires the securing of political liberty.

Perhaps most importantly, any stand other than the insistence that men can be feminists betrays the most radical potential of the movement. Under the slogan "Biology is not Destiny," the feminist movement challenged the regressive idea that one's biological make-up should have a role in determining one's social/political/economic role. The stance that men cannot be feminists is a regression back to a standpoint which feminism has surpassed.

Furthermore, part of the oppressive ideology of society is the myth that the divisions between groups have been total and absolute, that there has been all-out warfare between women and men, blacks and whites, Jews and Gentiles, etc. While acknowledging the overwhelming reality of oppression, it must nonetheless be said that this is a falsification of our history and a denial of our strengths. The support which the early feminists received from their husbands and male friends *is* part of the history of feminism. The fact that approximately one-third of the signatories to the 1848 Seneca Falls Declaration of the Rights of Women were men is as important a part of the history of feminism as the exploits of John Brown are part of the history of Abolitionism in the same century.

I have no doubt that the process of building male-female feminist alliances will be difficult. At times, men will more or less unconsciously continue to play out old patterns of domination and step on the toes of the women they are attempting to assist. When this occurs, I hope and trust it will be corrected. But how many opportunities to support feminist growth will be lost if we do not make efforts to establish such alliances?

I believe a male feminist theory and practice which can have any hope of success in mobilizing men in a politically effective way behind the clear moral imperatives supporting feminism must always remain simultaneously focused on both aspects of the personal/political dialectic. Men as a group benefit from the social powers which correlate with the male sex role. They reap the material rewards the society has to offer. But men individually pay too high a price for these benefits, and it is in their real personal interest to overthrow the system which creates and grants these privileges.[6] The male sex role is both unsatisfying and dangerous. The combination of breadwinner pressures, which make us neurotic, isolated competitors, and the restrictions on male emotional release for these pressures which are also part of the male role is a prescription for the earlier deaths and higher rates of tension-related health problems—heart attacks, ulcers, high blood pressure, suicides—we daily see men suffering from. Though not all men are aware of the source of their difficulties, I believe all men suffer from sexism. These are the disadvantages of the advantages men receive from a sexist system.

In these ways, the call for "Fraternity, Equality, and Liberty" presents us with the beginnings of a positive political analysis of and for changing men. I hope this becomes part of ongoing discussions of how to further feminist brotherhood.

NOTES:

[1] These hypotheses are among many popular in feminist theory, and one finds them in such frequently used women's studies texts as *Feminist Frameworks,* Alison M. Jaggar and Paula S. Rothenberg (Eds.), (2nd edition, McGraw-Hill, 1984) and *The Longest War,* by Carol Tavris and Carole Wade, (2nd edition, Harcourt Brace Jovanovich, 1984). See also the articles by Azizah al-Hibri, Eva Feder Kittay, Iris Marion Young, Pauline Bart, and Ann Ferguson in *Mothering: Essays in Feminist Theory,* Joyce Trebilcot (Ed.), (Rowman & Allanheld, 1984).

[2] Though he might well reject the analysis in this section, it is inspired by Albert Memmi's analysis of racism. See, for example, the section on "Racism and Oppression" in *Dominated Man,* (Beacon, 1968).

[3] See *Capitalist Patriarchy and the Case for Socialist Feminism,* Zillah R. Eisenstein (Ed.), (Monthly Review Press, 1979).

[4] I am indebted to Maria Papacostaki for clarifying discussions on this topic.

[5] See Jon Snodgrass, *For Men Against Sexism: A Book of Readings,* (Times Change Press, 1977, p. 9).

[6] These points are developed in two brief articles of mine: "Feminism for Men: Beyond Liberalism", *Brother: The Newsletter of the National Organization for Changing Men,* (3:3, 1985), and a review of Leo Kanowitz's *Equal Rights: The Male Stake* and William and Laurie Wishard's "Men's Rights" in *M.: Gentle Men for Gender Justice* (12, Spring 1984).

A New Vision of Masculinity

by Cooper Thompson

I was once asked by a teacher in a suburban high school to give a guest presentation on male roles. She hoped that I might help her deal with four boys who exercised extraordinary control over the other boys in the class. Using ridicule and their status as physically imposing athletes, these four wrestlers had succeeded in stifling the participation of the other boys, who were reluctant to make comments in class discussions.

As a class we talked about the ways in which boys got status in that school and how they got put down by others. I was told that the most humiliating put-down was being called a "fag." The list of behaviors which could elicit ridicule filled two large chalkboards, and it was detailed and comprehensive; I got the sense that a boy in this school had to conform to rigid, narrow standards of masculinity to avoid being called a fag. I, too, felt this pressure and became very conscious of my mannerisms in front of the group. Partly from exasperation, I decided to test the seriousness of these assertions. Since one of the four boys had some streaks of pink in his shirt, and since he had told me that wearing pink was grounds for being called a fag, I told him that I thought he was a fag. Instead of laughing, he said, "I'm going to kill you."

Such is the stereotypic definition of strength that is associated with masculinity. But it is a very limited definition of strength, one based on dominance and control and acquired through the humiliation and degradation of others.

Contrast this with a view of strength offered by Pam McAllister in her introduction to *Reweaving the Web of Life:*

> The 'Strength' card in my Tarot deck depicts, not a warrior going off to battle with his armor and his mighty sword, but a woman stroking a lion. The woman has not slain the lion nor maced it, not netted it, nor has she put on it a muzzle or a leash. And though the lion clearly has teeth and long sharp claws, the woman is not hiding, nor has she sought a protector, nor has she grown muscles. She doesn't appear to be talking to the lion, nor

flattering it, nor tossing it fresh meat to distract its hungry jaws.

The woman on the 'Strength' card wears a flowing white dress and a garland of flowers. With one hand she cups the lion's jaws, with the other she caresses its nose. The lion on the card has big yellow eyes and a long red tongue curling out of its mouth. One paw is lifted and the mane falls in thick red curls across its broad torso. The woman. The lion. Together they depict strength.

This image of strength stands in direct contrast to the strength embodied in the actions of the four wrestlers. The collective strength of the woman and the lion is a strength unknown in a system of traditional male values. Other human qualities are equally foreign to a traditional conception of masculinity. In workshops I've offered on the male role stereotype, teachers and other school personnel easily generate lists of attitudes and behaviors which boys typically seem to not learn. Included in this list are being supportive and nurturant, accepting one's vulnerability and being able to ask for help, valuing women and "women's work," understanding and expressing emotions (except for anger), the ability to empathize with and empower other people, and learning to resolve conflict in non-aggressive, non-competitive ways.

Learning Violence

All of this should come as no surprise. Traditional definitions of masculinity include attributes such as independence, pride, resiliency, self-control, and physical strength. This is precisely the image of the Marlboro man, and to some extent, these are desirable attributes for boys and girls. But masculinity goes beyond these qualities to stress competitiveness, toughness, aggressiveness, and power. In this context, threats to one's status, however small, cannot be avoided or taken lightly. If a boy is called a fag, it means that he is perceived as weak or timid—and therefore not masculine enough for his peers. There is enormous pressure for him to fight back. Not being tough at these moments only proves the allegation.

Violence is learned not just as a way for boys to defend allegations that they are feminized, but as an effective, appropriate way for them to normally behave. In "The Civic Advocacy of Violence" [*M.,* Spring 1982] Wayne Ewing clearly states:

I used to think that we simply tolerated and permitted male abusiveness in our society. I have now come to understand rather, that we advocate physical violence. Violence is presented as effective. Violence is taught as the normal, appropriate and necessary behavior of power and control. Analyses which interweave advocacy of male violence with 'Super Bowl Culture' have never been refuted. Civic expectations—translated into professionalism, financial commitments, city planning for recreational space, the raising of male children for competitive sport, the corporate ethics of business ownership of athletic teams, profiteering on entertain-

ment—all result in the monument of the National Football League, symbol and reality at once of the advocacy of violence.

Ultimately, violence is the tool which maintains what I believe are the two most critical socializing forces in a boy's life: *homophobia,* the hatred of gay men (who are stereotyped as feminine) or those men believed to be gay, as well as the fear of being perceived as gay; and *misogyny,* the hatred of women. The two forces are targeted at different classes of victims, but they are really just the flip sides of the same coin. Homophobia is the hatred of feminine qualities in men while misogyny is the hatred of feminine qualities in women. The boy who is called a fag is the target of other boys' homophobia as well as the victim of his own homophobia. While the overt message is the absolute need to avoid being feminized, the implication is that females—and all that they traditionally represent—are contemptible. The United States Marines have a philosophy which conveniently combines homophobia and misogyny in the belief that "When you want to create a group of male killers, you kill 'the woman' in them."

The pressures of homophobia and misogyny in boys' lives have been poignantly demonstrated to me each time that I have repeated a simple yet provocative activity with students. I ask them to answer the question, "If you woke up tomorrow and discovered that you were the opposite sex from the one you are now, how would you and your life be different?" Girls consistently indicate that there are clear advantages to being a boy—from increased independence and career opportunities to decreased risks of physical and sexual assault—and eagerly answer the question. But boys often express disgust at this possibility and even refuse sometimes to answer the question. In her reports of a broad-based survey using this question, Alice Baumgartner reports the following responses as typical of boys: "If I were a girl, I'd be stupid and weak as a string;" "I would have to wear makeup, cook, be a mother, and yuckky stuff like that;" "I would have to hate snakes. Everything would be miserable;" "If I were a girl, I'd kill myself."

The Costs of Masculinity

The costs associated with a traditional view of masculinity are enormous, and the damage occurs at both personal and societal levels. The belief that a boy should be tough (aggressive, competitive, and daring) can create emotional pain for him. While a few boys experience short-term success for their toughness, there is little security in the long run. Instead, it leads to a series of challenges which few, if any, boys ultimately win. There is no security in being at the top when so many other boys are competing for the same status. Toughness also leads to increased chances of stress, physical injury, and even early death. It is considered manly to take extreme physical risks and voluntarily engage in combative, hostile activities.

The flip side of toughness—nurturance—is not a quality perceived as masculine and thus not valued. Because of this boys and men experience a greater emotional distance from other people and few opportunities to participate in meaningful interpersonal relationships. Studies consistently show that fathers spend very small amounts of time interacting with their children. In addition, men report that they seldom have intimate relationships with other men, reflecting their homophobia. They are afraid of getting too close and don't know how to take down the walls that they have built between themselves.

As boys grow older and accept adult roles, the larger social costs of masculinity clearly emerge. Most women experience male resistance to an expansion of women's roles; one of the assumptions of traditional masculinity is the belief that women should be subordinate to men. The consequence is that men are often not willing to accept females as equal, competent partners in personal and professional settings. Whether the setting is a sexual relationship, the family, the streets, or the battlefield, men are continuously engaged in efforts to dominate. Statistics on child abuse consistently indicate that the vast majority of abusers are men, and that there is no "typical" abuser. Rape may be the fastest growing crime in the United States. And it is men, regardless of nationality who provoke and sustain war. In short, traditional masculinity is life threatening.

New Socialization For Boys

Masculinity, like many other human traits, is determined by both biological and environmental factors. While some believe that biological factors are significant in shaping some masculine behavior, there is undeniable evidence that cultural and environmental factors are strong enough to override biological impulses. What is it, then, that we should be teaching boys about being a man in a modern world?

- Boys must learn to accept their vulnerability, learn to express a range of emotions such as fear and sadness, and learn to ask for help and support in appropriate situations.
- Boys must learn to be gentle, nurturant, cooperative and communicative, and in particular, learn non-violent means of resolving conflicts.
- Boys must learn to accept those attitudes and behaviors which have traditionally been labeled feminine as necessary for full human development—thereby reducing homophobia and misogyny. This is tantamount to teaching boys to love other boys and girls.

Certain qualities like courage, physical strength, and independence, which are traditionally associated with masculinity, are indeed positive qualities for males, provided that they are not manifested in obsessive ways nor used to exploit or dominate others. It is not necessary to completely disregard or unlearn what is traditionally called masculine. I believe, however, that the three areas above are crucial for developing a broader view of masculinity, one which is healthier for all life.

These three areas are equally crucial for reducing aggressive, violent behavior among boys and men. Males must learn to cherish life for the sake of their *own* wholeness as human beings, not just *for* their children, friends, and lovers. If males were more nurturant, they would be less likely to hurt those they love.

Leonard Eron, writing in the *American Psychologist,* puts the issue of unlearning aggression and learning nurturance in clear-cut terms:

> *Socialization is crucial in determining levels of aggression. No matter how aggression is measured or observed, as a group males always score higher than females. But this is not true for all girls. There are some girls who seem to have been socialized like boys who are just as aggressive as boys. Just as some females can learn to be aggressive, so males can learn not to be aggressive. If we want to reduce the level of aggression in society, we should also discourage boys from aggression very early on in life and reward them too for others' behaviors; in other words, we should socialize boys more like girls, and they should be encouraged to develop socially positive qualities such as tenderness, cooperation, and aesthetic appreciation. The level of individual aggression in society will be reduced only when male adolescents and young adults, as a result of socialization, subscribe to the same standards of behavior as have been traditionally encouraged for women.*

Where will this change in socialization occur? In his first few years, most of a boy's learning about masculinity comes from the influences of parents, siblings and images of masculinity such as those found on television. Massive efforts will be needed to make changes here. But at older ages, school curriculum and the school environment provide powerful reinforcing images of traditional masculinity. This reinforcement occurs through a variety of channels, including curriculum content, role modeling, and extracurricular activities, especially competitive sports.

School athletics are a microcosm of the socialization of male values. While participation in competitive activities can be enjoyable and healthy, it too easily becomes a lesson in the need for toughness, invulnerability, and dominance. Athletes learn to ignore their own injuries and pain and instead try to injure and inflict pain on others in their attempts to win, regardless of the cost to themselves or their opponents. Yet the lessons learned in athletics are believed to be vital for full and complete masculine development, and as a model for problem-solving in other areas of life.

In addition to encouraging traditional male values, schools provide too few experiences in nurturance, cooperation, negotiation, non-violent conflict resolution, and strategies for empathizing with and empowering others. Schools should become places where boys have the opportunity to learn these skills; clearly, they won't learn them on the street, from peers, or on television.

Setting New Examples

Despite the pressures on men to display their masculinity in traditional ways, there are examples of men and boys who are changing. "Fathering" is one example of a positive change. In recent years, there hs been a popular emphasis on child-care activities, with men becoming more involved in providing care to children, both professionally and as fathers. This is a clear shift from the more traditional view that child rearing should be delegated to women and is not an appropriate activity for men.

For all of the male resistance it has generated, the Women's Liberation Movement has at least provided a stimulus for some men to accept women as equal partners in most areas of life. These are the men who have chosen to learn and grow from women's experiences and together with women are creating new norms for relationships. Popular literature and research on male sex roles is expanding, reflecting a wider interest in masculinity. Weekly news magazines such as *Time* and *Newsweek* have run major stories on the "new masculinity," suggesting that positive changes are taking place in the home and in the workplace. Small groups of men scattered around the country have organized against pornography, battering and sexual assault. Finally there is the National Organization for Changing Men which has a pro-feminist, pro-gay, pro-"new man" agenda, and its ranks are slowly growing.

In schools where I have worked with teachers, they report that years of efforts to enhance educational opportunities for girls have also had some positive effects on boys. The boys seem more tolerant of girls' participation in co-ed sports activities and in traditionally male shops and courses. They seem to have a greater respect for the accomplishments of women through women's contributions to literature and history. Among elementary school aged males, the expression of vulnerable feelings is gaining acceptance. In general, however, there has been far too little attention paid to redirecting male role development.

Boys Will Be Boys

I think back to the four wrestlers and the stifling culture of masculinity in which they live. If schools were to radically alter this culture and substitute for it a new vision of masculinity, what would that look like? In this environment, boys would express a full range of behaviors and emotions without fear of being chastized. They would be permitted and encouraged to cry, to be afraid, to show joy, and to express love in a gentle fashion. Extreme concern for career goals would be replaced by a consideration of one's need for recreation, health, and meaningful work. Older boys would be encouraged to tutor and play with younger students. Moreover, boys would receive as much recognition for artistic talents as they do for athletics, and, in general, they would value leisure-time, recreational activities as highly as competitive sports.

In a system where maleness and femaleness were equally valued, boys might no longer feel that they have to "prove" themselves to other boys; they would simply accept the worth of each person and value those differences. Boys would realize that it is permissable to admit failure. In addition, they would seek out opportunities to learn from girls and women. Emotional support would be commonplace, and it would no longer be seen as just the role of the female to provide the support. Relationships between boys and girls would no longer be based on limited roles, but instead would become expressions of two individuals learning from and supporting one another. Relationships between boys would reflect their care for one another rather then their mutual fear and distrust.

Aggressive styles of resolving conflicts would be the exception rather than the norm. Girls would feel welcome in activities dominated by boys, knowing that they were safe from the threat of being sexually harassed. Boys would no longer boast of beating up another boy or of how much they "got off" of a girl the night before. In fact, the boys would be as outraged as the girls at rape or other violent crimes in the community. Finally, boys would become active in efforts to stop nuclear proliferation and all other forms of military violence, following the examples set by activist women.

The development of a new conception of masculinity based on this vision is an ambitious task, but one which is essential for the health and safety of both men and women. The survival of our society may rest on the degree to which we are able to teach men to cherish life.

IV SPIRIT AND SOUL

Under Capricorn

by Jerah Chadwick

Our hands are holy
five pointed stars
our bouyant bodies
the circles of our arms
are blessings
and our cocks, aspects
of the Horned One
god of crossroads
and crossed fingers
of thresholds
we cross breathless
as climbers
          the mountains
in us like coral
a history rising
from the dark
toward the blue light
element we hunger for
toward air

The Men Of The Wound

by Shepherd Bliss

Nearly 100 men gathered at the beginning of last summer in a lodge in the Mendocino redwoods—much as men have assembled for centuries, to sail the sea, to tame the wilds, to play music, to be together.

An elder man, the poet and story-teller Robert Bly, had called us together. He invited another elder to teach with him—psychologist James Hillman. One of Bly's close friends—the forty year old drummer and story-teller Michael Mead—was there as Bly's right-hand man. A younger man, about half Bly's age—the dancer Martin Keogh—was our chief organizer. They brought us together.

We drummed, told each other stories, ate and drank, recited poetry, sweated, challenged and entertained each other. We were soon outside our regular daily experiences and into "mythological time."

Telling the story of what happened in those seven days has not been easy. Much happened. Writing about what happened is difficult. Perhaps focusing on my small group and its gift to the larger group will provide a sense of what occurred.

Each man chose a number, which randomly assigned him to one of a dozen groups. I was the leader of the "Men of the Wound" group. We were seven. We began by telling our stories to each other. Our task was to offer a gift to the group. We decided to weave our individual stories into a collective story.

In addition to our own stories, I also told the stories of two wounded Greeks—the god Hephaestus and the hero Philoctetes. Hephaestus was the only one of the 12 Olympian gods and goddesses who worked, as a smith; he was lame. Two distinct stories tell of his laming. In one his mother, Hera, kicked him out of heaven. In the other, his father, Zeus, expelled him. So the origins of his wound are unclear. He was either father-wounded or mother-wounded.

The source of Philoctetes' wound is clear. The great military commander Odysseus abandons him on an island on the way to Troy after a snake bites him and his screaming becomes so terrible and the wound so smelly that the men can no longer stand his grief. The community of men throws him out.

So these stories entered us—our individual stories and the mythological stories which have remained these thousands of years. We entered a sweat together—rocks fired to heat us—and more of our wounds emerged. There were conflicts in our group. But we came together.

We decided to offer a gift to the other men—to render our wounds and the wounds of all men into a form which would communicate. So we spent part of each day working on a play to present for our brothers. We rehearsed it— repeating each sound and movement carefully. Changing them. Talking to each other. Disagreeing. What should the mood be? Our emotions and feelings were various—confusion, anger, fear, love.

The night to tell our story had arrived—our last night together at the lodge. Dinner had included much toasting. Some of the other groups had presented their plays. Most were humorous—deeply humorous—reaching into profound places and shaking the body with laughter. Ours was not intended to be funny.

We darkened the room, covering up even the fireplace light. The men began to clap, rhythmically, demanding our presence. We entered by voice, announcing ourselves: "The Men of the Wound." Still dark, I said, "Mom and Dad have a baby Boy."

The lights rise to a boy being given birth by a "woman." The father cuts the "umbilical cord." Casting has been careful. Tom played the father; he never knew his father. The "mother" was one of the more nurturing, sensitive men in the group.

Our Greek chorus was composed of four—shirtless, barefoot, masked. Our leader was a dark, full bearded, masculine-voiced man. One of us played a constant drum beat throughout the play. Who were these men? How did they get here? You thought you knew everyone at the camp. You did not know who these men were.

Ritualistically, Dad took the knife to his son's penis, carefully, cutting it. "This is for your own good," the chorus announces, and the boy is circumcised. One man dashes out from the chorus—virtually invisible—and splashes blood on his groin. Another chorus member hits a cutting board with a meat cleaver. The sound sends a shock through the group. A few had laughed at the circumcision, thinking that perhaps it would be another humorous play. There would be no more laughter during this play.

The Boy regains his senses, begins to crawl about, entering the outer world. His mother goes for him, restraining him, retying the cord about his ankles. "The world is not a safe place," the chorus announces. Blood is splashed on his feet. He remains bound, crawling about on his knees. The men are visibly moved, leap back, when he is wounded, lamed, damaged in his grounding. He receives an Hephaestus-Philoctetes wound to his foot.

The Boy regains his senses again, plays, as boys are drawn to. He hurts his elbow, comes to his Dad for comfort. "Big boys don't cry," announces the chorus. Blood on his mouth, he receives a wound to his mouth—to his capacity to articulate.

Further diminished, he rallies again, finds a football, goes to his Dad to play. "Not now, I'm busy." This wound is to the heart, hitting him in the middle of his being.

Yet he rallies again, finding a sword this time. Plays with it. Transforms it into a baseball bat. The father, reading his newspaper, takes it: "You don't really want that," he casts a spell on his son. "You want this," he shoves the newspaper to his son. This wounding is to the head, as the meat cleaver comes. Sounds can be heard from the other men: open weeping, signs of recognition.

The words spoken by the chorus come from the real life experiences of the men in the group. They were words spoken to us as we grew up—spells cast upon us which needed to be broken.

Dad and Mom, arm in arm, begin to walk off. They stop for a moment, and Dad speaks, his first words to his son: "Now be a man!" The chorus joins the parents and walk off stage.

The final scene is the Boy alone, on his knees, his hands in the air—confused. The lights darken.

This play was one of the vehicles through which the grief of these men—seven in the skit and the nearly 100 present—was acknowledged.

As I write this, Father's Day is a few days off. It's been almost exactly two weeks since we presented the play. Rejoining daily, secular time has been hard for me. I still feel somewhat in the mythological time of that week together in the woods. I need to tell the story of the play to be free of it. It really did happen—the wounding. I sent my father a nice gift this year—an article I had written about "Fathers and Sons." No blaming, just a re-telling of part of my story—our story.

After the play, we were proud. Walked a little taller. Proud of the discipline that had pulled it off. Of our closeness to our feelings—and of the distance which enabled us to put them into such a form. Proud to have told our story. Proud to have moved our brothers. Proud to be men. And still wounded. Wounded men. But somehow more free of those wounds by having expressed them.

What Men Really Want
an interview with Robert Bly

by Keith Thompson

Keith Thompson: After exploring the way of the goddess and the matriarchs for many years, lately you've turned your attention to the pathways of male energy—the bond between fathers and sons, for example, and the initiation of young males. You're also writing a book relating some of the old classic fairy tales to men's growth. What has your investigation turned up? What's going on with men these days?

Robert Bly: No one knows! Historically, the male has changed considerably in the past thirty years. Back then there was a person we could call the '50s male, who was hard-working, responsible, fairly well disciplined; he didn't see women's souls very well, though he looked at their bodies a lot. Reagan still has this personality. The '50s male was vulnerable to collective opinion: if you were a man, you were supposed to like football games, be aggressive, stick up for the United States, never cry, and always provide. But this image of the male lacked feminine space. It lacked some sense of flow, it lacked compassion, in a way that led directly to the unbalanced pursuit of the Vietnam War, just as the lack of feminine space inside Reagan's head now has led to his callousness and brutality toward the poor in El Salvador, toward old people here, the unemployed, schoolchildren, and poor people in general. The '50s male had a clear vision of what a man is, but the vision involved massive inadequacies and flaws.

Then, during the '60s, another sort of male appeared. The waste and anguish of the Vietnam War made men question what an adult male really is. And the women's movement encouraged men to actually look at women, forcing them to become conscious of certain things that the '50s male tended to avoid. As men began to look at women and at their concerns, some men began to see their own feminine side and pay attention to it. That process continues to this day, and I would say that most young males are now involved in it to some extent.

Now there's something wonderful about all this—the step of the male bringing forth his own feminine consciousness is an important one—and yet I have the sense there is something wrong. The male in the past twenty years has become more thoughtful, more gentle. But by this process he has not become more free. He's a nice boy who now not only pleases his mother but also the young woman he is living with.

I see the phenomenon of what I would call the "soft male" all over the country today.

Sometimes when I look out at my audiences, perhaps half the young males are what I'd call soft. They're lovely, valuable people—I like them—and they're not interested in harming the earth, or starting wars or working for corporations. There is something favorable toward life in their whole general mood and style of living.

But something's wrong. Many of these men are unhappy. There's not much energy in them. They are life-preserving but not exactly life-giving. And why is it you often see these men with strong women who positively radiate energy? Here we have a finely tuned young man, ecologically superior to his father, sympathetic to the whole harmony of the universe, yet he himself has no energy to offer.

KT: It seems as if many of these soft young men have come to equate their own natural male energy with being macho. Even when masculine energy would clearly be life-giving, productive of service to the community, many young males step back from it. Perhaps it is because back in the '60s, when we looked to the women's movement for leads as to how we should be, the message we got was the new strong women wanted soft men.

RB: I agree. That's how it felt! The women did play a part in this. I remember a bumper sticker at the time that read "WOMEN SAY YES TO MEN WHO SAY NO." We know it took a lot of courage to resist or to go to Canada, just as it took some courage also to go to Vietnam. But the women were definitely saying they preferred the softer receptive male, and they would reward him for being so. "We will sleep with you if you are not too aggressive and macho." So the development of men was disturbed a little there; nonreceptive maleness was equated with violence, and receptivity was rewarded.

Also, as you mention, some energetic women chose soft men to be their lovers—and in a way, perhaps, sons. These changes didn't happen by accident. Young men for various reasons wanted harder women, and women began to desire softer men. It seems like a nice arrangement, but it isn't working out.

KT: How so?

RB: Recently I taught a conference for men only at the Lama Community in New Mexico. About forty men came, and we were together ten days. Each morning I talked about certain fairy tales relating to men's growth, and about the Greek gods that embody what the Greeks considered different kinds of male energy. We spent the afternoon being quiet or walking and doing body movement or dance, and then we'd all come together again in the late afternoon. Often the younger males would begin to talk and within five minutes they would be weeping. The amount of grief and anguish in the younger males was astounding! The river was deep.

Part of the grief was a remoteness from their fathers, which they felt keenly, but part, too, came from trouble in their marriages or relationships. They had learned to be receptive, and it wasn't enough to carry their marriages. In every relationship, something fierce is needed once in a while; both the man and the woman need to have it.

At the point when it was needed, often the young man didn't have it. He was nurturing, but something else was required—for the relationship, for his life. The male was able to say, "I can feel your pain, and I consider your life as important as mine, and I will take care of you and comfort you." But he could not say what he wanted, and stick by it; that was a different matter.

In The Odyssey, Hermes instructs Odysseus, when he is approaching a kind of matriarchal figure, that he is to lift or show Circe his sword. It was difficult for many of the younger males to distinguish between showing the sword and hurting someone. Do you understand me? They had learned so well not to hurt anyone that they couldn't lift the sword, even to catch the light of the sun on it! Showing a sword doesn't mean fighting; there's something joyful in it.

KT: You seem to be suggesting that uniting with their feminine side has been an important stage for men on their path toward wholeness, but it's not the final one. What is required? What's the next step?

RB: One of the fairy tales I'm working on for my *Fairy Tales for Men* collection is a story called "Iron John."[1] Though it was first set down by the Grimm Brothers around 1820, this story could be ten or twenty thousand years old. It talks about a different development for men, a further stage than we've seen so far in the United States.

As the story starts, something strange has been happening in a remote area of the forest near the king's castle; when hunters go into this area, they disappear and never come back. Three hunters have gone out and disappeared. People are getting the feeling that there's something kind of weird about that part of the forest, and they don't go there anymore. Then one day an unknown hunter shows up at the castle and says, "What can I do around here?" I need something to do." And he is told, "Well, there's a problem in the forest. People go out there and they don't come back. We've sent groups of men to see about it and they disappear. Can you do something about it?"

Interestingly, this young man does not ask for a group to go with him—he goes into the forest alone, taking only his dog. And they wander about in the forest, they come across a pond. Suddenly a hand reaches up from the pond, grabs the dog and drags it down. The hunter is fond of the dog and he's not willing to abandon it, in this way. His response is neither to become hysterical, nor to abandon his dog. Instead, he does something sensible, he goes back to the castle, rounds up some men with buckets and then they bucket out the pond.

Lying at the bottom of the pond is a large man covered with hair all the way down to his feet. He's kind of reddish—he looks a little like rusty iron. So they capture him and bring him back to the castle, where the king puts him in an iron cage in the courtyard.

Now, let's stop the story here a second. The implication is that when the male looks into his psyche, not being instructed what to look for, he may see beyond his feminine side, to the other side of the "deep pool." What he finds at the bottom of his psyche—in this area that no one has visited in a long time—is an ancient male covered with hair. Now, in all of the mythologies, hair is heavily connected with the instinctive, the sexual, the primitive. What I'm proposing is that every modern male has, lying at the bottom of his psyche, a large primitive man covered with hair down to his feet. Making contact with this wildman is the step the '70s male has not yet taken, this is the process that still hasn't taken place in contemporary culture.

As the story suggests very delicately, there's a little fear around this ancient man. After a man gets over his initial skittishness about expressing his feminine side, he finds it to be pretty wonderful, he gets to write poetry and go out and sit by the ocean, he doesn't have to be on top all the time in sex anymore, he becomes empathetic. It's a beautiful new world. But Iron John, the man at the bottom of the lake, is quite a different matter. This figure is even more frightening than the interior female, who is scary enough. When a man succeeds in becoming conscious of his interior woman, he often feels warmer, more alive. But when he approaches what I'll call the "deep male," that's a totally different situation!

Contact with Iron John requires the willingness to go down into the psyche and accept what's dark down there including the sexual. For generations now, the business community has warned men to keep away from Iron John, and the Christian Church is not too fond of him either. But it's possible that men are once more approaching that deep male. Freud, Jung, and Wilheim Reich are three men who had the courage to go down into the pond and accept what's there, which includes the hair, the ancientness, the rustiness. The job of modern males is to follow them down. Some of that work has already been done, and in some psyches (or on some days in the whole culture) the Hairy Man or Iron John has been brought up and stands in a cage "in the courtyard." That means he has been brought back into the civilized world, and to a place where the young males can see him.

Now, let's go back to the story. One day the king's eight-year-old son is playing in the courtyard and he loses his beloved golden ball. It rolls into the cage, and the wildman grabs it. If the prince wants his ball back, he's going to have to go to this rusty, hairy man who's been dying at the bottom of the pond for a very long time and ask for it. The plot begins to thicken.

KT: The golden ball, of course, is a recurrent image in many fairy stories. What does it symbolize in general, and what is its significance here?

RB: The golden ball suggests the unity of personality that we have as children—a kind of radiance, a sense of unity with the universe. The ball is golden, representing light, and round, representing wholeness, like the sun, it gives off a radiant energy from inside.

Notice that in this story, the boy is eight. We all lose something around the age of eight, whether we are girl or boy, male or female. We lose the golden ball in grade school if not before; high school finishes it. We may spend the rest of our lives trying to get the golden ball back. The first stage of that process I guess would be accepting—firmly, definitely—that the ball has been lost. Remember Freud's words? "What a distressing contrast there is between the radiant intelligence of the child and the feeble mentality of the average adult."

So who's got the golden ball? In the '60s, males were told that the golden ball was the feminine, in their own feminine side. They found the feminine, and still did not find the golden ball. That step that both Freud and Jung urged on males and the step that men are beginning to undertake now, is the realization that you cannot look to your own feminine side, because that's not where the ball was lost. You can't go to your wife and ask for the golden ball back. She'd give it to you if she could, because women are not hostile in this way to men's growth, but she doesn't have it anyway and besides, she has lost her own. And heaven knows you can't ask your mother!

After looking for the golden ball in women and not finding it, then looking into his own feminine side, the young male is called upon to consider the possibility that the golden ball lies within the magnetic field of the wildman. Now, that's a very hard thing for us to conceive the possibility that the deep nourishing and spiritually radiant energy in the male lies not in the feminine side, but in the deep masculine. Not the shallow masculine, the macho masculine, the snowmobile masculine, but the deep masculine, the instinctive one who's underwater and who has been there we don't know how long.

Now, the amazing thing about the "Iron John" story is that it doesn't say that the golden ball is being held by some benign Asian guru or by a kind young man named Jesus. There's something connected with getting the golden ball back that is incompatible with niceness. And the frog only turns into a prince when it is thrown against the wall in a fit of what New Age people might call "negative energy." New Age thought has taught young men to kiss frogs. That doesn't always work. You only get your mouth wet. The women's movement has helped women learn to throw the frog against the wall, but men haven't had this kind of movement yet. The kind of energy I'm talking about is not the same as macho, brute strength which men already know enough about; it's forceful action undertaken, not without compassion, but with resolve.

KT: It sounds as if contacting the wildman would involve in some sense a movement against the forces of "civilization."

RB: It's true. When it comes time for a young male to have a conversation with the wildman, it's not the same as a conversation with his minister or his guru. When a boy talks with the hairy man, he is not getting into a conversation about bliss or mind or spirit, or "higher consciousness," but about something wet, dark and low—what James Hillman would call "soul."

And I think that today's males are just about ready to take that step, to go to the cage and ask for the golden ball back. Some are ready to do that, others haven't gotten the water out of the pond yet, they haven't yet left the collective male identity and gone out into the wilderness alone, into the unconscious. You've got to take a bucket, several buckets. You can't wait for a giant to come along and suck out all the water for you; all that magic stuff isn't going to help you. A weekend at Esalen won't do it either! You have to do it bucket by bucket. This resembles the slow discipline of art; it's the work that Rembrandt did, that Picasso and Yeats and Rilke and Bach all did. Bucket work implies much more discipline than many males have right now.

KT: And of course, it's going to take some persistence and discipline, not only to uncover the deep male, but to get the golden ball back. It seems unlikely that this "un-nice" wildman would just hand it over.

RB: You're right; what kind of story would it be if the wildman answered: "Well, OK, here's your ball—go have fun." Jung said that in any case, if you're asking your psyche for something, don't use yes or no questions—the psyche likes to make deals. If part of you for example is very lazy and doesn't want to do any work, a flat-out New Year's resolution won't do you any good; it will work better if you say to the lazy part of yourself, "You let me work for an hour, then I'll let you be a slob for an hour—deal?" So in "Iron John," a deal is made, the wildman agrees to give the golden ball back if the boy opens the cage.

At first, the boy is frightened and runs off. Finally, the third time the wildman offers the same deal, the boy says, "I couldn't open it even if I wanted to because I don't know where the key is." The wildman now says something magnificent, he says, "The key is under your mother's pillow."

Did you get that shot? The key to let the wildman out is lying not in the toolshed, not in the attic, not in the cellar—it's under his mother's pillow! What do you make of that?

KT: It seems to suggest that the young male has to take back the power he has given to his mother and get away from the force field of her bed. He must direct his energies away from pleasing Mommy and toward the search for his own instinctive roots.

RB: That's right, and we see a lot of trouble right there these days, particularly among spiritual devotees. A guru may help you skip over your troubled relations with your mother, but one doesn't enter the soul by skipping; one's personal history is also history in the larger sense. In the West our way has been to enter the soul by consciously exploring the relationship with the mother—even though it may grieve us to do it, even though it implies the incest issue, even though we can't seem to make any headway in talking with her.

KT: Which would explain why the boy turns away twice in fright before agreeing to get the key from his mother's bed. Some longtime work is involved in making this kind of break.

RB: Yes, and it also surely accounts for the fact that, in the story, the mother and father are always away on the day that the boy finally obeys the wildman. Obviously, you've got to wait until your mother and father have gone away. This represents not being so dependent on the collective, on the approval of the community, on being a nice person, or essentially being dependent on your own mother because if you went up to your mother and said "I want the key so I can let the wildman out," she'd say, "Oh no, you just get a job" or "Come over here and give Mommy a kiss." There are very few mothers in the world who would release that key from under the pillow because they are intuitively aware of what would happen next—namely, they would lose their nice boys. The possessiveness that some mothers exercise on sons—not to mention the possessiveness that fathers exercise toward their daughters—cannot be overestimated.

And then, we have a lovely scene in which the boy succeeds in opening the cage and setting the wildman free. At this point, one could imagine a number of things happening.

The wildman could go back to his pond, so that the split happens over again: by the time the parents come back, the wildman is gone and the boy has replaced the key. He could become a corporate executive, an ordained mininster, a professor, he might be a typical 20th century male.

But in this case, what happens is that the wildman comes out of the cage and starts toward the forest and the boy shouts after him, "Don't run away! My parents are going to very angry when they come back." And Iron John says, "I guess you're right; you'd better come with me." He hoists the boy up on his shoulders and off they go.

KT: What does this mean, that they take off together?

RB: There are several possible arrangments in life that a male can make with the wildman. The male can be separated from the wildman in his unconscious by thousands of miles and never see him. Or the male and the wildman can exist together in a civilized place, like a courtyard, with the wildman in a cage, and they they can carry on a conversation with one another, which can go on for a long time. But apparently the two can never be united in the courtyard, the boy cannot bring the wildman with him into his home. When the wildman is freed a little, when the young man feels a little more trust in his instinctive part after going through some discipline, then he can let the wildman out of the cage. And since the wildman can't stay with him in civilization, he must go off with the wildman.

This is where the break with the parents finally comes. As they go off together the wildman says, "You'll never see your mother and father again," and the boy has to accept that the collective thing is over. He must leave his parents' force field.

KT: In the ancient Greek tradition a young man would leave his family to study with an older man the energies of Zeus, Apollo, or Dionysius. We seem to have lost the rite of initiation, and yet young males have a great need to be introduced to the male mysteries.

RB: This is what has been missing in our culture. Among the Hopis and other Native Americans of the Southwest, a boy is taken away at age twelve and led down into the kiva (down!): he stays down there for six weeks, and a year and a half passes before he sees his mother. He enters completely into the instinctive male world, which means a sharp break with both parents. You see, the fault of the nuclear family isn't so much that it's crazy and full of double binds (that's true in communes too—it's the human condition), the issue is that the son has a difficult time breaking away from the parents' field of energy, especially the mother's field, and our culture simply has made no provision for this initiation.

The ancient societies believed that a boy becomes a man only through ritual and effort—that he must be initiated into the world of men. It doesn't happen by itself, it doesn't happen just because he eats Wheaties. And only men can do this work.

KT: We tend to picture initiation as a series of tests that the young male goes through, but surely there's more to it.

RB: We can also imagine initiation as that moment when the older males together welcome the younger male into the male world. One of the best stories I've heard about this kind of welcoming is one which takes place each year among the Kikuyus in Africa. When a young man is about ready to be welcomed in, he is taken away from his mother and brought to a special place the men have set up some distance from the village. He fasts for three days. The third night he finds himself sitting in a circle around the fire with the older males. He is hungry, thirsty, alert, and frightened. One of the older males takes up a knife, opens a vein in his arm and lets a little of his blood flow into a gourd or bowl. Each man in the circle opens his arm with the same knife as the bowl goes around, and lets some blood flow in. When the bowl arrives at the young male, he is invited in tenderness to take nourishment from it.

The boy learns a number of things. He learns that there is a kind of nourishment that comes not from his mother only, but from males. And he learns that the knife can be used for many purposes besides wounding others. Can he have any doubts now that he is welcome in the male world?

Once that is done, the older males can teach him the myths, the stories, the songs that carry male values, not fighting only, but spirit values. Once these "moistening myths" are learned, they lead the young male far beyond his personal father and into the moistness of the swampy fathers who stretch back century after century.

KT: If young men today have no access to initiation rites of the past, how are they to make the passage into their instinctive male energy?

RB: Let me turn the question back to you: as a young male, how are *you* doing it?

KT: Well, I've heard much of my own path described in your remarks about soft men. I was 14 when my parents were divorced, and my brothers and I stayed with our mom. My relationship with my dad had been remote and distant anyway, and now he wasn't even in the house. My mom had the help of a succession of maids over the years to help raise us, particularly a wonderful old country woman who did everything from changing our diapers to teaching us to pray. It came to pass that my best friends were women, including several older, energetic women who introduced me to politics and literature and feminism. These were platonic friendships on the order of a mentor-student bond. I was particulary influenced by the energy of the Women's Movement, partially because I had been raised by strong yet nurturing women and partially because my father's absence suggested to me that men couldn't be trusted. So for almost ten years, through about age 24, my life was full of self-confident, experienced women friends and men friends who, like me, placed a premium on vulnerability, gentleness, and sensitivity. From the standpoint of the '60s -'70s male, I had it made! Yet a couple of years ago, I began to feel that something was missing.

RB: What was missing for you?

KT: My father. I began to think about my father. He began to appear in my dreams, and when I looked at old family photos, seeing his picture brought up a lot of grief—grief that I didn't know him, that the distance between us seemed so great. As I began to let myself feel my loneliness for him, one night I had a powerful dream. I was carried off into the woods by a pack of she-wolves who fed and nursed and raised me with love and wisdom, and I became one of them. And yet, in some unspoken way, I was always slightly separate, different from the rest of the pack. One day after we had been running through the woods together in beautiful formation and with lightning speed, we came to a river and began to drink. When we put our faces to the water, I could see the reflection of all of them but I couldn't see my own! There was an empty space in the rippling water where I was supposed to be. My immediate response in the dream was panic—was I really *there,* did I even *exist?* I knew the dream had to do in some way with the absent male, both within me and with respect to my father. I resolved to spend time with him, to see who we are in each other's lives now that we've both grown up a little.

RB: So the dream deepened the longing. Have you seen him?

KT: Yes. I went back to the midwest a few months later to see him and my mom, who are both remarried and still live in our hometown. For the first time I spent as much, if not more time with my dad than with my mom. He and I took drives around the county to places we'd spent time during my childhood, seeing old barns and tractors and fields which seemed not to have changed at all. I would tell my mom, "I'm going over to see dad. We're going for a drive and then having dinner together. See you in the morning." That would *never* have happened a few years earlier.

RB: That dream is the whole story. What has happened since?

KT: Since reconnecting with my father I've been discovering that I have less need to make my women friends serve as my sole confidantes and confessors. I'm turning more to my men friends in these ways, especially those who are working with similar themes in their lives.

What's common to our experience is that not having known or connected with our fathers and not having older male mentors, we've tried to get strength second-hand through women who got *their* strength from the Women's Movement. It's as if many of today's soft young males want these women, who are often older and wiser, to initiate them in some way.

RB: I think that's true. And the problem is that, from the ancient point of view, women *cannot* initiate males, it's impossible.

When I was lecturing about the initiation of males, several women in the audience who were raising sons alone told me they had come up against exactly that problem. They sensed that their sons needed some sort of toughness, or discipline, or hardness—however it is to be said—but they found that if they tried to provide it, they would start to lose touch with their own femininity. They didn't know what to do.

I said that the best thing to do when the boy is twelve is send him to his father, and several of the women just said flatly, "No, men aren't nourishing, they wouldn't take care of them." I told them that I had experienced tremendous reserves of nourishment that hadn't been called upon until it was time for me to deal with my children. Also, I think a son has a kind of body-longing for the father which must be honored.

One woman told an interesting story. She was raising a son and two daughters. When the son was fourteen or so he went off to live with his father but stayed only a month or two and then came back. She said she knew that, with three women, there was too much feminine energy in the house for him. It was unbalanced, so to speak, but what could she do?

One day something strange happened. She said gently, "John, it's time to come to dinner," and he knocked her across the room. She said, "I think it's time to go back to your father." He said, "You're right." The boy couldn't bring what he needed into consciousness, but his body knew it. And his body acted. The mother didn't take it personally either. She understood it was a message. In the U.S. there are so many big muscled high school boys hulking around the kitchen rudely, and I think in a way they're trying to make themselves less attractive to their mothers.

Separation from the mother is crucial. I'm not saying that women have been doing the wrong thing necessarily. I think the problem is more that the men are not really doing their job.

KT: Underneath most of the issues we've talked about is the father or the absence of the father. I was moved by a statement you made in *News of the Universe* that the love-unit most damaged by the Industrial Revolution has been the father-son bond.

RB: I think it's important that we not idealize past times and yet the Industrial Revolution does present a new situation because as far as we know, in ancient times the boy and his father lived closely with each other, at least in the work world, after age twelve.

The first thing that happened in the Industrial Revolution was that boys were pulled away from their fathers and other men and placed in schools. D.H. Lawrence described what this was like in his essay, "Men Must Work and Woman As Well." What happened to his generation as he describes it, was the appearance of one idea: that physical labor is bad. Lawrence recalls how his father enjoyed working in the mines, enjoyed the camaraderie with the other men, enjoyed coming home and taking his bath in the kitchen. But in Lawrence's lifetime the schoolteachers arrived from London to teach him and his classmates that physical labor is a bad thing, that boys and girls both should strive to move upward into more "spiritual" work—higher work, mental work. With this comes the concept that fathers have been doing something wrong, that men's physical work is low, that the women are right in preferring white curtains, and a sensitive, elegant life.

When he wrote *Sons and Lovers,* Lawrence clearly believed the teachers: he took the side of "higher" life, his mother's side. It was not until two years before he died, when he had tuberculosis in Italy, that he began to realize it was possible that his mother hadn't been right on this issue.

A mental attitude catches like a plague. "Physical work is wrong." And it follows from that that if father is wrong, if father is crude and unfeeling, then mother is right and I must advance upward, and leave my father behind. Then the separation between fathers and sons is further deepened when those sons go to work in an office, become fathers, and no longer share their work with their sons. The strange thing about this is not only the physical separation, but the fact that the father is not able to explain to the son what he's doing. Lawrence's father could show his son what he did, take him down in the mines, just as my own father, who was a farmer, could take me out on the tractor, and show me around. I knew what he was doing all day and all the seasons of the year.

In the world of offices this breaks down. With the father only home in the evening, and women's values so strong in the house, the father loses the son five minutes after birth. It's as if he had amnesia and can't remember who his children are. The father is remote, he's not in the house where we are, he's somewhere else. He might as well be in Australia.

And the father is a little ashamed of his work, despite the "prestige" of working in an office. Even if he brings his son there, what can he show him? How he moves papers? Children take things physically, not mentally. If you work in an office, how can you explain how what you're doing is important, or how it differs from what the other males are doing? The German psychologist Alexander Mitscherich writes about this situation in a fine book called *Society Without The Father.* His main idea is that if the son does not understand clearly, physically what his father is doing during the year and during the day, a hole will appear in the son's perception of his father, and into the hole will rush demons. That's a law of nature; demons rush in because nature hates a vacuum. The son's mind then fills with suspicion, doubt, and a nagging fear that the father is doing evil things.

This issue was dramatized touchingly in the '60s when rebellious students took over the president's office at Columbia looking for evidence of CIA involvements with the "university." It was a perfect example of taking the fear that your father is demonic and transferring the fear to some figure in authority. I give the students all the credit they deserve for their bravery, but on a deeper level they weren't just making a protest again the Vietnam War, they were looking for evidence of their father's demonism. A university, like a father, looks upright and decent on the outside, but underneath somewhere you have the feeling that he's doing something evil. And it's an intolerable feeling that the inner fears should be so incongruous with the appearances. So you go to all the trouble to invade the president's office to make the outer look like the inner, to find evidence of demonic activity. And, then, naturally given the interlocking relationships between establishments, you do discover letters from the CIA and demonic links are found! But the discovery is never really satisfying, because the image of the demons inside wasn't real in the first place. These are mostly imagined fears: they come in because the father is remote, not because the father is wicked. Finding evidence doesn't answer the deep need we spoke to in the first place—the longing for the father, the confusion about why I'm so separate from my father, where is my father, doesn't he love me, what's going on?

KT: Once the father becomes a demonic figure in the son's eyes, it would seem that the son is prevented from forming a fruitful association with *any* male energy, even positive male energy. Since the father serves as the son's earliest role model for male ways, the son's doubts will likely translate into doubts toward the masculine in general.

RB: It's true, the idea that male energy, when in authority, could be good has come to be considered impossible. Yet the Greeks understood and praised that energy. They called it Zeus energy which encompasses intelligence, robust health, compassionate authority, intelligent, physical, healthy authority, good will, leadership—in sum, positive power accepted by the male in the service of the community.

The Native American understood this too—that this power only becomes positive when exercised for the sake of the community, not for personal aggrandizement. All the great cultures since have lived with images of this energy, except ours.

Zeus energy has been disintegrating steadily in America. Popular culture has destroyed it mostly, beginning with the "Maggie and Jiggs" and "Dagwood" comics of the 1920s in which the male is always foolish. From there the stereotype went into animated cartoons, and now it shows up in TV situation comedies. The young men in Hollywood writing these comedies have a strong and profound hatred for the Zeus image of male energy. They believe that they are giving the audience what it wants or simply that they're working to make a buck, whereas in fact what they are actually doing is taking revenge on their fathers, in the most classic way possible. Instead of confronting their father in Kansas, these television writers attack him long distance from Hollywood.

This kind of attack is particularly insidious because it's a way of destroying not only all the energy that the father lives on but the energy that he has tried to pass on. In the ancient tradition, the male who grows is one who is able to contact the energy coming from older males—and from women as well, but especially male spiritual teachers who transmit positive male energy.

KT: I find in your translations of the poems of Ranier Maria Rilke, as well as in your own most recent book of poems, *The Man in the Black Coat Turns,* a willingness to pay honor to the older males who have influenced you—your own father and your spiritual fathers. In fact, in the past few years, you seem to have deliberately focused on men and the masculine experience. What inspired this shift in emphasis away from the feminine?

RB: After a man has done some work in recovering his wet and muddy feminine side, often he still doesn't feel complete. A few years ago I began to feel diminished by my lack of embodiment of the fruitful male or the "moist male," I found myself missing contact with the male—or should I say my father?

For the first time, I began to think of my father in a different way. I began to think of him not as someone who had deprived me of love and attention or companionship, but as someone who himself had been deprived, by his mother or by the culture. This process is still going on. Every time I see my father I have different and complicated feelings about how much the deprivation I felt with him came willfully and how much came against his will—how much he was aware of and unaware of. I've begun to see him more as a man in a complicated situation.

Jung made a very interesting observation, he said that if a male is brought up mainly with the mother, he will take a feminine attitude toward his father. He will see his father through his mother's eyes. Since the father and the mother are in competition for the affection of the son, you're not going to get a straight picture of your father out of your mother. Instead, all the inadequacies of the father are well pointed out. The mother tends to give the tone that civilization and culture and feeling and relationship are things which the mother and the son and the daughter have together. Whereas, what the father has is something inadequate. Still, maybe brutal, unfeeling, obsessed, rationalistic, money-made, uncompassionate.

So the young male often grows up with a wounded image of his father—not necessarily caused by the father's action, but based on the mother's observation of these actions.

I know in my own case I made my first connection with feeling through my mother, she gave me my first sense of human community. But the process also involved picking up a negative view of my father and his whole world.

It takes a while for a man to overcome this. The absorption with the mother may last ten, fifteen, twenty years, and then, rather naturally, a man turns toward his father. Eventually, when the male begins to think it over, the mother's view of the father just doesn't hold up.

Another way to put all this is to say that if the son accepts his mother's view of his father, he will look at his own masculinity from a feminine point of view. But eventually the male must throw off this view and begin to discover for himself what the father is, what masculinity is.

KT: What can men do to get in touch with their male energy—their instinctive male side? What kind of work is involved?

RB: I think the next step for us is learning to visualize the wildman. And to help that visualization. I feel we need to return to the mythologies that today we only teach children. If you go back to ancient mythology, you find that people in ancient times have already done some work in helping us to visualize the wildman. I think we're just coming to the place where we can understand what the ancients were talking about.

In the Greek myths, for example, Apollo is visualized as a golden man standing on an enormous accumulation of dark, dangerous energy called Dionysius. The Bhutanese bird men with dog's teeth is another possible visualisation. Another is the Chinese tomb guardian, a figure with enormous power in the muscle and the will, and a couple of fangs sticking out of his mouth. In the Hindu tradition this fanged aspect of the Shiva is called the Bhairava. In his Bhairava aspect, Shiva is not a nice boy. There's a hint of this energy with Christ going wild in the temple and whipping everybody. The Celtic tradition gives us Cuchulain—smoke comes out of the top of his head when he gets hot.

These are all powerful energies lying in ponds we haven't found yet. All these traditions give us models to help us sense what it would be like for a young male to grow up in a culture in which the divine is associated not only with the Virgin Mary and the blissful Jesus, but with the wildman covered with hair. We need to tap into these images.

KT: These mythological images are strong, almost frightening. How would you distinguish them from the strong but destructive male chauvinistic personality that we've been trying to get away from?

RB: The male in touch with the wildman has true strength. He's able to shout and say what he wants in a way that the '60s-'70s male is not able to. The approach to his own feminine space that the '60s-'70s male has made is infinitely valuable, and not to be given up, but as I say in my poem, "A Meditation on Philosophy," "When you shout at them, they don't reply. They turn their face toward the crib wall and die."

However, the ability of a male to shout and to be fierce is not the same as treating people like objects, demanding land or empire, expressing aggression— the whole model of the '50s male. Getting in touch with the wildman means religious life for a man in the broadest sense of the phrase, the '50s male was almost wholly secular so we are not talking in any way of a movement back.

KT: How would you envision a movement forward?

RB: Just as women in the '70s needed to develop what is known in the Indian tradition and Kali energy—the ability to really say what they want, to dance with skulls around their neck, to cut relationships when they need to—what males need now is an energy that can face this energy in women, and meet it. They need to make a similar connection in their psyches to their Kali energy— which is just another way to describe the wildman at the bottom of the pond. If they don't they won't survive.

KT: Do you think there's any hope?

RB: I feel very hopeful. Men are suffering right now—young males especially. But now that so many men are getting in touch with their feminine side, we're ready to start seeing the wildman and to put its powerful dark energy to use. At this point many things can happen.

NOTE:

[1] Called "Iron Hans" in *The Complete Grimm's Fairy Tales,* Pantheon Books, 1972.

The Wildman In The Cage: Comment

by James Hillman

There are many kinds of strength. The strength of experience (Bogart), of endurance (Stallone), of moral rectitude (Spencer Tracy) and idealism (Jimmy Stewart), of the martial arts and of the street and the woods. When the word strength comes up in analysis, we have to get to the image, the figure of it. I always try to qualify generalized nouns by working with the patient on imagining what act or what person he is seeing as "strong." There is a great difference between Lorne Green and James Dean.

Strength of penis, of throat (words, expression, talking), of nose (common sense, direction), strength of legs—these four "bodies" frequently appear as dream images and symptom locations in the men I see in practice. Some men haven't found their legs and they dream of growing legs or they feel paralyzed in the legs. This sort of strength bears on the ability to work (and not only to stand up); legwork, pound the pavement, move on. Others have blockages in the nasal-throat passages. They have to "clear their heads" of coagulated gook, the young sap that clogs their breath. They require operations (in their dreams) to open the throat. I take this not only as opening downward the connection so that the lower "breath" can rise up and be "expressed," but also that they begin to tongue words, taste events, allow connections within their own heads between what they hear and what they say, what they take in and what they swallow. Developing strength of throat is a work on what the kundalini yoga refers to as the Visuddha chakra, that center of consciousness, where the power of words becomes more and more real.

So much has been said about the penis in the last 100 years of psychology that I don't want to gild the lily. Still, we all know the strength of confidence that seems to stem from it. Gaining confidence from it seems to require giving it confidence—confiding in it, letting it confide in you.

What do you want from it? use it for? expect? What does it want from you? Men need to notice its inherent requirements and whether they really originate in the penis or derive from propaganda about what it should be feeling and doing. Men begin to discover its inherent freedom, one's own Statue of Liberty (hence license and licentiousness and libido). Many men feel they get their penis confidence back only from a woman. This is so overwhelming for them that they can leave wife and children, risk livelihood and life just for its sake. This "strength" seems what they have waited for all their lives. I respect these happenings in the patients even while ironically reflecting them against their archetypal nature: foolishness of the Trickster, antisocial Donjuanism, psychopathic. The penis body has the great virtue of putting a man in touch with his psychopathy—and this is the wildman too, and needs to be recognized, else it becomes utterly inhuman.

Before taking up the fourth body, the nose, I want to say something about anger. The hairy man in the cage has been here a very long time. He is angry. We are all sons of Jacob, not Esau his hairy brother. Civilization looks back to Gilgamesh, the hero, not to Enkidu, his hairy companion who dies. As Bly says, the wildman is the repressed, and always threatening, and threatening in therapy as anger. What can we do with him?

First of all, we have to watch out that our professional style doesn't keep him out: the modulated voice, the quizzical gaze, the understanding manner. He does *not* want to be "understood," because understanding, he feels, always tends to undermine his wants. Mirroring is not enough. To engage him, we have to raise our voices, grunt and growl. As a therapist I have to allow Esau and Enkidu into the armchair. If I repress, what the patient learns in the hour from my role-modeling is my style of repression. If I avoid the wildman, how can the patient be expected to let him in?

Anger. As a son of Mars I easily become angry and the wildman comes into my therapy sessions directly. Handling this anger in front of the patient, our handling it together, letting it walk in, walk by, walk out—and not explaining it or apologizing for it—this is a "martial art." It serves to depotentiate the fear in the patient of his own wildman. It shows him that rage and outrage belong and have a place in human intercourse. I don't mean simply his sitting with me through an outburst of *Heilige Zorn* (the holy rage fathers were proud to indulge in the German family). Nor do I mean putting him through trial by ordeal. Rather I mean recognizing anger as an impersonal factor in nature, recognizing that it brings with it—not only scorn or senseless tempestuousness, but a strength and warmth, something mineral like iron, like flint. It contributes something proud and noble, and not only mean-spirited viciousness. Much of my rage in analysis has to do with stupidity and shallowness; rage at the patient's weak, unfelt, self-indulgent reactions. His being "personal" rather than "intelligent." My anger seems to put a claim on the patient for "more" or "better."

For a long time I was ashamed at this anger over the other's inferiority: Should I not be giving that inferiority shelter? Does my angry superiority not polarize us so I become wildman and he scared victim? S-M? But I have since found that even after I recognized the anger that rises from my own anxiety over inferiority, my own anxiety over therapy being so ineffective, I also recognized in this anger, and even in this anxiety, a certain ambition that we get somewhere and that what we are doing together, and life too, really matters. Sometimes the anger emerges from the teacher banging down his ruler, sometimes maybe Captain Bligh, sometimes from my retarded frustrated adolescent whose feelings appear in an unsorted lump—anger simply as intensity. But sometimes, too, it is the wildman inside the cage of therapy who cannot bear its politeness and its routines. He seems to explode whenever things get too set and taken for granted. By envisioning my anger at his attack—not on the patient but on the therapeutic vessel—I keep the wildman therapy minded. He gives it huge value just because of his anger with it. Of course, my anger gets caught up on moralisms, in personal opinions, in peeves. A certain distortion or perversion comes with it, just as distortions and perversions come with sexuality, eating, or making art. This is the amusing part. From iron to irony. And, of course, the personal part of my anger is destructive, that is, attacking the other person personally or taking an attack only personally—egocentric anger. When you are attacked personally you identify with the fault under attack (defense identification) and this is hardly therapeutic!

I have found that my anger is a kind of love: It appears over social injustice, at insults the patient has not noticed, as an expression of concern (and not only frustration or envy). If we didn't get angry, we would never sense what was "wrong."

Part of developing anger is extending its expression—cursing rather than bitching, sharpening the emotion's point rather than a general hostile mood, active rather than passive aggression, holding with it (like Jacob wrestling the angel) rather than letting it all fly away. So long as the anger stays focused on the parents or on the system or on me, the therapist, it has nothing much to do. It stays stuck and is chained with guilt. By extending the horizon of anger, the patient does begin to wake up to the world. It is a way into *Gemeinschaftsgefühl* (social feeling of Alfred Adler).

I've found that this wildman also comes as an ethnic ancestor. That is, the wildman is not only savage and hairy, or threateningly remote from the soft male. He may be your own grandfather. He often brings with him an Irish or Swedish or Russian memory. Not necessarily a personal memory of your own grandfather or great uncle (whom you may never have actually known), but a memorial image or family legend of a Great Strong Ancestor. By recounting (or inventing) tales of this ancestor, place is made for a giver of strength. The strength of the ancestor, by the way, is usually not Macho; the strength is tempered with folly. The ancestor from Cork and how he got to be a policeman because of his huge hands; the Russian Jew and what he did when he landed in Hoboken; the mistakes of the Swede on the wrong train. Machoism hasn't the humor and can't take being ridiculous. But in fairy-tales the giant, fearful as he is, is also a character you laugh at, uneasily maybe, but there is a laugh there.

As soon as possible and wherever possible in therapy, I try to circumvent discussion of the parents for discussion of the ancestors. I want to reconstruct the Family Tree. What strength there! Jung refers to the ancestor as the 2,000-year-old man. We each carry him within our instinctual reactions, our natural wisdom. And to reach him, the key is under the mother's pillow, as Bly's tale says. Where the mother's cushion is, is where the key lies hidden.

Now this is not merely the longing to be back in bed with Mother—really, for most men that is a revolting idea and not a repressed wish at all. No, it is rather that mother's strength—the archetypal fairy-tale mother—rests comfortably pillowed on the ancestors. She derives her strength from the great forces beneath her that dream onward in her mind. Jungian psychology and mythology speak of the "phallic mother." Where does she get her strength from? From her ancestors. So one goes back to that mother's pillow, feels beneath the sleepiness and passive regression, gets below it, under it, where resides the secret of the mother's strength: her ambition, her drive, her fantasies for her sons, her forebodings and hopes, fantasies from ancestral roots, their ancient claims on life arising again into life through her dreaming head on the pillow.

The wildman as ancestor shifts the prejudice that he is merely a grunt with a club. The waking ego defends itself with prejudices, assuming the wildman is just a big cock, or has no language, or has dumb simple perceptions, unschooled. Our notions of instinct are loaded with notions of this sort. Actually animals are terribly refined in their perceptions, their receptivity, their social relations, and their forms of expression. Just look at their tails. The hairy part of us partakes in this animal refinement. This idea, that it is the animal that is refined, produces a wonderful realization, freeing a patient tangled up in the civilized prejudices about the wild.

Ancestral strength brings forms with it. Bly and I have talked about this just this past summer in Maine where my wife and I were honored to take part in his seminars. I was saying there that we fear the wildman, perhaps, not so much because he will be spontaneous and uncontrolled, but because he is conservative and formal. Instinct is formal, form giving and form fulfilling. The wildman is the radical in us, the radical takes strength from the roots (*radix* = root), and the roots are embedded in solid old forms. So a man fears his Russian—Jewish Shtetl, another his Sicilian peasantry because of the restrictive ritualistic formalisms. The wildman brings the beauty of the old ways. I think he ushers in a life that is more aesthetic because it is more animal. But we may not experience this until we first strike a deal with him, as Bly says. And the first exchange in the deal is to bring to him your softness. You have to admit your fear and weakness, your lostness, your pseudo-strength. Admit your love of cushions. That gives him an opening to be more comprehensive and compassionate than your prejudice about him as only savage.

All of which take me back to the nose.

The soft male has a soft nose. He has lost his direction. As Bly says about these men, "They could not say what they wanted and stick by it. They could not lift the sword." Some core of intention has been enucleated. The leprosy of the nuclear age has eaten away at the nose. Or at least the soft male blames the nuclear age: Any moment we will all be blown up. So life is led as if after the catastrophe, a blown-away life: blown-up subjectivism in self-important inflations and depressions, blown about by this or that novelty, experience, woman.

I tend to see blaming the nuclear blow-up in these men not as a literal prediction but as a catatonic dissociation from their own explosive vitality. However, to say to these men, "What do you want, what do you think, what do you feel?" only backs them further into lostness. Nose to the wind, introspective meditation, sniffing all sorts of possibilities, but no true scent and sticking to its track. These questions only force them into a psychology of will: "making up their minds," "decisions." But will-power is powerless without its animal vehicle; and, without a nose, the will doesn't know where to go. Besides, Bly's soft males have anyway asked themselves what they want a thousand times over and have been asked by their parents and their women a thousand times over.

In fairy-tales the witch has a long nose and so do the animals that come to help. The giants have a keen sense of scent too. The hero often has to get his nose on straight, that is, find his sense of direction. It's these soft males who go to the "ironmasters," the gurus of the will, like Werner Erhard and Don Juan and the Orient. They have no orientation and so they are suckers for spiritual directors.

Once there was no question for a young man about his direction if life. You did what your forefathers did and were lucky to be apprenticed. Caste and tradition. We are glad to be free of that confinement today; but if you take the idea of caste less literally it means that we are born with a congenital sense of direction which is given with our ancestors and/or our animal totem of the clan. Hence my insistence on the wildman as ancestor. In the emotions rising from him comes a sense of direction.

I feel strongly about this "nose-body," having been a 97-lb weakling myself for many years. I had a nose for the wind and followed hunches and gambles and felt in touch with the Great Invisibles that soft males pick up on in our Great Spirit quests (meditations, introspections, and confessional poems). But what the soft male needs is closeness with the softness, first of all. Under the mother's pillow is a mole; also, if you look closely enough, a rabbit, a furry creature who has a nose that is not Magical and Marvelous but concrete, shortsighted, and particular. A nose that not so much desires ("What do you want, really; what's your goal in life?") as it does more surely keep you awake and on track. Without the nose you have to plan a direction and force yourself to stick with it— psychology of willpower. With a nose you don't need those awful American moralisms about commitment and responsibility and choice. Did you ever see a responsible rabbit or a committed mole? But are they ever determined! The nose is not an instrument of will, but of keening knowledge, pursuit, and survival. As Jimmy Durante used to say: "Only the nose knows."

shaman psalm

by James Broughton

Listen   Brothers   Listen
The alarms are on fire
The oracles are strangled
Hear the pious vultures
condemning your existence
Hear the greedy warheads
calling for your death
Quick while there's time
Take heed   Take heart
Claim your innocence
Proclaim your fellowship
Reach to each other
Connect one another
and hold

Rescue your lifeline
Defy the destroyers
Defy the fat vandals
They cry for a nation
of castrated bigots
They promise a reward
of disaster and shame
Defy them   Deny them
Quick while there's hope
Renovate man
Insist on your brotherhood
Insist on humanity
Love one another
and live

Release your mind from
the handcuffs of guilt
Take off your blinders
Focus your insight
Take off the bandages
that infect your fears
See your wounds heal when
you know your birthright
Men are not foes
Men are born loving
welcome being tingled by
the touch of devotion
Honor one another
or lose

Come   Brothers   Waken
Uproot hostility
Root out the hypocrites
Warm up your phoenix
to arouse a new era
Disarm the cutthroats
Sever the loggerheads
Offset the history
of torment and curse
Man is the species
endangered by man
Quick while there's time
Abandon your rivalries
or mourn

Deflate pugnacity
Magnify friendliness
Off with your mask
Off with your face
Dump the false guides
who travel the warpaths
Uncover your loving
Discover surrender
Rise in your essence to
the tender occasion
Unwrap your radiance
and brighten your crew
Value one another
or fail

Come forth unabashed
Come out unbuttoned
Bury belligerence
Resurrect frolic
Only through body can
you clasp the divine
Only through body can
you dance with the god
in every man's hand
the gift of compassion
in every man's hand
The beloved connection
Trust one another
or drown

Banish animosity
Summon endearment
You are kindred to
each one you greet
each one you deal with
crossing the world
Salute the love ability
in all those you meet
Elicit the beauty that
hides in all flesh
Let freedom of feeling
liberate mankind
Love one another
at last

Hold nothing back
Hold nothing in
Romp and commingle
out in the open
Parade your peculiar
Shine your monkey
Rout the sourpuss
Outrage the prig
Quick while there's room
Revel in foolhardy
Keep fancies tickled
Grow fond of caress
Go forthright together
or fail

Affirm your affection
Be laughing in wisdom
You are a miracle
considered a moron
You are a godbody
avoiding holiness
Claim your dimension
insist on redemption
Love between men will
anachronize war
bring joy into office
and erogenate peace
Accept one another
and win

Relish new comrades
Freshen new dreams
Speak from the heart
Sing from the phallus
Keep holy bounce in
your intimate ballgames
Sexual fervor can
leap over galaxy
outburst the sun
football the moon
Give way to love
Give love its way
Ripen one another
or rot

Extend your vision
Stretch your exuberance
Offer your body to
the risks of delight
where soul can run naked
spirit jump high
Taste the divine on
the lips of lover
Savor the divine on
the thigh of a friend
Treasure the divinity
that ignites the orgasm
Surprise the eagles
and soar

Let the weapons rust
Let the powers crumble
Open your fists
into embraces
Open your armslength
into loving circles
Be champions of hug
Be warriors of kiss
Prove in beatitude
a new breed of man
Prove that comradeship
is the crown of the gods
Cherish one another
and thrive

Listen   Brothers   Listen
The alarms are too late
This is the hour for
amorous revolt
Dare to take hold
Dare to take over
Be heroes of harmony
bedfellow bliss
Man must love man
or war is forever
Outnumber the hawks
Outdistance the angels
Love one another
or die

Buried Treasure:
Bringing Gay Spirit To Light
an interview with Don Kilhefner

by Fred Green

Fred Green: It seems to me that *we're* at the moment, *in a period of apathy in the gay movement*. There seems to be a lack of direction, a lack of interest.

Don Kilhefner: I think you've put your finger on something that is a key issue. What is going on in the gay community? Why is there an absence of any kind of vitality? Where's the Life? When I look around, I see pretty much a corpse. I mean, when I talked to the Lesbian and Gay Academic Union (LGAU) a couple of months ago, the name of the talk was really "Necrophilia." And it was carefully chosen. There was the idea that all the ideas, all the strategy, all the tactics that our community is using, it's like this fucking corpse left over from the late sixties, early seventies. Everybody keeps trotting out these old corpses, and wanting them to do the job, and they just won't do it. I happen to think that our community is in a major crisis today, and it has nothing to do with what the L.A. Times tells us, that we've made tremendous strides. I see it more in terms of, uh, how to put it? Maybe in terms of gay soul-making. That sense of vision, that sense of excitement of discovering who we are as a people is no longer there. Since you were at that LGAU meeting, our movement has been taken over by an assimilationist ideology. Right now we're dominated by an ideology that says that we're no different than anybody else. All we want to do is to be basically just like straight people. Other than what we do sexually, we're just like they are. That ideology has very subtly crept into most of our movement today. And if that is the case, we end up with what we have right now: a community that really is in crisis, because we have no sense of who we are, there's no encouragement to continue exploring our identity.

FG: Is that because we're beginning to feel comfortable in a way?

DK: Well, I think it deals with a much bigger issue. I think we're dealing here with a theme that's been with us as a people at least for the past century, if not more. If you study, for instance, the development of the gay community here in this country, there's always been that tension, between those people who have said "What does it mean to be gay? Why are there gay people? What's this gayness all about? What are we doing? Why are we here?" as opposed to those who were saying, "Well, it's just a sex act. Other than that, there's no special reason why we're here, there's nothing special that we're doing, we're just like everybody else." That tension has always been there. You can go back to the time of Walt Whitman and see that tension. You could see that drama playing itself out in Victorian England with Edward Carpenter. You could see that here in Los Angeles in the forties and fifties and early sixties with Gerald Heard, and what he represented, and let's say, *One, Incorporated* and the *Homophile Movement* and what it represented. And you see that with the gay liberation movement, between those people who were really moving towards a vision of what it might mean to be gay as opposed to, say, the "gay-normals" who in about the mid-seventies, put a brake on that, and started to clean up the act. Well, they cleaned up the act all right, and in the process, I think we've become a dispirited people.

FG: The reception to your talk was so energetic, the applause was so sustained, that it makes me feel that you touched something in all those people.

DK: Sure. This is one of the things I've noticed myself. You know, I've been talking this line for a long time. I mean, when we were down on Wilshire Boulevard I was probing this way. What does it mean to be gay? Where does that meaning come from? Is that something that's coming from you, or is it something that somebody just handed you? And so, this talk has been going on for a long time. I'm finding that all through that period there were people who were willing to listen, but more recently, in the last three or four years, there's been much more receptivity.

FG: Are you saying, Don, that because of our oppression, we have lost touch with who we are?

DK: Not so much oppression. It has to do more with suppression. There have been parts of ourselves that we have hidden out of sight to the point that they're almost hidden from us. We've forgotten where we put these things. Somewhere back around age 3, 5, 7 or 9 we hid these things. We put them away. I don't know where we put them inside of ourselves, but we buried them. It's like buried treasure. So when we talk about this it's like remembering that there's buried treasure somewhere inside. Are you familiar with the Gnostic "Hymn of the Pearl?"

FG: No, but tell me. I love it already.

DK: It's a famous Gnostic tale in which this person was sent by his parents, the King and the Queen, out of heaven down to earth to find the pearl that was buried there. When he got down here, he was so seduced by all the worldly pleasures, drink and dance and this bauble and that bangle and all of that, that he forgot why it was that he was here. He got into this unconscious state where he just kind of survived. Then the King and Queen sent down a bird with a message reminding him that there was something that he was here for. And he sort of woke up and remembered that there was this pearl that was lying down at the bottom of the ocean. But there was a big dragon that was curled around it. So the idea was how do you get down there and recover that pearl? He had to use trickery, to do that, to recover it and to get back to heaven. But it's here! This buried Treasure! Somehow we have to find a way to come awake to realize that there is a treasure buried deep inside us. But we have to be willing to go into that ocean, and confront that dragon. Much of the work that Mitch Walker, Chris Kilbourne and others of us are doing with Treeroots is, in a sense, activities which help to reclaim that pearl.

FG: What is Treeroots?

DK: Treeroots is a non-profit corporation that Mitch and I have been working on for some time. It's primarily an organization, on one level, to help gay men reclaim the pearl. To help them to become spiritual archeologists. To go down into those layers that are covered with dirt and see what's down there.

FG: So you're saying that we have to get back to that person that we were, as children, before we decided we had to change, to cut it off?

DK: We might be cutting it off today. All of those queer ideas we used to have. I don't know if you had them as a kid. When I was in the first, second, third grade, I would come home from school. I lived on a farm. After my chores were finished, what I did was build some little bird feeders. I took them out into the forest. I had my little route of bird feeders. I would go out and feed the birds. Now, my brothers and sisters, they all had fucking slingshots. And when they went out in the woods, they were out there to kill the birds. I was out there with a different sentiment towards what was going on. I never revealed that to them. I never told anyone. Nobody in my family knew that I was building bird feeders and going out and feeding the birds. 'Cause in my family that was considered queer. So you learn to hide these queer feelings. You learn to hide the way you see the world, and what's going on inside of you. And that stuff is hidden very, very deep in most of us.

FG: If I were to get involved with Treeroots, what kind of activity could I expect?

DK: Right now we're doing workshops. There's something called the "Gay Voices and Visions" workshop, where one of the things we do is look at the development of gay consciousness in the West, let's say in the last one hundred years. We take some of the writings of the gay visionaries and gay mystics and look at what they had to say. What are gay people telling us about what gayness might be about? And to bounce that material off our own lives, our own understanding....

FG: For example....

DK: For example, let's take Edward Carpenter and his book *The Intermediate Type Among Primitive Folk*. In that book for the first time, Carpenter puts out the fact that almost consistently, if you look at the anthropological literature around the world, you will see that gayness is often associated, sometimes almost entirely associated, with shamanism, with some kind of magical, spiritual, illuminating role that gay people play in almost every culture in which they are found. Now that comes as a shock to most gay people. That kind of information has been kept from us. It's very important, because it helps gay people to understand some of the reasons why we do the things we do.

FG: When I was just starting college, I must've been 18 or 19, I took an art history class. The first paper I ever did was on cave painters and the shaman as artist and healer. Isn't that something? I hit on that immediately.

DK: That is interesting, and I think it is significant. There's something there, possibly in our genetic make-up. But we have no context in this culture, no context that will honor that, encourage that, draw it out of us. I think we've been living it, though, most of us, throughout our lives. But we're not fully aware of it. There's something about our sense of idealism, our sense of altruism, our ability to work as the healers, the mediators, the magicians, the spirit people and the medicine people that's very important to our culture. We are the facilitators. We are the helpers in many ways. Almost wherever you see us, you will find us doing those kind of helping, service-like roles. And that certainly parallels our own experience. One of the first awakenings I had around this was when I was in the Peace Corps in the early sixties, and the place was filled with gay men and lesbians. It seems that wherever we're found throughout the world, that there's some kind of queer role that we're playing. It's beneficial to the community and other people recognize it.

FG: You used the word idealism. That's real true for me. In my paintings, for some reason, I try to express the essence of things, the way things might be, the ideal state, rather than the way things are now.

DK: Sure, that's the visionary. Seeing out the possibilities that other folks aren't seeing. Indeed, when we get right down to it, when we ask what is the definition of gay today, it might be that there are these people who see differently. It might be that simple. There are these people who have a different vision, a different consciousness. Not better or worse, just a different consciousness.

FG: Our task, then, is first to get in touch with that consciousness, and then to share it?

DK: We've been sharing it all along. We're doing it all the time. I would imagine that you're being your gay self wherever you are. Somehow that vision, that consciousness permeates your experience. For most of us, anyhow. But often, the key is that we don't know it. We must begin to get some sense of this ourselves. Then we can begin to start communicating it to the larger culture. Straight people can't do this for us. Many of them don't understand a word of what you and I might be talking about here. We understand it. When I talked about idealism, something clicked inside you that you could identify with. I have some really close, good friends who are straight, and I would talk to them sometimes about things which I considered to be such elementary, such basic concepts, and we would get into these long, horrendous arguments. I realized that finally we weren't seeing the same way. I could talk about the same stuff with a rap group at the Center and people would say, "Ho, hum, of course." But somehow straight people don't see the way we do. That's part of what we're dealing with. Something that's deep inside of us. It's a gift that we have. It's our gift to the species.

FG: So, in a way, we have a great responsibility.

DK: Yes, there's much potential, if we don't fall into the big sleep. The big gay sleep. When have you heard a community leader or an activist talk about our soul? They don't. What's happening? We're three years into this AIDS crisis. Major, major crisis, and still people are silent about what's going on with us as people. What is this telling us? I think it's an issue that most people are afraid to deal with. I think there's a lot of fear around. They don't know how to get into this. We hear a lot of talk about gay spirit, but in terms of people actually getting into it, getting into their own darkness, getting into their own soul? What is gay soul-making all about? That's something else. Treeroots is one attempt to make this available to gay men who will take advantage of it.

By the way, one of the other things that Treeroots is doing, we're going to be sponsoring a faerie gathering this coming Labor Day weekend up in the forest outside of Los Angeles. It'll give a chance for gay men, let's say in southern California, to come to one of these gatherings and maybe kind of hang out with each other for three or four days in a way that we very rarely have a chance to do.

FG: And what's going to happen there?

DK: Usually, what goes on are things like workshops; people who have skills to share with other people. Lots of just talking and visiting with each other, small circles where we begin to share the work that we're doing. You as an artist might come and talk about the work that you're doing. Other people would be sharing with you the work that they're doing. Find true love. (Laughter) So those are some of the things that Treeroots is up to. It's providing a resource that's not available anywhere else in the gay community, here in Los Angeles if not in the country. What we're doing here is in many ways unique. There are lots of places around the country where these ideas, these feelings are beginning to bubble up, but it's here, pretty much, in Los Angeles, where we've been able to give some kind of structure to it. It's a little more visible, a little more organized. And there's something about this that deals with the health and well-being of our community. It's no longer Fred or Don getting our act together. Sure, that needs to happen. But on a community-wide level, we need this cleansing, this going deeper. For the sixties and the seventies, there was a real need for the gay warrior. For the eighties and the nineties, it's the gay shaman. It isn't that one's better than the other. At a certain time, there was a need for the warrior to come forward. Now there's a need for the shaman to help to facilitate that exploration of the soul. It's a different kind of work, a different kind of gay liberation work that needs to be done right now.

We need to regain contact with our gay spirit. There are all sorts of deliciously queer things that will happen when we open ourselves to it.

Towards The New Frontiers of Fairy Vision... subject-SUBJECT Consciousness

by Harry Hay

This last Summer (1979) that wonderful Gay brother, Don Kilhefner, together with John Burnside, Mitch Walker, and I evoked a SPIRITUAL CONFERENCE FOR RADICAL FAIRIES to be held in the Arizona Desert over the Labor Day weekend. At the opening of that Gathering, we called upon Gay Brothers to tear off the ugly green frog-skin of Hetero-male imitation—in which we had wrapped ourselves in order to get through school with a full set of teeth—to reveal the beautiful Fairy Prince hidden beneath. In this discussion the writer shall be addressing himself only to the Fairy Prince because the Gay Women have not as yet shared with us SHE whom they perceive in themselves, *as Gay Women,* beneath the Hetero-male-AND-female-derived-and-evolved distortions they for so long have had to endure. Parenthetically, I might add—that the concept of Fairy *Kings* and Fairy *Queens* was never more than a mistaken Hetero Stereotype ... as usual. Ole Pops attempting pompously to explain something he could never possibly understand. In a Fairy Circle, who is at the head and who is at the foot?

Perhaps—before I go any further—I should explain what I mean by Fairy Spirituality. To me the term "spiritual" represents the accumulation of all experimental consciousness from the division of the first cells in the primeval slime, down through all biological political social evolution to your and to my latest insights through gay Consciousness just a moment ago. What else can we call this everwhelmingly magnificent inheritance other than spiritual?

The pathways we explored, during our Desert Retreat, to transform ourselves from Hetero-imitating Gays into Radical Fairies were many. Because the old ways of fairy transformation were obliterated during the night-marish centuries of Judeao-Christian oppression, we felt ourselves free to invent new ones. So—to begin with—

- we reached out to re-unite ourselves with the cornered, frightened, rejected little Sissy-kids we all once were;
- we reached out to recapture, and restore in full honors, that magick of

"being a different species perceiving a different reality" (so beautifully projected almost a century ago by J.M. Barrie's *Peter Pan)* which may have encapsulated our boyhoods and adolescences;

• we told that *different* boy that he was remembered ... loved ... and deeply respected;

• we told him we now recognized that he, in true paradox, had always been the real source of our Dream, of our strength to resist, of our stubborn endurance ... a strength, again in true paradox, that few Hetero Males can even begin to approach, let alone *match;*

• we told that beloved little Sissy that we had experienced a full paradigm shift and that he could now come home at last to be himself in full appreciation.

Carl Jung, in this respect, proved to be absolutely right. When the Fairies reached out to make re-union with that long-ago-cast-out shadow-self so long suppressed and denied, the explosive energies released by the jubilations of those re-unions were ecstatic beyond belief. When we caught up that lonely little Sissy-boy in an ecstatic hug of re-uniting, we were recapturing also the suddenly-remembered sense of awe and wonder of the Marvelous Mother Nature who in those years so powerfully surrounded him. We were—yes—even recapturing the glowing innocence of that Sissy-boy's Dream. And in that Dream, the glowing non-verbal dream of young Gayhood, may lie the key to the enormous and particular contribution that Gay People may have to make to our beloved Humankind ... a key known as *subject-SUBJECT Consciousness.*

How to infect other Fairies with the same excitement we bubbled with in the Desert, and have soared and circled with ever since? One way would be to share the steps by which *we* made the breakthroughs to the riveting perceptions hereinafter to be known as subject-SUBJECT Consciousness. And then, beyond that, to share some of the gleaming insights these new dimensions to the Gay Vision lend to problems that heretofore have locked us in.

To begin: How old were you when you first began to be aware that you held a sense of beauty, an excitement, within you that was different from what other boys felt? I must have been about four when one night I inadvertently beheld my father's genitals: I thought they were the most beautiful things I'd ever seen and—equally—in that flashing instant I knew I could never tell this *to anybody!* I was nine when my Father attempted to *unmake* the Sissy in me by teaching me to use a pair of boxing gloves ... and I simply *couldn't* understand why he wanted me to hit somebody else (sixty years later I can still feel the stifling paralysis of that bewilderment). I didn't want to hurt the other boys, I wanted to be tender to them in the same way I wanted them to be tender to me—*even as I also knew,* in that very same moment, that here again I couldn't share such heresies WITH ANYONE. All this time I would pretend that I had a friend who felt the same way as I did, *and who understood everything:* But of course I knew there was really no such a person. I knew that I was the only one like this in the whole world!

And then came that wonderful day—that shattering day, full of glitter and glisten and fireworks in my head and tumult of thunder and trumpets in my blood—when I discovered ... a word ... a name (even though it was not yet in ordinary dictionaries) for me ... FOR US! I wasn't the ONLY one after all: I wasn't a wicked genii, I wasn't possessed by Evil or—maybe—crazy. There had been *others*—maybe even now others—maybe even one whom someday I could meet. ANOTHER—*just like me*—who would understand *everything.* And he would reach for my hand and we would run to the top of the hill to see the sun rise ... and we'd never be lonely again. My source of course was a book by Edward Carpenter in the locked glass cabinet behind the Lady Librarian's desk. There was another book in that case—about grass—by a man named Whitman, which I would discover on another day when the Librarian had to step out on an errand.

I suppose I was about eleven when I began first thinking about—and then fantasizing about—HIM! And, of course, I perceived him *as subject.* I knew that all the other kids around me thought of girls as sex-OBJECTS to be manipulated ... to be lied to in order to get them to "give in" ... and to be otherwise (when the boys were together without them) treated with contempt. And strangely, the girls seemed to think of the boys as objects, too. But HE whom I would *love* would be another ME ... we wouldn't manipulate each other, *we would SHARE* and we'd always understand each other completely *and forever!*

Then came that second shattering day IN THE LIFE ... when I first met that—*OTHER.* And suddenly—between us—that socially-invisible Arc flashed out and zapped into both our eagerly-ready bodies *total systems of knowledge* ... perhaps one of those inheritable consciousnesses for which Dr. Ralph Sperry of Cal Tech has recently been rewarded for discovering ... a system of knowledge of which our flesh and brains had always been capable of but never—until that moment of imprinting—had actually contained. Like two new-hatched chicks whose incubator-attendant has now sharply tapped on their tray so that their feet, registering the vibrations, suddenly trigger body-mechanisms by which the chicks can know to peck at the ground around their feet thereby triggering further, in turn, how to feed and drink ... so we two young Fairies knew—through that flashing Arc of Love—the tumult of Gay Consciousness in our vibrant young bodies in ways that we—in the moments before could never have imagined—and now would never again forget for as long as we lived. AND THIS—*in ourselves and, simultaneously, in each other*—WE ALSO KNEW ... *SUBJECT - TO - SUBJECT!*

We must not suppose that we share subject-SUBJECT vision *only* in the spheres of Love, and personal relations. Actually—almost at once we began to become aware that we had been accumulating bits and pieces of subject-SUBJECT perceptions and insights all our lives, talking to trees and birds and rocks and Teddy Bears and remembering what all we had shared by putting it down in poetry, storing it all up for the wonderful day when we finally would flash on to what it all meant. The personal collecting, and storing up of these secret treasures—these beautiful beckoning not-as-yet comprehensible secret sacra—is part of the hidden misery-cum-exaltation of growing up gay. For the world we inherit, the total Hetero-Male-oriented-and-dominated world of Tradition and of daily environment, the SUMMUM BONUM of our history, our philosophy, our psychology, our culture, our very languages of communication... *all* are totally subject-OBJECT in concept—in definition—in evolving—in self-serving orientation. Men and Women are—sexually, emotionally, and spiritually—*objects* to one another.

Under the "Fair-Play without-which-there-ain't-no-game" rules of the Hetero-Male aggressive territoriality, even the Hetero-Males—precisely because they conceive of themselves as in life-long competition each with the others—engage themselves endlessly in tug-of-war games of Domination and Submission. The most lofty systems of governance the Hetero-Male has devised—Democracy—must be seen as a domination of Minorities by a Majority, a tyranny of the Majority if you will. Domination-submission, subject-OBJECT. Fair play, the Golden Rule, Equality, Political Persuasion, give-and-take, all of these are conditions of subject-OBJECT thinking. In each case, a given person is the *OBJECT* of another person's perceptions... to be influenced, persuaded, cajoled, jaw-boned, manipulated and therefore, in the last analysis, *controlled*. In the parliaments of government, the game of administration is to persuade Minorities to make of themselves *objects of approval* instead of objects of DISapproval... but *OBJECTS* regardless.

To all of this—we fairies should be, essentially, alien. Because that OTHER... THOSE OTHERS... with whom we seek to link, to engage, to slip into, to merge with... is another LIKE ME... is SUBJECT—*LIKE ME!* I say "we fairies *should be* alien—to as many aspects of our Hetero-Male-dominated surround as we can be sensitive to" because we also know—all too glumly—just how easily and how often we fall prey to self-invited oppressions: How often do we allow ourselves—through fuzzy thinking—to accept, or to identify with, Hetero-originating definitions or misinterpretations of ourselves. The Hetero-male, incapable of conceiving that there could possibly be a window on the world other than his own, is equally incapable of perceiving that we Gay People might not fit in *either* of his Man-Woman categories, might be equally incapable of perceiving that we Gay People might turn out to be classifications very else: He might not be able to handle perceiving that the notion of all persons being only varying combinations of male and female is simply a Hetero-male-derived notion suitable only to Heteros and *holding nothing of validity insofar as Gay people are concerned.* Yet we fairies allow Bully-boy to persuade us to search out the "feminine" in ourselves... "after all, good ole Bully-boy used to tell us we threw balls like a girl" (Right Fielders of the World—UNITE!). Wow—that surely is pretty sexist thinking we've internalized right there. Did you ever ask the girls back then if they thought you threw a ball like them? *THEY'D* have straightened you out in nothing flat! THEY'D have told you you didn't throw a ball like a girl but like something OTHER. You were *not* a Sissy—like the boys said. You were—*OTHER!*

What *OTHER?* Let us enter this brave new world of subject-SUBJECT consciousness, this new planet of Fairy-vision, and find out. All kinds of our friends would like to hear what we see. For instance, the Women of Women's Liberation would give their eye-teeth to know how to develop some measure of subject-to-SUBJECT relations with their men: And we who have known the jubilation of subject-to-SUBJECT visions and visitations *all our lives* have neither shared nor even spoken!

Of course we haven't as yet spoken because we haven't as yet learned how to communicate subject-SUBJECT realities. Subject-SUBJECT is a multi-dimensional consciousness which may never be readily conveyable in the Hetero-male-evolved two-dimensional, or Binary, language to which we are presently confined in terms of communication. And we need more than mere words and phrases. We need what Scientists invent out of whole cloth when they attempt to desscribe and communicate new concepts: We need working models, a whole new mathematics, perhaps, a new poetry—allegories—metaphors—a music—a new way of dancing. *We must re-examine every system of thought heretofore developed,* every Hetero-male-evolved subject-OBJECT philosophy, science, religion, mythology, political system, language...divesting them every one of their binary subject-OBJECT base and re-inserting a subject-SUBJECT relation. Confronted with the loving-sharing Consensus of subject-SUBJECT relationships *all Authoritarianism must vanish.* The Fairy Family Circle, co-joined in the shared vision of LOVE (which is the granting to any other, and all others, that total space wherein each may grow and soar to his own freely-selected full potential), reaching out to one another subject-to-SUBJECT, *becomes for the first time in history the true working model of a Sharing Consensus!*

To even begin to prepare ourselves for a fuller participation in our gay subject-SUBJECT inheritance, we must—both daily and hourly—practice throwing off all those Hetero-imitating habits, compulsions, ways of misper-ceiving, which we constantly breathe in from our environmental surround. For this practice we need the constant company of our Fairy Families. We need the spiritual and emotional support of that non-verbal empathy which Sociologists assure us comprises almost seven-eighths of the communication in any culture, that empathy we now refer to as Body Language. We need the marvelous input of each other's minute-by-minute new discoveries, as each of us begins to explore this vast new universe...this subject-SUBJECT frontier of human consciousness. As ours are the first deliberate feet upon this pristine shore, there are no guide-posts as yet erected nor maps to have been found in ̄ottles ̄or even the prospectuses of ancient visionary seers.

Well—not *quite* right. SUFI was, for instance, a philosophical discipline capable of bringing its students to subject-SUBJECT ways of relating and perceiving the landscapes of earth and heaven around them. It was invented and developed by gay Persian mystic poets and kindred Islamic scholars, such as the great philosopher-poet Omar Khayyam, during the 9th-10th centuries A.D. It has long been generally recognized that SUFI vision was a capacity open only to a few—though theory never went on to say *why*. For those capable of cultivating subject-to-SUBJECT vision, explanations were not necessary: For the Heteros who were incapable of subject-to-SUBJECT perceptions, explanations could only have been incomprehensible.

In the last decade, Hetero Flower Children have revived some of SUFI's trance-inducing rituals *without*, however, comprehending the spiritual prerequisite that the participants be capable of relating *to each other*—as well as to the landscape and skyscape around—subject-to-SUBJECT, physically *as well as* emotionally and intellectually. Now—it is time for FAIRIES to reclaim these penetrating exercises and restore to SUFI its liberating and transcendant capacities for subject-to-SUBJECT thought and perception.

Re-working all previously developed systems of Hetero thought will mean, of course, that all the data we previously have gathered concerning Shamanism and Magick must also be *re*-examined, *re*-worked, and *re*-organized along subject-SUBJECT evaluations. Which is just as well because, for instance, failing to perceive the *lethal* subject-OBJECT character of most traditionally-evolved *Berdache* ritualism and priestcraft, Gay scholars have tragically *misled* brothers and sisters of vulnerable minorities and thereby, in consequence, toxified themselves at precisely those moments when we desperately needed their most crystalline of clarifications.

It is time, therefore, that we FAIRIES faced the reality that *no* Hetero-dominated culture, geared as each of them is to subject-OBJECT conformities, is ever about to discover acceptable Gay-Consciousness-tolerances within themselves—left to their own devices. *Only* when we Fairies begin to validate the contributions Gay Consciousness is capable of developing and delivering, are the Heteros going to begin to sit up and take notice. Only when we begin to manifest the new dimensions of subject-SUBJECT relationships superimposed over the now-obsolete Hetero subject-OBJECT traditions—*and the Heteros begin to perceive the value of that super-imposition*—will they begin to see a value in altering their priorities. Only when they begin to become aware of their need of our contributions to their world-visions (and when they equally discover that *their laws are in our way,* impeding our further output in their favor) will they find themselves sufficiently challenged to restructure their perceptions of essential human variations.

In the meantime, Fairies everywhere must begin to stand tall and beautiful in the sun. Fairies must begin to throw off the filthy green frog-skin of hetero-imitation and discover the lovely Gay-Conscious notMAN (as the quite discerning early Greeks called us) shining underneath. Fairies must begin creating their new world through fashioning for themselves supportive Families of Conscious Choice within which they can explore, in the loving security of shared consensus, the endless depths and diversities of the newly-revealed subject-SUBJECT inheritances of the Gay Vision!

Let us gather therefore—
> in secure and consecrated places . . .

to re-invoke from ancient ashes our Fairy Circle . . .

to dance . . .

to meditate—not in the singular isolation of hetero subject-OBJECT praxis,
> but rather—In Fairy Circles reaching out to one another in subject-
> SUBJECT evocation.

to find new ways to cherish one another . . .

to invent new rhyme and reason and ritual
> replacing those obliterated in the long nightmare of our Oppression, *and
> so*—in fact—*re-invent ourselves* . . .

to break through to ever more spiritually-encompassing and emotionally-
resurrective Gay Families and Fairy Family Collectives,
> who by the very mutuality of their subject-SUBJECT sharing
> are strengthened to reach out contributively *to the Hetero Community
> around them* . . .

AND SO FINALLY—

TO PENETRATE EVER MORE COMPREHENSIVELY THE ESSENTIAL
NATURE OF COVENANTS NEEDED TO LAY THE GROUND-
WORK OF A NEW WORLD-WIDE SUBJECT-SUBJECT CON-
SCIOUSNESS SHARABLE BY ALL!

Desert Circle:
Passages and Images
From The Spiritual Conference

by Will Roscoe

> *. . . the ceremony I had just witnessed was performed after a battle in case any of the boys who had just been killed wished to return and that those who had lost their hands might wish to do so since the body is born whole. However most of the spirits would have gone to the Blue Desert of Silence.*
> Wild Boys, *William Burroughs*

How is it love comes to fill your mind? Where does this love come from?: Something you can hold in the eye of your mind, a place faraway in an ancient space—from faraway you see movement, white moving up and down, a circle of people dancing faraway can barely see and don't hear the music—where does this love come from?—from a time and a place but it feels like the way you love a person and can long for him—white sails in the desert, wings of twenty feet or more in length—moving silent and huge close to desert face, jackrabbits stop in path sit still watch fearlessly waft of wind, a breath of dry brittle desert air, of sun and day, air of the earth of the desert breathing—lover of the dance, lover of flight, lover of this bright blue jewel, shimmering, throwing off flashes of light bright and clean like knife edges—like one most beautiful, meditative, sublime insight, like a concept of love and birth—the several days and events are merged into one lovely memory-jewel in my mind, an image that brings a love and yearning feeling to the fore—I've been to a very special little-boy space, I've been to the edges of a dream, I danced with the fairy-spirits there, I slipped away unnoticed and did not once bother to touch the earth the whole time—white sails in the desert, on the horizon, in the haze-wavey heat of the valley plain edge you see white figures move around a white sail there, barely see the motion, the prepaiations, the packing and fluffing of a journey to come—I'm sure I wasn't missed . . . .

Our first ritual—the Ritual of the Naming or the Ritual to invoke the Fairy Circle Family: In this ritual fairies in the circle announce themselves, present their images and body-forms, using all their gentle wit and humor, expressing a love and an understanding at that same time—the fairies make offerings of themselves through their images (and take such terrible risks!)—yet it is a time of great laughter and vulnerability—expressions are offered as gifts of vision of the total image—many devices can be used, story-telling, confession, singing, dancing, talking, touching, chanting, even disagreeing sometimes—it is important still that the fairies avoid what the mortals call "one-sided" presentations of themselves—in the spirit of contradiction, diverse-unique-conflicting combinations of who/what fairies are, this is the greatest act of vulnerability, of self-disclosure—and it is this ritual-process by which we are known to each other, by which we initiate a transition out of hetero-modes of relating and create a subject/subject space, giving space for individuality, taking space to share and express secrets—by the natural end of the ritual the focus of communication shifts from the spoken word/image context to the subjective mode, where body language, emotion, attitude, and empathy are relied on to communicate more, much more, in a compact form, than what the mortal word can convey, word-by-word patterns—in this sense the fairies slip into a new dimension, the space between, the magical space where contradictions, where individuality and group feeling, where trust and differences all abound—this is a space of absolute unpredictability, of near-pure creativity and spontaneity—out of this terrific possibility, this sparkling mixture could come nearly anything.

Glow of moon slices over aura of skin: blue august moon: came to a place in the desert—moon white smooth brush tip of cock bead of clear fluid there—"bodies fit together in so many nice ways" he said—said slipping cool evening legs between each other skin frictionless lubricated cool dry—feel two cocks balls pressed together warm soft mixing rubbing pressure—feel leg with leg, stomach with stomach, smooth heart, warm hand, soft smile, dark corners, cool smooth even light—sound of crickets chirring—blue august moon—bodies fit together—passing hand along side silent sound of skin touching not touching floating, sliding—swoosh along form—so many ways—cool edge to the night—sun warmed desert air—on lawn head in lap, moon in corner of eye rises to straight above lawn and this desert sanctuary—lips press around head of cock, lick at tip, tongue swirls down throat opens to swallow cock and life giving pleasure pressure of leg against leg—bodies fit together—dusk slipping in, inside, voices in the dusk, quiet conversations around us—cricket chirring against blue moon—white light cool dry fluid pours over form—moves together under blue august moon light air warm dusk skin yields to gentle pressure passing time in the evening perpetual casual eternal suspended moment of time hung from a thread above the breathing desert—arms, arms, arms slip through arms quiet smooth perfect to embrace this world-moment, love-of-you-of-all 'neath the moon's light in arms of a loving community—resting passing time this great fairy circle dusk of magic drawn from the sky by couples in arms licking kissing smelling pyramids of blue light around them—glittering dusk settles on all, all are blessed by this sensuality under moon light this quiet time together outside time forever permanent and perfect forever bliss forever warmsoft skin forever birth of culture and light and hope of the person—eye turned to blue moon above, clear and seeing—"real possibilities in our lives"—couples in arms on the cool green lawn under the rising moon (passing time before tonight's great fairy circle ritual).

WE ARE A SUBJECT/SUBJECT PEOPLE: Fairies sitting and sprawled on lawn in circles around Harry sitting on a stool, in the growing dusk and Harry in a light-colored kaftan, a glowing, animated shape in the dusk, a voice coming from the darkness: WE ARE A SUBJECT/SUBJECT PEOPLE: it's in the knowing, the *knowing* of the Other, we, as fairies know the other as ourselves, don't think *about* the Other but think *of* him: we know him because we know ourselves and he is like us—it's a whole different basis for bonding than the dualism, the wrestling and manipulating of hetero bonding, it's based on affinity, likenesses, it's not opposites or either-or/good-bad/man-woman splintering of the psyche: suddenly the mind soars free!—you think so much faster in subject/subject mode—you're thinking in picture images, personal symbols, in likeness and similarity, in what you identify with, associations, sensations, key phrases, feelings, you're thinking without fear of the different or the unknown, the mind open, receptive to possibility....

Little boys playing in the mud, fingers toes squirmy, slap and splash of mud glopping and slipping down back, break of laughter: MUD RITUAL: a glimpse between bushes on old creek bed—a hundred fairies blackened and caked in mud eyes shine out electric, white glowing, lit up from inside like a bobcat at night—coming toward you, sticks, mud, white eyes, handfuls of straw, in bowlegged swagger, walk of an ape, arms swinging from sides mud drips from elbows: rolling up from the creek bed and gully below, a break in time, wind and crickets suddenly silent, from the green clump of the desert sanctuary nestled below, screams, whoops, chants, and hollering, the wild shouts rolling up the foothills, the sound of the mud ritual, rushing on toward the mountains ahead: ACT-OUT: act-out the erasing of your personality. Act-out the return to the mineral elements. Act-out the discovery of your form as the mud is washed off. Act-out the disengagement from your image.

Whether the fairy-spirit has always been in us waiting to be activated, or whether it entered us (our bodies) from the outside at some time, we know that it is an ancient, timeless spirit. Rituals, raw image-making, primitive rituals create the images that bring associations back to our primordial sensations and functions: we're creating pictures, images like hieroglyphs, three-dimensional living pictures that unlocked spirit memories and ancient visions: a circle of people on a plain, moon overhead slides behind clouds, spills white glow through sky, pyramid shaped mountain hulking in the dark: a circle of people each hugging the other: naked boys swimming in pool, splashing and playing, other boys lay sunning, naked at pool-side, eyes heavy in late afternoon still dry heat and low sun: circles around circles of fairies in rings running in circles, each ring in alternating directions, running in circles holding hands around an altar, a great cloud-carpet of dust rises in the air to engulf us: these rituals are touchstones to remind us, to invoke the fairy spirit in us. (As we learn more, perhaps we can transcribe these basic images into incantations and glyphs that release the fairy-spirit and free the person from Word/Image bondages.)

The secret of levitation has to be laughter: moment at the very beginning of the Great Fairy Circle, when David read the invocation "this is to you O Walt Whitman"—he stood in the center of a circle of two hundred fairies, standing right over a ring of candles around an altar in the center of the circle, his long white robe only inches above candle flame—there's a sudden hushed anxiety— no one wants to break the silent wonderment of the moment—shifting from foot to foot around the circle—then at that moment, exactly one queen (Bill) in a sari broke ranks and with light, quick, efficient steps crosses the center of the Circle from behind David, knelt to the ground, bent forward and with a feather held in his hand, delicately lifted David's robe back away from the flame, David, the whole time unaware and reading from *Democratic Vistas*—crisis solved— just another queen doing what had to be done—and at the moment I thought the repressed giggles and cackles around the circle would lift us all right up, levitating there, and in one final sublime chuckle rise off the desert floor in a great sigh of the earth upward into the night air.

Oh such pasing, fleeting moment—glimpses of what we really are—why is it is brief?—why just this one afternoon of hundreds of days of cities and streets, of hard work in fields and offices, of schools, of buildings, of small apartments in edges of ghettos?—yet who could doubt that this is where our hearts are forever drawn: where does this love come from?—from a place and a time but it feels like the love of a person—as if we spent every afternoon of our days relaxing in the spinning culture of our own creating, music, light, gentle touch, play and preparation—we are here together—we are here in a dream—we are invisible— oh, oh, I know we have left the poor planet earth far behind, I know we have soared beyond our bodies at last, understood at last we were not born there, we were not meant to "be" there, were not meant to stay—still, yet, the final reason of our time on this planet just slipping around the corner ahead—something we've always known, something forgotten like a dream you wake up from, it's in there, in the body, you feel it, strain to finally hold and know it fully.

Brother to Brother

by Joseph Beam

I know the anger that lies inside me like I know the beat of my heart and the taste of my spit. It is easier to be angry than to hurt. Anger is what I do best. It is easier to be furious than to be yearning. Easier to crucify myself in you than to take on the threatening universe of whiteness by admitting that we are worth wanting each other.[1] (Audre Lorde)

I, too, know anger. My body contains as much anger as water. It is the material from which I have built my house: blood-red bricks that cry in the rain. It is what pulls my tie and gold chains taut around my neck, fills my penny loafers and Nikes, molds my Calvins and gray flannels to my torso. It is the face and posture I show the world. It is the way, sometimes the only way, I am granted an audience. It is sometimes the way I show affection. I am angry because of the treatment I am afforded as a Black man. That fiery anger is stoked additionally with the fuels of contempt and despisal shown me by my community because I am gay. *I cannot go home as who I am.*

When I speak of home, I mean not only the familial constellation from which I grew, but the entire Black community: the Black press, the Black church, Black academicians, and the Black left. Where is my reflection? I am most often rendered invisible, perceived as a threat to the family, or am tolerated if I am silent and inconspicuous. I cannot go home as who I am and that hurts deeply.

Almost every morning I have coffee at the same donut shop. Almost every morning I encounter the same Black man who used to acknowledge me from across the counter. I can only surmise that it is my earrings and earcuffs that have tipped him off that I am gay. He no longer speaks, instead looks disdainfully through me as if I were glass. But glass reflects, so I am not even that. He sees no part of himself in me—not my Blackness nor my maleness. "There's nothing in me that is not in everyone else, and nothing in everybody else that is not in me."[2] Should our glances meet, he is quick to use his *Wall Street Journal* as a shield while I wince and admire the brown of the coffee in my cup.

I do not expect his approval—only acknowledgement; the struggles of Black people are too perilous and too pervasive for us to dismiss each other, in such cursory fashion, because of perceived differences. Gil Scott-Heron called it "dealing in externals," that is, giving great importance to visual information and ignoring real aspects of commonality. Aren't all hearts and fists and minds needed in this struggle, or will this faggot be tossed into the fire? In this very critical time everyone from the corner to the corporation is desperately needed.

> [Brother] the war goes on
> respecting no white flags
> taking no prisoners
> giving no time out for women and children
> to leave the area
> whether we return their fire
> or not
> whether we're busy attacking each other
> or not.[3]

If you could put your newspaper aside for a moment, I think you too would remember that it has not always been this way between us. I remember. I remember the times before different meant separate, before different meant outsider. I remember Sunday School and backyard barbeques and picnics in the Park and the Avenue and parties in dimly lit basements and skateboards fashioned from two-by-fours and b-ball and . . . I remember. I also recall secretly playing jacks and jumping rope on the back porch, and the dreams I had when I spent the night at your house.

But that was before different meant anything at all, certainly anything substantial. That was prior to considerations such as too light/too dark; or good/bad hair; before college/army/jail; before working/middle class; before gay/straight. I am no longer content on the back porch; I want to play with my jacks on the front porch. There is no reason for me to hide. Our differences should promote dialogue rather than erect new obstacles in our paths.

Dream: 2/15/84

We have all gathered in the largest classroom I have ever been in. Black men of all kinds and colors. We sit and talk and listen, telling the stories of our lives. All the things we have ever wanted to say to each other, but did not. There is much laughter, but also many tears. Why has it taken us so long? Our silence has hurt so much.

On another day:

I am walking down Spruce/Castro/Peachtree[4] Street on my way to work. A half block away, walking towards me, is another Black gay man. We have seen each other in the clubs. Side by side, and at the precise moment that our eyes should meet, he studies the intricate detail of a building. I check my white sneakers for scuff marks. What is it that we see in each other that makes us avert our eyes so quickly? Does he see the same thing in me that the brother in the donut shop sees? Do we turn away from each other in order not to see our collective anger and sadness?

The same angry face, donned for safety in the white world, is the same expression I bring to you. I am cool and unemotive, distant from what I need most. "It is easier to be furious than to be yearning. Easier to crucify myself in you . . . ." And perhaps easiest to ingest that anger until it threatens to consume me, or apply a salve of substitutes to the wound.

But real anger accepts few substitutes and sneers at sublimation. The anger-hurt I feel cannot be washed down with a Pesi or a Colt 45; cannot be danced away, cannot be mollified by a white lover, nor lost in the mirror reflections of a Black lover; cannot evaporate like perspiration after a Nautilus workout, nor drift away in a cloud of reefer smoke. I cannot leave it in Atlantic City, or Rio, or even Berlin when I vacation. I cannot hope it will be gobbled up by the alligators on my clothing, nor can I lose it in therapeutic catharsis. I cannot offer it to Jesus/Allah/Jah. So, I must mold and direct that fiery cool mass of angry energy—use it before it uses me!

Anger unvented becomes pain, pain unspoken becomes rage, rage released becomes violence.

Use it to create a Black gay community in which I can build my home surrounded by institutions that reflect and sustain me. Concurrent with that vision is the necessity to repave the road home, widening it, so that I can return with all I have created to the home which is my birthright.

NOTES:

[1] Audre Lorde, "Eye to Eye: Black Women, Hatred, and Anger," *Sister Outsider* (Crossing Press, 1984) p. 153.

[2] James Baldwin, "Go the Way Your Blood Beats," *Village Voice,* (Vol. 29, No. 26.) p. 14.

[3] Julie Blackwomon, "Love Poem for Sister Sonia," *Revolutionary Blues and Other Fevers,* (self-published, 1984; distributed by Giovanni's Room, 345 S. 12th Street, Philadelphia, PA 19107).

[4] "Gay" streets in Philadelphia, San Francisco, and Atlanta, respectively.

Outlaws (The Work Ahead)

by Daniel Garrett

These days language shakes down
to elementals: pride, history,
activism, tomorrow, you and
expectation flows in my veins,
unhalting, knowing it's the darkness
of you I have wanted to melt into.

We love as outlaws
men in search of our own constitution.

Martin, Malcom and Harvey's dying let us know
there is work to do,
not to hope or grieve for
laugh away or moan through,
simply to do.

With no land for our harvests
we must free the earth
and with rake, shovel and spade
turn the dirt, drop the seeds,
looking out for rain, sun, weeds
and for the hard rows we hoe
our crops gain from sweated, tender effort,
schools, dance halls, theatres rising tall,
and in our hot black hands
we'll take the law
as with glass
stretching it clear and glistening
shining with freedom.

Androgynies

by Franklin Abbott

The perfect hostess will see to it that the works of male and female authors be properly separated on her bookshelves. Their proximity unless they happen to be married should not be tolerated.

Lady Gough, *Etiquette,* 1863

And when you make the inner
as the outer, the outer as the inner,
and the upper as the lower,
and when you make male and female
into one, so the male shall not be
male and the female shall not
be female, then shall you enter
paradise.

The Gospel of Thomas

These words are from the Gospel of Thomas and are recorded there as sayings of Jesus. Thomas' gospel was excluded from the New Testament scriptures by the fathers of the Christian Church. I suppose they had enough to explain already even with Paul's letters attached. What if these words had been accepted as God's own? That they were not did not limit speculation by theologians in and outside of Christian time and space. Maximus the Confessor believed that though in birth and death Jesus was a man, in the Resurrection Jesus was androgynous. Scot Erigena perceived original sin as the division into sexes. When Adam was alone s/he was androgynous. Taking Eve from his side (removing the feminine) resulted in the fall from grace and the expulsion from paradise into duality: the knowledge of good and evil. Scot Erigena believed that when the sexes reunited so would the sphere of earth reunite with the circle of paradise. This reunion of the sexes, this coincidence of opposites, was the least imperfect definition of God according to Nicholas of Cusa. Heraclitus said, "God is day and night, winter, summer, war, peace, satiety, hunger—all the opposites. This is the meaning."

* * * * *

These observations were culled from scholarly texts which I read alternating paragraphs with glances out the window of a train travelling west from Atlanta to Birmingham. The train was moving faster than the cars on the parallel road, fast through the green Piedmont, fast past myriad white blackberry blooms ready for the rain of May and the sun of June to make berries dark and sweet as any bee's honey.

I sat beside a white haired, white skinned woman aging and proper on her way to Meridian, Mississippi to visit her third daughter. Her first question was did I go to church in my neighborhood. My affirmation was all she needed to take a nap and for me to resume reading about how Christ and Satan were brothers and of God's fondness for Mephistopheles.

I tired of reading and walked the train back to the car on the end where irritated Black men fed up with white folks cooked and served them breakfast. The car was full and I asked the two men waiting ahead if I could sit with them. They nodded and sat opposite me. We put our orders in, were told there was no orange juice and I asked them their destination. New Orleans, they said and just as we began to talk about New Orleans, the dining car porter seated at our table a fortyish woman with teased hair and an alcoholic manner. No water, she complained she couldn't get a glass of water. She ignored us, we ignored her and introduced ourselves. Jack and Bill were from Washington. Bill called Jack Gerard. Jack looked like Jack but sounded like Gerard, a gentle Jewish man full of his mother's wisdom. We talked about music and ate our pancakes. Bill would get uncomfortable if I looked at Jack too long so I made a point to alternate my focus. Bill was studying to be a nurse and Jack sold telephone equipment. I told them how I made my living and that I'd leave the train in Birmingham for a visit with my grandparents. The woman at our table was satisfied with neither the food nor the company and never got a glass of water. The irritation of the Black men cooking and waiting intensified and Bill said we'd better get out of their way.

I walked the train back and told the white haired, white skinned lady what I'd eaten and then the train slowed briefly and stopped for only a minute in homage to Anniston, Alabama. It lurched forward and I returned to reading a tale about how Satan was created out of God's spittle and how every saint worth his salt had had to overcome the temptations of a she-devil. After half an hour Jack walked through the car, said hi and three minutes later walked back by and said hi again and that there were no Cokes in the cars in front. Our eyes met briefly, he blushed just slightly, I wished the seat beside me was empty and he kept walking. The white haired, white skinned lady beside me was asleep under a white blanket dreaming no doubt of her daughter in Meridian, Mississippi who would pick her up at the depot in a completely air-conditioned station wagon full of grandchildren all raised Christian and polite. I put my book in my lap, closed my eyes, took off Jack's shirt, found Gerard and imagined sodomy dark as blackberries and sweet as any bee's honey. The conductor called out "Birmingham, twenty minutes." Mrs. Whitehair stirred and said, "I guess we're almost to Birmingham." I smiled, kissed my fantasy farewell and said, "Twenty minutes, we're almost there." Having repeated all we knew in common, we were quiet until we said good-bye.

* * * * *

In the old Persian cosmology the gods of good and evil were both born of boundless time. An old Greek myth shows the goddess of all things rising naked from chaos, separating sea from sky, dancing on the waves and making love with the north wind. She transformed into a pregnant dove hovering over the waters and when the time was right, laid the cosmic egg from which, when hatched, the universe was born. The Maoris say that from the void, vast burning, unposessing and delightful, came the night, hanging, drifting and moaning, and from the night came the daughter of troubled sleep and from her the dawn, the abiding day and the bright day and from the day came space. From space evolved moisture, male, and the great expanse of heaven, female. From their union came a boy, the heavens and a girl, the earth. The heavens and the earth are the parents of their gods and goddesses and their gods and goddesses are the parents of the Maoris.

* * * * *

My grandparents' house in Mt. Olive, Alabama is on Meadowview Lane though the view is of woods, other houses and a cornfield. The house is brick painted white with pink trim. My grandfather made the carport into a porch where he sits in his 83rd year and watches his neighbors. The porch is off the kitchen where my grandmother orchestrates a host of smells and bubbling sounds that culminate in her saying, "Anybody hungry better come to the table." We do and my grandfather drones, "Smile on us heavenly father for the blessings we are about to receive..." and then we pass bowls of okra, corn, beans, potatoes, turnip greens, peas and then plates of biscuit and cornbread. At the point a stomach might easily burst, my grandmother manifests apple pies, pound cake and cookies and starts us off by eating some herself. We meekly follow suit moaning of the stomach's pain and the tongue's ongoing delight.

My grandmother is on the verge of eighty. This winter her nerves went bad and she went for the first time in her life to the hospital to suffer every medical indignity meant to prognosticate the body's future. They told her what she told them at the start, it was her nerves. She said she'd get better when the weather did and she could get out and dig in her flowers. She was right again. Her yard was full of flowers. Even still she looked tired and sometimes seemed to drift far away. I think she was taking inventory, remembering every flower she ever coaxed to blossom.

My grandfather has suffered three losses of late. Lonnie, his brother, Ruth, his brother Roy's wife, and with them his sense of humor. He digs in his garden, smokes his pipe, reads his paper. He says Herbert Hoover was the last good president. He says people don't know the value of a dollar, that people who won't work shouldn't be fed, that the world is full of crooks and fools. He knows that he is right: he lives a righteous life. He is honest in his action and grows a garden bigger than his own needs and from it still feeds his children. He used to joke and play the fiddle, used to sing of rocks of ages, grace amazing and the wonder working power of the blood of the lamb. Now he does his digging early, then he sits by the window while he waits for the postman who is a woman.

*   *   *   *   *

The Upanishads say the female and male are two halves of a split pea. If this be the truth we are not surprised at other androgynous eruptions in myth. Venus has been worshipped bald and bearded and Zeus with six breasts arranged in a triangle on his chest. Even that classical paragon of virility, Hercules, along with his young male initiates would don women's clothing to promote vigor and make them immortal.

Kuan Yin and Avalokiteshvara are female and male aspects of the Buddhist Bodhisativa of Compassion, a being whom upon enlightenment paused on the edge of bliss and vowed assistance to all who ask liberation from suffering. It is to this great saint the mantra, OM MANI PADMA HUM is directed. The Bodhisativa of Compassion encloses all pain and all pleasure thus resolving all paradox. OM MANI PADMA HUM means the jewel of liberation is in the lotus that holds both birth and death. In Tibet the female principle is called YUM and functions in time. The male principle is called YAB and functions in eternity. The union of YUM and YAB produces the world in which all things are temporal and eternal. To unite the YUM and the YAB within is to know that the two are the same, that each is both, that their duality is an illusion and a source of enlightenment at the same time. In a Jivan Mukta, a person within whom this paradox is resolved, opposites do not hold and absolute liberty allows that person to fly, to be in two places at once, to walk on water and produce other assorted miracles.

*   *   *   *   *

Much to my surprise, my grandmother has planted daisies and petunias in my grandfather's garden and my grandfather has planted Irish potatoes in my grandmother's flower beds. They took turns showing me these travesties. Twenty years ago when they lived in a little white house on the Bon Secour River my grandfather's garden was up the drive, his own domain, row after row, practical and inviolable. My grandmother grew her flowers close to the house in circular beds around tall pine trees cascading Spanish moss. In these beds my grandfather neither dug nor planted. He looked, just as my grandmother only tasted from his labors. Now there are petunias in the corn, daisies through the cantaloupes and vines of potatoes curl toward Sweet Williams and impatiens.

And when we make
the fruit as the flower,
the flower as the fruit,

and when we taste fragrance
and know the scent
that nurtures life,
and when we make
the blossom and the harvest
one in the same,
ripe as berries
and sweet as honeysuckle,
then shall we abide in paradise
and then shall paradise abide
in each and all.

CONTRIBUTORS

Franklin Abbott is a poet and a psychotherapist in private practice with Ansley Therapy Associates in Atlanta, Georgia. He edits poetry for *Changing Men* and *RFD* and edited this book.

Jimmy Santiago Baca lives with his family in New Mexico. His poems have appeared in *The Sun* and *Changing Men*. A book of his poetry, *Immigrant In A Strange Land*, has been published by Louisiana State University.

Joseph Beam is editor of *In The Life: A Black Gay Anthology*. He is a board member of the National Coalition of Black Lesbians and Gays and is editor of their magazine, *Black/Out*.

Lou Becker lives with his wife Jennie West and their son Jacob in rural central Georgia where they helped co-found Eskenosen, Inc., a non-profit organization that assists low income people in organizing their communities.

Shepherd Bliss teaches men's studies and psychology at JFK University. He co-edits *The Men's Studies Review* and edited *The New Holistic Health Handbook*.

Robert Bly is a major American poet who lives in Minnesota. His works include *This Tree Will Be Here for A Thousand Years* and *Collected Poems*.

Harry Brod is an assistant professor in the Program for the Study of Women and Men in Society at the University of Southern California. He is spokesperson of the National Organization for Changing Men.

James Broughton is the author of many volumes of poetry including *Ecstasies, A Long Undressing*, and *Graffiti for the Johns of Heaven*. He is also the maker of many widely acclaimed films; among them are *The Pleasure Garden, The Bed*, and *Devotions*.

John Ceely is the author of a book of poems, *The Country is Not Frightening*, and a collection of translations from Nahwatl, *Eleven Aztec Songs*.

Jerah Chadwick lives in Fairbanks, Alaska after spending 3½ years in the Aleutian Islands. He is author of two books of poems, *The Dream Horse*, and *Absence Wild: Aleutian Poems*.

Louie Crew a.k.a. Li Min Hua is the Director of the Writing Program at the Chinese University in Hong Kong. He is a widely published poet.

Ken Fremont-Smith is a member of the Movement for a New Society, a men's movement activist and childcare worker.

Daniel Garrett grew up in the South and now lives in New York. He was a member of the Blackheart Collective and is coordinating editor for *Other Countries*, a new literary journal by Black gay men.

John Gill is a publisher with The Crossing Press. His own books of poetry include *From the Diary of Peter Doyle, Country Pleasures*, and *Erotic Poems* translated from the Greek anthology.

Fred Green is an artist and illustrator. He recently completed a series of 3 large paintings of Hollywood seen from a spiritual perspective. He has illustrated numerous children's books.

Craig G. Harris is a journalist, poet and fiction writer whose work has been published in *In The Life: A Black Gay Anthology, Gay Life* and numerous other publications.

Harry Hay is a pioneer of the gay movement in the U.S., having founded the Mattachine Society in 1950 and co-founded the radical faerie movement. He lives with his lover, John Burnside, in Southern California.

Essex Hemphill has lived in Washington, D.C. for over 20 years. His poetry has appeared in *Essence, Callaloo, Black Light, RFD,* and *Changing Men. Conditions,* a book of his poetry, was published in 1986 by BeBop Books.

James Hillman is an analyst in private practice and author of *Suicide and The Soul, Dream and the Underworld,* and *Revisioning Psychology.*

Clinton Joyce Jessner is a professor of sociology at Northern Illinois University. He has published in the areas of sociology theory, sexology and gender.

Sam Julty is the publisher/editor of *M/R* magazine. He has been writing on men's issues since 1972 and taught men's studies at N.Y.U. in 1978.

Don Kilhefner is a pioneer gay liberationist and founder of Los Angeles' Gay and Lesbian Community Service Center and Treeroots. He works as Jungian-oriented psychotherapist in Los Angeles and is engaged in research in gay archetypal psychology.

Michael S. Kimmel teaches sociology at Rutgers University. He is Book Review Editor for *Changing Men: New Directions In Research on Men and Masculinity* (Sage, 1987). His articles have appeared in *Psychology Today, The Village Voice* and *The Nation.*

Jim Long is a landscape architect, herbalist and farmer. He is editor and publisher of *The Ozark Herbalist Newsletter.*

Louis W. McLeod is a psychotherapist in private practice in Atlanta. He has worked with men in maximum security prison mental health units.

Mike Messner teaches sociology at California State University, Hayward. He is sports editor of *Changing Men.*

John Mifsud is a native of Malta and has been working as a performer/writer/director of socially conscious, ethnic theatre for over ten years. He currently lives in Seattle.

Thomas Moore practices archetypal psychotherapy in Dallas, Texas and Massachusetts. He is on the faculty of the Dallas Institute, International College, and he teaches archetypal psychology at Lesley College.

Gordon Murray is a San Francisco Bay area therapist and third world cross cultural trainer.

John R. Nierenberg became involved in liberationist politics when studying at the University of Pittsburgh. He now lives in San Francisco and is a freelance writer.

Bruce Pemberton lives with his wife, Judy, and two teenagers in Atlanta. He is in private practice as a psychotherapist and helped form the Men's Experience, an on-going support network for changing men.

Eric Stephen Peterson is currently living in Eugene, Oregon. He was a junior at Roseburg High School when he wrote this journal.

Joseph H. Pleck has been active in the men's movement since 1971. He is author of *The Myth of Masculinity.*

Robert Earl Price is a native of Atlanta, Georgia. He is a winner of the Broadside Award For Poetry and the William Wyler Award For Screenwriting. His writings have appeared in many magazines including *Essence* and *Changing Men.*

Lewis Rich-Shea lives in Massachusetts with his wife Aviva and their (thus far) four children.

Steven Riel served as President of Gay People at Georgetown University in 1980. He is currently working on a graduate degree in Library Science at Simmons College.

Rick Ritter is a counselor and co-founding board member of Men For Nonviolence in Ft. Wayne, Indiana. He is a readjustment counseling specialist with the Vietnam Veteran Outreach Program of the Veteran's Administration.

Will Roscoe is a San Francisco based writer and community organizer. In 1975 he co-founded the first gay organization in Montana. He is currently editorial coordinator for *The Gay American Indian Anthology.*

Don Sabo researches and writes about men's lives from a feminist perspective. He is co-author of *Jock: Sports and Male Identity* and an associate professor of Sociology at D'-Youville College in Buffalo, New York.

Sy Safransky lives in Chapel Hill, North Carolina, where he edits *The Sun*.

Assotto Saint was born and raised in Haiti. He is author of several theatre pieces on Black gay men and a book of poems, *Triple Trouble.* He is lead singer of the band Xotika based in New York City.

Kendall Segal-Evans is a licensed marriage, child and family counselor. He has been a speaker for the Los Angeles Chapter of the National Organization for Changing Men in Schools and on radio and TV.

John Stoltenberg is a writer and magazine editor living in New York City. He is chair of the Task Group on Pornography of the National Organization for Changing Men and co-founder of Men Against Pornography.

David Sunseri was born and raised in San Francisco where he currently lives, writes poems and practices Zazen.

Mutsuo Takahashi is Japan's foremost gay poet. His latest book, *A Bunch of Keys,* was translated by **Hiroaki Sato** who won the P.E.N. Translation Prize for 1982.

Cooper Thompson is director for Resources for Change, a Cambridge, Massachusetts organization providing training on masculinity, sex roles, and homophobia. He is a member of the National Council of the National Organization for Changing Men.

Keith Thompson lives and writes in Mill Valley, California.

Allan Troxler is an artist, folkdancer and political activist in Durham, North Carolina.

Jim Warters lives with his wife, Nancy, in Pittsburgh where he attends classes at the University of Pittsburgh and enjoys the benefits of retirement.

Tom Wilson Weinberg is a singer and songwriter living in Boston with his lover, John Whyte. His albums are *Gay Name Game* and *All American Boy* and he is author of the musical show "Ten Percent Review."

James R. Whipple is a public health and medical investigator and volunteer group facilitator in the Detroit Area Crisis Center.

Carl Wittman was a dance teacher, scholar, writer and political activist. He died of AIDS in January, 1986.

MAGAZINES

RFD: A Country Journal For Gay Men Everywhere. Box 68, Liberty, TN 37095. Subscription (4 issues) $15.00.

Changing Men: Issues In Gender, Sex and Politics. 306 N. Brooks St., Madison, WI 53715. Subscription (4 issues) $16.00.

BIBLIOGRAPHY

FATHERS:

"American Family" © 1986 Essex Hamphill. In: Conditions, BeBop Books, Washington, D.C.

"The Lost Father" © 1984 *Voices: The Art and Science of Psychotherapy*—Vol. 20, No. 3, Fall 1984, Issue #77.

"Letter to My Father" © *Changing Men*, Issue #10, Spring 1983.

"Healing the Wounded Father" © 1985, Joseph H. Pleck, *The Men's Journal.*

"My Father" © 1986 Sy Safransky In: *A Bell Ringing in the Empty Sky: The Best of the Sun*, 412 W. Rosemary St., Chapel Hill, N.C. 27514.

"The Co-Parenting Father" © 1984 *Changing Men*, Issue #12, Spring-Summer 1984.

"An Older Father's Letter to His Young Son" © 1987 Lou Becker.

STORIES

"Having Sons" © 1982 John Gill, *From the Diary of Peter Doyle and Other Poems*, Alambic Press.

"Ah, Ya Throw Like a Girl!!!" © 1984 *Changing Men*, Issue #11, Winter 1983-1984.

"Backwoods Boyhood" © 1980 Jim Long, *RFD, Issue #22*, Winter 1979/80.

"Pigskin, Patriarchy and Pain" © 1986 Don Sabo, *Changing Men*, Issue #16, Summer 1986.

"A Month In the Life of a High School Homo" © 1983 Eric S. Peterson, *RFD*, Summer 1983.

Stories To Antonio © 1987 Jimmy Santiago Baca.

"Some Scars Don't Show" © 1984 Ken Fremont-Smith, *Changing Men*, Issue #13, Fall 1984.

"Rape, A Personal Account" © 1985, *changing Men*, Issue #14, Spring 1985.

"Circumcision Controversy" © 1984, *Changing Men*, Issue #12, Spring-Summer 1984.

"On the Job: Excerpts from A Working Man's Journal" © 1984 John Ceely, *Changing Men*, Issue #13, Fall 1984.

"Mad As Hell" © 1984 Craig G. Harris, *New York Native*, Vol. 4, Issue #24, 101, 10/22 - 11/4/84.

"Haiti: A Memory Journey" © 1986 Assotto Saint, *New York Native*, March 3, 1986.

"Singing Off The Beat" © 1984 Tom Wilson Weinberg, *RFD*, Issue #39, Summer 1984.

"Thriving As an Outsider, Even as an Outcast in Small Town America" © 1981 Proceedings of the Third Annual Conference on the Small City, Vol. 3, 1981. University of Wisconsin/Stevens Point, Center fdor the Sm 'l City.

"Loving Dance" © 1975 Carl Witman, *RFD*, Issue #4, Summer 1975.

"Men Together in Group Therapy" © 1984 *Voices: The Art and Science of Psychotherapy*, Vol. 20, No. 3, Issue #77, Fall 1984.

"Retired" © 1986 Jim Warters, *Changing Men*, Issue #16, Summer 1986.

"Walking in the Woods in a Season of Death" © 1985 Allen Troxlar. First published in the *Independent*, 9/27/85, reprinted in *RFD*, Issue #45, Winter 1985-86.

ISSUES:

"Myself as King of the Wood" English translation © 1984 Hiroaki Sato. From *A Bunch of Keys: Selected Poems* by Mutsuo Takahashi, translation by Hiroaki Sato, The Crossing Press.

"Rape Prevention and Masculinity" © 1986 Kendall Segal-Evans.

"Bringing War Home: Vets Who Batter" © 1981 *Changing Men*, Issue #5, Spring 1981.

"Misogyny: Gay and Straight" © 1985 *Changing Men*, Issue #14, Spring 1985.

"Other Men" © 1983, 1986 John Stoltenberg, *Changing Men*, Issue #11, Winter 1983-84.

"Oh My Loving Brother" © 1981 *Changing Men*, Issue #6, Fall 1981.

"Men and Their Health: A Strained Alliance" © 1982 *Changing Men*, Issue #7, Winter 1981-81.

"The Gay Side of Manhood" © 1985 *Changing Men*, Issue #14, Spring 1985.

"Men Cooperating for A Change" © 1984 *Changing Men*, Issue #12, Spring-Summer 1984.

"Fraternity, Equality, Liberty" © 1986 Harry Brod, *Changing Men*, Issue #16, Summer 1986.

"A New Vision of Masculinity" © 1985 Cooper Thompson, *Changing Men*, Issue #14, Spring 1985.

SPIRIT AND SOUL

"Under Capricorn" © 1982 Jerah Chadwick, *Catch the Fire*, Album by Charlie Murphy, Good Fairy Records.

"The Men of the Wound" © 1986 Shepherd Bliss, *The Men's Journal*, Summer 1986.

"What Men Really Want" © 1982 Keith Thompson. *Dromenon*, Vol. III, No. 4., Summer-Fall 1982.

"The Wildman in the Cage" © 1987 James Hillman, *Voices: The Art and Science of Psychotherapy*, Vol. 20, No. 3, Issue #71, Fall 1984.

"Shamanpsalm © 1983 James Broughton. In: *Ecstasies*, Syzygy Press.

"Buried Treasure: Bringing Gay Spirit to Light" © 1984, Fred Green, Greater Los Angeles Chapter, Lesbian and Gay Academic Union Newsletter, Vol. 6, Issue #4, Summer 1984.

"New Frontiers of Fairy Vision ... Subject-Subject Consciousness" © 1980 Harry Hay, *RFD*, Issue #24, Summer 1980.

"Desert Circle: Passages and Images from the First Spiritual Conference on Radical Fairys" © 1980 Will Roscoe, *RFD*, Issue #22, Winter 1979-80.

"Brother to Brother: Words from the Heart" © 1987 Joseph Beam, excerpts from *In The Life: A Black Gay Anthology*, Alyson Press.

"Outlaws (The Work Ahead)" © 1986 Daniel Garrett.

"Androgynies" © 1987 Franklin Abbott, © 1985 *Changing Men*, Issue #14, Spring 1985.